Landscapes and Communities on the Pacific Rim

A Study of the
Maureen and Mike Mansfield Center

The Maureen and Mike Mansfield Foundation, established in 1983 as a 501(c)(3) nonprofit organization incorporated in Montana, was created to perpetuate the values embodied in Mike Mansfield's distinguished career and to enhance and carry forward the ideals of Maureen and Mike Mansfield by fostering United States-Asia relations, education in Asian Studies, and ethics in public affairs.

The Foundation supports the Maureen and Mike Mansfield Center at The University of Montana, an academic center focusing on Asian Studies and ethical questions that include Asian contexts and Asian ways of thinking, and the Mansfield Center for Pacific Affairs, designed to promote understanding and improved relations between the United States and the nations of the Asian-Pacific Rim.

LANDSCAPES AND COMMUNITIES ON THE PACIFIC RIM
Cultural Perspectives from Asia to the Pacific Northwest
Edited by Karen K. Gaul and Jackie Hiltz

REMEMBERING THE "FORGOTTON WAR"
The Korean War Through Literature and Art
Edited by Philip West and Suh Ji-moon

AMERICA'S WARS IN ASIA
A Cultural Approach to History and Memory
Edited by Philip West, Steven I. Levine, and Jackie Hiltz

Landscapes and Communities on the Pacific Rim

Cultural Perspectives from Asia to the Pacific Northwest

Karen K. Gaul and Jackie Hiltz
Editors

An East Gate Book

M.E.Sharpe
Armonk, New York
London, England

An East Gate Book

Copyright © 2000 by the Maureen and Mike Mansfield Center

Quote on page 187 from Roger Ames, "Putting the *Te* Back into Taoism," in *Nature in Asian
Traditions of Thought: Essays in Environmental Philosophy*, ed. J. Baird Callicott and
Roger T. Ames (Albany: State University of New York Press, 1989), p. 117, is reprinted
by permission of the State of University of New York Press © 1989, State University of
New York. All rights reserved.

Poem on page 95 is ten lines from "Summons for a Recluse" by Zhao Yin Shi (p. 244) from
The Songs of the South translated by David Hawkes (Penguin Classics, 1985).
Copyright © David Hawkes, 1985.

Library of Congress Cataloging-in-Publication Data

Landscapes and communities on the Pacific Rim: Cultural Perspectives from Asia to the
Pacific Northwest / Karen K. Gaul & Jackie Hiltz (editors).
     p. cm. — (A study of the Maureen and Mike Mansfield Center)
"An East Gate book."
Includes bibliographical references.
    ISBN 0-7656-0511-2 (cloth : alk. paper) — ISBN 0-7656-0512-0 (pbk. : alk. paper)
     1. Human ecology—Asia—Pacific Coast. 2. Human ecology—Northwest, Pacific. 3.
Landscape changes—Asia—Pacific Coast. 4. Landscape changes—Northwest, Pacific. 5.
Sustainable development—Asia—Pacific Coast. 6. Sustainable development—Northwest,
Pacific. 7. Pacific Coast (Asia)—Environmental conditions. 8. Northwest,
Pacific—Environmental conditions. I. Gaul, Karen K., 1961–. II. Hiltz, Jackie. III. Series.

GF651.L36 1999
304.2′091823—dc21

                                             99-050049

Printed in the United States of America

Contents

Preface
Philip West   vii

Foreword
Cliff Montagne   ix

Introduction
Karen K. Gaul, Jackie Hiltz, Joseph Moll, and Philip West   xv

Part I: Northwest Voices

1. Focusing the Countryside
Daniel Kemmis   3

2. The Instability of Stability
Jack Ward Thomas   20

Part II: Historical Overviews

3. Asian Perceptions of and Behavior Toward the Natural Environment
Rhoads Murphey   35

4. The New Concepts in Conservation
J. Baird Callicott and Karen G. Mumford   58

5. Mountain Islands, Desert Seas: Mountains in Environmental History
Dan Flores   75

Part III: Living a Landscape: Historical and Contemporary Cases

6. Idealizing Wilderness in Medieval Chinese Poetry
Xiaoshan Yang   91

7. The State Remains, but Mountains and Rivers Are Destroyed
   Allan G. Grapard 108

8. Big Water, Great River: Two Ways of Seeing the Columbia
   William L. Lang 130

9. The Role of Government Intervention in Creating Forest
   Landscapes and Resource Tenure in Indonesia
   Nancy Lee Peluso 147

10. China's Environment: Resilient Myths and Contradictory
    Realities
    Vaclav Smil 167

Part IV: Moving Beyond Boundaries

11. Dancing with Devils: Finding a Convergence of Science and
    Aesthetics in Eastern and Western Approaches to Nature
    Alan Graham McQuillan 185

12. Of Frogs, Old Ponds, and the Sound of Water: Building a
    Constituency for Environmental Literature in the United States
    and Japan
    Scott Slovic 219

Contributors 241

Index 247

Preface

The chapters in this volume were prepared for a symposium held in Missoula, Montana, in October 1995. The symposium was sponsored by the Maureen and Mike Mansfield Center at The University of Montana and was part of a joint research project supported by Akira Yamaguchi, president of KST (*Kinoshiro-Taisetsu*)-Hokkaido, a home-building company, Kuriyama, Japan. The purpose of the symposium was to integrate Asian realities and perspectives with the broad and vigorous discussion of environmental issues in the West, in particular the Pacific Northwest of the United States.

We began by acknowledging that environmental issues pivot on the broad-ranging question of the relationship between human beings and nature. To give focus to the question we found it helpful to refer to "landscapes" and "communities." In doing so we discovered several things. We first identified a tendency in the West to link nature with wilderness. But to regard wilderness as a starting point in the discussion is not typically shared in Asian ways of thinking.

In the course of the symposium we also discovered very divergent views about nature within the West as well as in Asian thought. Moreover, cultural orientations that shape ways of looking at landscapes and communities change over time, sometimes radically. If traditional Japanese and Chinese views of nature inspire an environmental ethic that speaks to us in the West, why do we see so little of that ethic expressed in practice in China and Japan today? And if the legacies of certain ways of thinking in the modern West, including economic modernization itself, are linked in our minds with environmental degradation, how are we to explain the strength of environmental awareness, scholarship, and practice in Western countries today?

In addition to the support of Akira Yamaguchi, we recognize the patience and hard work of Yahiro Ohkoda, director of the International Environmental Institute (IEI), which is the research arm of KST-

Hokkaido. The Maureen and Mike Mansfield Foundation supports the operation of the Mansfield Center at The University of Montana and oversees the endowment from the Burlington-Northern Foundation that funds the annual Mansfield Conference, with which the symposium was linked.

As a Mansfield Fellow, Joe Moll, a graduate student in the Wildlife Biology Program, worked closely with the center from the beginning in implementing the joint research with IEI and in the organization of the symposium. Hank Harrington in the Environmental Studies Program at The University of Montana and Cliff Montagne, associate professor of Soil Sciences at Montana State University, helped in the design of the symposium. Even before the joint research was begun, Steve Siebert and Alan McQuillan in the Forestry Department helped the center conceive its larger project on "Asia and the Environment." Bill Bevis and Karen Gaul cotaught a course that ran in conjunction with the conference and symposium. I want to recognize the invaluable contributions of Fred Allendorf, Jill Belsky, Bill Bevis, Motoo Fujiki, Steve Lansing, and Anna Tsing who also participated in the symposium. William Lang and Scott Slovic were especially helpful in the early stages of editing, and Ashley Preston has carefully reviewed early versions of the Introduction.

For the preparation of the volume itself, the center is indebted to coeditors Karen Gaul and Jackie Hiltz. Our efforts toward producing a truly cross-cultural and cross-disciplinary volume is due in a major way to their perseverance and teamwork with others at the Mansfield Center and on campus.

Philip West, Director
Maureen and Mike Mansfield Center

Foreword

In the context of this collection of papers, it is fitting to acknowledge Akira Yamaguchi and his unique efforts at providing sustainable home-building for the particular landscapes and communities on Hokkaido, the northernmost island of Japan.[1] At latitudes comparable to Montana in the United States, Hokkaido experiences long winters with snow for up to six months of the year. For the last fifty years, Mr. Yamaguchi has been developing new technologies to meet the housing needs of Hokkaido residents and to use natural resources more responsibly.

In fact, in reference to his business, KST (*Kinoshiro-Taisetsu*)-Hokkaido, Yamaguchi resists the title "home construction company." Instead, Yamaguchi and his 1,300 employees view their work as the construction of a *context* for healthy living in terms of both a physical and cultural environment. Yamaguchi uses the term "Total Systems" to express this broader perspective, which his company aims to implement in the construction of KST homes. Today's KST-Total Systems approach and the unique features of KST homes stem from the vision and hard work of Yamaguchi, a lifelong resident of Hokkaido who believes in the blending of traditional craft, modern technology, and wisdom gained from experience.

Akira Yamaguchi's grandfather emigrated to Hokkaido from Honshu, the main island, in 1896 to become a farmer-soldier and to eke out a living in a mountainous land with long, snowy winters.[2] The Yamaguchi family developed a diversity of subsistence and business enterprises near the town of Chiyoshibetsu, which is situated where a mountain valley intersects the sea coast. Summer was the farming season, winter for logging, and spring for fishing, with value added to the natural products through a sawmill and clog factory. The whole family worked together to produce the food they needed and enough extra products (fish, wood, clogs) to buy items from outside of the valley where they lived. They

improvised many tools themselves in order to be reasonably self-suffi-
cient in the ecological, social, and economic conditions of their environment. Akira Yamaguchi grew up in this small valley living a life
closely tied to the seasons.

As a youth, Yamaguchi was influenced by his father, who encouraged his interest in woodcraft and construction. He apprenticed as a
temple-builder, during which time he learned that much of the longevity
of Japanese temples depends on careful and painstaking internal struc-
tural work that remains invisible on the outside surface of a finished
building. He went to Sapporo as a carpenter and was shocked when
winter came and the construction industry came to a standstill. Carpen-
ters went on welfare and rested up for the coming season.

In Sapporo, Yamaguchi became a building subcontractor, and in 1959,
he became an independent contractor. He teamed up with a prominent
architect, Toshio Maeda, to build high-quality homes for the Sapporo
elite. Yamaguchi and Maeda developed a practical alternative to the traditional steeply sloping roofs that often caused slipping snow and numerous cases of injury or death each year. They developed the snow-duct
roof that gently slopes toward a center, so that the snow can melt and the
water percolate down the drain.

By the late 1960s, Yamaguchi consolidated the design and construction company into one firm, which was the beginning of the Total Systems concept. By 1972, Yamaguchi had evolved production of the
snow-duct roof, thermal insulation, and the adaptation of the traditional
Russian *petchka* stove as a unique housing response to Hokkaido winters.[3] In addition, he developed a system of working year round which,
although initially met with skepticism and reluctance, lent more finan-
cial stability to both company and employees. To spread the word about
his homes and their innovative features, Yamaguchi began an educational advertising campaign. In 1977 the operation moved to Kuriyama
where another innovation, the two-meter-high ferroconcrete semibase-
ment, was developed.

In the early 1980s, prolonged hospitalization prompted Yamaguchi
to think about his youth and his relationships with his extended family.
Seeing the extended family as a center of traditional family values, he
decided to design a three-story house that would bring together three
generations and would last for a long time as well. The KST homes of
the 1990s incorporate all of these features that have been slowly integrated over decades of hard work.

The KST operation itself embodies the life work and philosophy of Yamaguchi. Rather than a specialized plant focusing on one aspect of home construction, KST creates the total physical home and a healthy living environment (*kinoshiro*, translated as "wooden castle") for the people of Hokkaido. KST supplies almost every single feature necessary for the house: from beams and frames to furnishings and curtains. This reduces the amount of energy and transportation necessary to hire subcontractors to provide various elements of the house. At the same time, KST encourages multigenerational living in the same large home. As well as potentially strengthening family ties, fewer homes need to be built, and fewer appliances and utilities used. Additionally, by aspiring to use timber primarily from Hokkaido forests, and by developing technologies for increased use of small-diameter timber (for example, by utilizing a carefully developed lamination process) KST sees its work as bioregionally oriented.[4] In the last few decades, KST-Hokkaido has built a total of 15,000 houses on Hokkaido, averaging 700 per year. On these several different levels, KST's Total Systems approach addresses environmental and cultural concerns of the people of Hokkaido.

Hokkaido has only been settled and developed by Japanese citizens since 1868. Like many other areas around the world, Hokkaido's rush to colonize and then to modernize has been expensive, both monetarily and environmentally. In this time the native Ainu population has been greatly diminished, and an agricultural, silvacultural, and urban-industrial infrastructure has developed.[5] The forests of Hokkaido have been replaced by single- or double-species tree plantations; major rivers have been channeled; and some native fauna species have decreased. For example, the herring fishery of Chiyoshibetsu was depleted by a combination of overfishing and erosion from tree harvest.[6]

For most of the last century much of Hokkaido's development has been directed from the central government in Tokyo. Many residents feel that Hokkaido is still like a colony, controlled by the Tokyo-based national government and other economic and industrial interests largely centered in the nation's capital. Like other colonies, Hokkaido's natural resources are exploited by residents and outsiders alike, often with little attention to long-term sustainable use. Often, ideas are implemented without considering the unique cultural and environmental setting of Hokkaido. Most home construction on the island, for example, is an import from the south where snowfall is significantly less or nonexistent.

Many people of Hokkaido are ready to find new models for self-sufficiency, including a more equal partnership with the rest of Japan. The current set of goals for the development of Hokkaido, recommended by the Hokkaido Regional Development Authority in 1996, emphasizes reduction of Tokyo's control over the regional, economic, political, and social life of Hokkaido as part of the process of decentralizing the nation. Yamaguchi's company seeks to address the need for regionally appropriate housing, a goal that seems to fit within the vision for Hokkaido but which has met with considerable resistance from politicians and the media who criticize him for his attacks on mass consumption and mass production, as well as other home builders who rely on cheaply imported wood.

There are a number of features that make the KST homes and their production process different from all other home construction on Hokkaido. In combination, these features and properties support KST's claims of sustainability.

The milling and every aspect of KST production has been carefully developed over many years. The evolution of these technologies has meant perfecting—after some long processes of trial and error—all stages of the construction process. The KST factory cures and mills both hard and soft woods, utilizing state-of-the-art laser-beam-guided machinery, and then uses every bit of the tree: Planks and beams are made from the core of the tree, laminated beams from scrap pieces of lumber, plywood and furniture fill from smaller parts, and sawdust and chips fuel the boiler for the kilns for the curing process. Research for the development of the lamination process, and even more efficient uses of small pieces of wood, continues to be carried out.

The foundation of the KST home is a high-walled ferroconcrete box, rather than an open cement foundation. The height of the walls keeps piling and drifting snow away from the wooden structure of the house, and its top concrete layer prevents moisture from seeping into the wooden structure mounted on this ferroconcrete base. Many homes in the Hokkaido climate, with its cold damp winters, suffer from mold which often causes the inhabitants to become ill. The wooden "temple" frame fixed on the reinforced ferroconcrete box foundation provides long-lasting strength and flexibility against shaking.

The inverted slope on the roof directs melting snow down a duct and into tanks in the ground. The absence of typically slanted roofs eliminates snowslide hazard, and the duct can collect rainwater in drought.

KST developed a unique heating system, adapted from the Russian *petchka* stove, to meet the needs presented by the long, cold winters on Hokkaido. This single heating source uses little fuel, usually kerosene, and combined with an open design and well-insulated but breathable wall panels provides a pleasant ambient heat throughout the entire home.[7] Five panel windows contribute to efficient heating and cooling in all seasons.

The result of all of these efforts is a living space which is healthy, aesthetically pleasing, and durable. Given the realities of Hokkaido living, the KST home has many characteristics of sustainability. The KST home reflects a long process of research and implementation that makes these homes most suitable for their bioregion.

Given the careful consideration of environmental and cultural factors applied to every aspect of this home construction process, it is fitting that Yamaguchi and IEI have supported this academic exploration of "Landscapes and Communities in Asia and the Pacific Northwest" in Missoula, Montana.

Cliff Montagne
Associate Professor of Soil Sciences
Montana State University

Notes

1. For a detailed account of the life and accomplishments of Akira Yamaguchi, see his autobiography, *Mottainai* (Waste Not, Want Not) (Sapporo, Hokkaido: International Environmental Institute, 1994).

2. "Farmer-soldiers" were early settlers of Hokkaido who were sponsored by the Japanese government as farmers or homesteaders. The government also expected them to be available to perform as soldiers against potential Russian threats.

3. The Russian *petchka* heating stove is a small charcoal or oil-burning stove built into the base of a large brick wall thermal mass. The stove exhaust pipe winds through the brick mass, allowing for most of the heat in the exhaust gas to be transferred to the brick, providing moderate and constant heat.

4. Senior management at KST projects that, by the year 2010, KST will have mastered technologies and processes that may result in the exclusive use of Hokkaido materials in KST homes.

5. In 1980 there were fewer than 200 Ainu people without mixed Japanese ancestry, although there were 24,160 people of mixed Ainu and Japanese ancestry (*Kodansha Encyclopedia of Japan* [Tokyo: Kodansha, 1983]).

6. For example, soil scientist Masamichi Takahashi reports an overharvest of forest watersheds which flow into the sea along the coast of Hokkaido. Slow regeneration in the severe climate has led to erosion, turbidity, seaweed damage, and loss of much of the herring fishery. He further hypothesizes that government erosion dams are preventing nutrients and critical fulvic acids (carriers of iron) derived from forest soils from reaching the seaweed upon which the herring depend. The Science and Technology Agency rejected his 1995 proposal to study the hypothesis on the grounds that there is no money for forestry research. (Personal communication with Takahashi, Forest Soil Laboratory at the Hokkaido Research Center of the Forestry and Forest Products Research Institute, Sapporo University, July 1995.)

7. The amount of fuel required from this single source of heat is approximately one-fifth of that needed for the average Japanese home.

Introduction

Karen K. Gaul, Jackie Hiltz, Joseph Moll, and Philip West

On cold winter days people in downtown Missoula can look up and see herds of elk and mule deer wintering on the exposed south faces of the mountains that encircle the city. In the autumn of 1995 voters here supported a bond issue to purchase and protect part of that winter range as designated "open space." Approval came only after years of debate, several failed attempts, and campaigns coordinated by nonprofit land trust organizations. Reaching community consensus on the meaning and value of landscape is a difficult business.

The open space debate and other contested land management issues represent the latest round of collective reflection on how Missoulians perceive and inhabit their surroundings.[1] The local economy is responding to new constraints on development imposed by decreased forest production and environmental regulation, as well as to opportunities for new markets for diversified forest and agricultural products, tourism, and service-related industries. These changes are reflected in a reshuffled demography of the region and consequently in the attitudes expressed in public debate. As former Missoula Mayor Dan Kemmis notes, the city can serve as a center of activity, distilling regionwide effects of these changes.[2] Of course, such local adaptations to larger market and social forces are not limited to Missoula. Small cities and communities throughout the United States and throughout the world are struggling to maintain their unique traditions and landscapes while embracing the demands and opportunities of global commerce.

Local Places

Imagine sitting in the shade of a dense cluster of spruce and fir trees in the Kootenai National Forest surrounding the small town of Libby in the north-western corner of Montana.[3] Here you are nestled in a forest echoing with 100 years of intensive timber extraction. After an initial boom and bust cycle of gold mining in the mid-nineteenth century, timber (and related products such as Christmas trees) offered the most substantial livelihood choice for Libby's residents. But by the early part of this century the inhab-itants of Libby became increasingly concerned about their reliance on a single and diminishing resource. Sawmills in nearby towns closed up one after another. The community faced an impending crisis with a great deal of strife but also with some forethought: In 1946 they organized a study group to assess the situation and seek solutions to their problems.

Fifty years later, the community of Libby with a population of around 14,000 is perhaps more factionalized than ever. Loggers want to con-tinue "wisely" harvesting spruce and fir forests; timber families want to go on making a living from a resource that had supported generations before them. Hunters and others concerned about wildlife are alarmed by rapidly decreasing habitat, and environmentalists argue that the ram-pant exploitation must stop. In the face of these conflicting pressures, the community has followed its own historical precedent again by sit-ting down at the negotiating table as a community, and in conversation with the Forest Service, in an attempt to work out ways for healthy use of private and federal forests in the Kootenai drainage.

If we shift our seat to the hills above Chamba, a hill town of roughly 20,000 people in the northern state of Himachal Pradesh in India, the shade we would find beneath a cluster of trees would be fairly sparse.[4] Use by villagers for fuelwood, fodder, and hundreds of other household and animal husbandry purposes keeps "village forests," or those areas designated for common use, fairly heavily used. But village-level use is only the most visible in forests that will also see contract timber extrac-tion and immeasurable black market extraction of timber, herbs, and more, under the cover of night.

Here, too, the community is divided in terms of priorities for forest care and exploitation. A small group of activists work incessantly pro-viding environmental education for all residents of Chamba, using ev-ery strategy imaginable, including piggy-backing with the rural literacy outreach program. A few families work independently replanting seedlings for future fuel and fodder use. The Forest Department administers reforestation schemes such as Social Forestry to involve local people in forest protection and regeneration. But external funding often fosters a desire in people to do forest-related work for compensation rather than out of protection of their own resources. The end of funding can mean the end of some people's commitment to the project. And a great many others continue to cut and lop, seemingly without considering what their actions may mean for their children. Again, with forests as one of the kingpins of this area's economy, forest loss is met with a mix of confusion, argument, and apathy.

If we move on to Shimokawa, a small town of approximately 5,000 people in the rolling hills of north central Hokkaido, Japan, the surrounding forests would be surprisingly thick with small-diameter larch trees.[5] Here, in a 64,000–hectare township that is mostly forested, the price of labor to thin these forests is more costly in the long run than simply buying foreign wood.

A small copper mine closed down about fifteen years ago, severely limiting income possibilities for local residents. Some engage in small-scale agriculture. The Shimokawa Forest Co-op, called Kumiai, first started in 1943, provides over 100 local jobs. Of the 600 township land-owners, 388 are members of the co-op. Recently, national forest legislation called for forest management on a watershed level for 100 pilot watersheds throughout Japan. Kumiai took advantage of this opportunity to add national forest land to its management land base, increasing from 7,000 to 58,000 hectares of land managed. Through this new scheme, the co-op has access to the national forest resources such as machinery and research information, as well as timber contract arrangements previously denied to the co-op. But the "watershed management" concept is still being driven by timber harvest, rather than attention to the ecology of the watershed.

Each of these communities—Libby, Chamba, and Shimokawa—are involved in a struggle over livelihood within diminishing forests. Each area supplements timber-related income with agriculture, some small-scale industry, other resource extraction such as mining, and with minor products gathered from the forests such as herbs, mushrooms, bamboo, and so on. Interestingly, tourism is an option that has so far not gained much favor in any of these regions, primarily due to their distance from major throughways or large cities. However, each community is beginning to consider tourism as a way of broadening the base of livelihood possibilities.

In Libby, Chamba, and Shimokawa, local communities claim a long history of reliance on forest materials. In all three of these areas, federal and/or state management of forests has meant complex relationships among private landowners, government management, community use of public lands, and disagreement over revenues generated by forests. Yet on the community level, residents of each of these areas struggle to respond creatively to the forest dilemmas which have resulted from perhaps questionable management practices. Their lifestyles and livelihoods are closely tied to the natural resources that a forest environment provides, but which is in serious jeopardy. Only diligent, creative, and cooperative efforts by all interested and affected parties will enable these communities to come to terms with their resource management predicaments.

If members from each of these communities could visit one another what would they learn? Given the capabilities of today's communication technologies, combined with what are indeed serious local manifestations of global environmental crises, the sharing of information between various places in the world becomes both possible and essential. It is not only a matter of Americans drawing upon and learning from far away places, to perhaps apply ideas to our own ends, but rather an opportunity to exchange information and share experiences to the benefit of all parties. Examination of the situations in the Himalaya, the northern Rockies, and northern Hokkaido offers new insights for solutions and new perspectives to all.

Breaking Down Boundaries: Cross-disciplinary Approaches

Issues of environmental and cultural sustainability like those evident in the communities of Libby, Chamba, and Shimokawa have galvanized members of the academic community, as well as members of nongovernmental organizations and those in the private and public sectors, to move beyond the boundaries of their respective disciplines. A quick browse through any bookstore today will reveal growing stocks of books on shelves labeled Environment, Earth Sciences, Nature Writing, and Ecology. Other disciplinary sections such as history, anthropology, sociology, and biology are expanded to make room for environment-related studies. But the interdisciplinary nature of some of these works makes integration critical: How else to accommodate Simon Schama's multifaceted *Landscape and Memory* (1995)? Environment-related courses and multidisciplinary programs, which use such texts, are increasingly present in the curriculum of many colleges and universities across the United States.

Although the environmental movement of the late 1960s and 1970s was also informed and supported by intellectual activity, the seriousness with which these efforts are being made across the academy, through arts, sciences, and humanities in the 1990s, is unprecedented. The last decade or so has seen unparalleled struggles to come to terms with the swiftly changing and even disappearing cultural and biological diversity on the planet. As more and more species slip into extinction, and as cultures everywhere respond to rapid economic, political, and environmental change, what have been traditional disciplines are being forced to shift priorities, expand their focus, or break down boundaries. No one discipline alone is able adequately to explain, predict, or address the ever-changing cultural and environmental conditions that define who we are. Academic research can include not only studies of specific field situations, but a careful look at how we conceptualize our surroundings in particularly European and American castings of the "natural" world. These more self-conscious approaches, many suggest, will help us to view our current environmental problems in context and enable us to make informed decisions about our actions.

In all of these efforts, we might identify a common theme and perhaps a shared goal. Across these various fields and interdisciplinary approaches, we can trace the idea of integration. Whether this means integration of traditional disciplines, of different cultural perspectives, or of religious and ethical values, some effort and recognition of connections rather than insistence on discrete fields is a hallmark of these new paradigm shifts. Integration, however, does not lead to simplification; a related goal for some of these explorations is understanding and describing complexities of natural processes, of human cultures, and of human-environmental interactions.

Conservation biologists, ecological anthropologists, environmental philosophers, and others would each address the situations in Chamba, Libby, and Shimokawa in different ways. But these days, researchers in each of these fields are intentionally reaching toward overlap and common ground with others, generating areas for conversation and cooperation rather than mutually exclusive study. Despite obvious differences, in the mid- to late twentieth century, many disciplines have shared radical paradigm shifts. Certain notions about reality which had been assumed from Enlightenment science, under contemporary environmental, economic, and political conditions, have demanded re-examination. It is no accident that these intellectual crises parallel environmental and social ones. Basic Enlightenment faith in the ability of science to apprehend the true character of the natural world, of the transparency of language to explain that world, and the ability of humans to observe, record, and relay such information accurately or objectively have been deeply challenged from all sides. In academic disciplines, responses to these paradigm shifts have taken a number of forms.

In the sciences, heretofore rigidly defined fields are now drawing from one another and inventing new areas of inquiry and application. Aldo Leopold (1886–1948), for example, an early leader in wildlife conservation, articulated the connections between human beings and their environment. He characterized the community broadly to include the nonhuman biotic and abiotic components: geology and climate, vegetation and animals, the history of human settlement, the desires of the current society, and the dreams of coming generations. Today, conservation biology as a multidisciplinary field seeks to integrate principles of disciplines as diverse as genetics, biogeography, philosophy, landscape ecology, policy development, sociology, population biology, and anthropology.[6] Models of predictable, linear, and delimited systems have been abandoned for more open-ended, fluid, and constantly shifting realities that are not describable or containable in simple models. In this volume, Alan McQuillan addresses these issues in his chapter, "Dancing with Devils."

Ecological anthropology and other social science approaches have similarly moved from functionalist to process-oriented models.[7] New perspectives in these and other fields emphasize shifting and complex realities rather than stable, definitive ones. Here too, anthropologists have come to recognize the impossibility of focusing on one element of cultural practices to the exclusion of others. As Nancy Peluso points out in her chapter, deforestation cannot be understood apart from colonialism, economic pressures, social stratification, and more. Allowing for partial glimpses then, rather than whole and finished stories, reflects a respect for the complexity, the interrelatedness, and the messiness of real lives.

In the arts, the burgeoning fields of nature writing and environmental writing have contributed to expanding bookshelf stocks. These works, advocates argue, can guide us in our quest to develop a new system of values that will enable us to sustain what we love while producing what we need. In some instances, this has meant a reach across national and cultural boundaries for mutual explorations, such as in Scott Slovic's work exposing Japanese audiences to American environmental literature.[8]

These paradigm shifts are not accomplished without debate. In the humanities, for example, historians are conducting some intensive studies of place, of particular natural "resources," and of the social inequalities reflected in land use practices. Donald Worster's book, *Rivers of Empire: Water, Aridity, and the Growth of the American West* (New York: Pantheon Books, 1985), is one such example. But historians also are reflecting on intellectual history, and related social and environmental implications of the implementation of certain ideas. The "truth" of certain understandings of nature—whether as a conceptual construct of the "Western" mind, as an Edenic garden or paradise, or as a physical "reality" that needs protection from human destruction and interference— cannot be disputed conclusively.[9] But a recognition that all conceptualizations are contingent upon particular places, times, and cultural settings, as Allan Grapard illustrates in this volume, is essential.

Philosophers, too, are responding to and effecting paradigm shifts. One of the few efforts at a broadranging examination of Asian perspectives is the edited collection, *Nature in Asian Traditions of Thought* (Albany: State University of New York Press, 1989). Environmental and comparative philosophy, editors J. Baird Callicott and Roger Ames assert, are responses to a loss of faith in science and constantly shifting understandings about the world and the place of humans in it. An interesting outcome of this shift in philosophy has been a closer look at "Eastern" thought and some effort to include these perspectives into Western philosophy curricula.

In not only environmental ethics, but in everything from regional and place histories to quantum physics, from conservation biology to a recent deluge of nature writing, from new ecological economics to ecological anthropology, academicians are taking on this "crisis of thought."

Breaking Down Boundaries: Cross-cultural Approaches

Today's communication and transportation technologies force an attention to a global scale of economy, environmental conditions, and shared predicaments—the "big picture." A panoramic view demands that we not only look at other cultures, but learn from them. Paradoxically perhaps, returning to local places illustrates the point. In the dramas of

Libby, Chamba, and Shimokawa, some of the most important actors are those far from and invisible to these small towns: the purchasers and consumers who drive the rates of timber extraction and related regional and international transport. In this sense, the extraction, processing, transport, and consumption of timber spans not only local communities but across continents. Timber trade is only one example of ways in which the many reaches of the globe are interconnected. And so we can think simultaneously of global as well as local situations in an interdependence of culture and scale.

This ability to shift our gaze in terms of scale, from local, across regional, national, and international boundaries, is one of the ways this project encourages moving beyond or breaking down boundaries. In the midst of debates about the general merits of "global" versus "local" scales of analyses of cultural and environmental change, we recognize the need for multilevel scales of analysis. Attempting to address global environmental or economic problems can be overwhelming, making local action seem more appealing and perhaps more manageable. Yet we cannot deny the ties between localities, or assume them to be discrete, impenetrable entities. Thus, a simultaneous focus on local processes and the flows between them through broader regional, national, and international interactions is necessary for more realistic assessments and effective action.

Scholars and activists in other countries are rigorously pursuing work on the environment. India may well be at the forefront in terms of both scholarship and activism. Scholars such as Madhav Gadgil and Ramachandra Guha offer integrated analyses of historical, as well as current, social and economic factors involved in environmental struggles in India.[10] For decades Japan, with its unprecedented development in the wake of World War II, has grappled with the results of environmental problems, such as the Minamata Disease. China, with its burgeoning population and developing economy, is beginning to re-examine its historical infatuation with nature. Xiaoshan Yang suggests that such an inquiry may provide perspectives from which to explore remedies for some of the recent serious abuse of China's environment (Chapter 6, this volume). Facing massive extraction of their forest resources, residents of Southeast Asia are actively confronting the socioeconomic and political entanglements of extractive, external powers from Japan.

Western understandings of human-environmental interactions might benefit from both the mistakes and the successes that these other perspectives offer. This collection of essays presents such a mix of perspectives. By focusing on situations in America's Northwest, across the Pacific Rim, and throughout Asia, using the methods, approaches, and languages of a variety of disciplines, these essays explore particular contexts within and comparative cases across these areas.

Asia and the Pacific Northwest

We see the upper arc of the Pacific basin as a useful area for comparative and integrative purposes. Although Asia and the Pacific Northwest are themselves somewhat artificially described areas, this investigation focuses within and across them in order to explore shared issues such as increased demands on natural resources and rapid economic change, as well as the ways these cultural and environmental challenges are uniquely addressed in different areas. More pointedly, this collection, as sponsored and administered through the Maureen and Mike Mansfield Center at the University of Montana, seeks to address those connections that Ambassador and Senator Mike Mansfield himself pursued across the Pacific Rim, from the mountains and communities of Montana to those in Japan and beyond.

In October 1995, scholars and practitioners from a number of disciplines gathered for a three-day symposium in Missoula, Montana. They were invited to consider the ways in which various communities of people on both sides of the Pacific envision their landscapes as well as environmental challenges such as natural resource development, economic diversification, and environmental protection. Under the broad title, "Landscapes and Communities in Asia and the Pacific Northwest," the symposium attempted to facilitate cross-disciplinary and cross-cultural communication.

The essays in this collection arise from presentations and discussions during that symposium, and they offer ways to consider the complexities that we sum under the terms "landscape" and "community." The papers do not suggest that there is a unified way of discussing the interactive relationship between people and environments. Quite the contrary, they reflect a variety of approaches and often include varying degrees of optimism or pessimism about the future (contrast, for example, essays by Vaclav Smil and Rhoads Murphey, in this volume).

Because numerous interrelated themes are woven through these papers, the chapters could have been organized in any number of ways.

We chose to arrange them in four broad sections. The essays offer parameters for dialogue as well as examples of how disciplines are beginning to share approaches, methods, and languages.

Through ethnographic and historical case studies, textual, cartographic, and narrative analysis, and critical examination of our own discourses and methods, the papers in this volume engage in a cross-disciplinary and cross-cultural discussion of ways that various groups envision and inhabit their environments.

The pieces contribute to environmental considerations in the study of Asia—on both sides of the Pacific. They also help to broaden the discussion of environment in the United States by exploring Asian perspectives and case studies, in particular those of Indonesia, China, and Japan. The effort to expand cross-cultural communication is limited, we admit, as all papers were written in English and presented in a particular place and time. Our hope is that this effort can contribute to a fuller cross-cultural discussion, where papers on related topics in Asian languages will continue to be exchanged and translated into English and other Asian languages.

In the end, the collection of essays does not constitute a step-by-step manual for resolving crises of natural environments and human cultures. Rather, we offer them as a beginning step in the process: that of first defining the challenges and refining our questions. The complexity of the crises demands participation across academic and professional disciplines, and across cultures. This volume demonstrates that such collaboration is both possible and productive.

Notes

1. See Dan Flores, "Place: An Argument for Bioregional History," *Environmental History Review* 18 (Winter 1994): 1–18; Bill Kittredge, *Owning It All* (Minneapolis: Graywolf Press, 1987); Yi-Fu Tuan, *Space and Place: The Perspective of Experience* (Minneapolis: University of Minnesota Press, 1977); Wallace Stegner, *The American West as Living Space* (Ann Arbor: University of Michigan Press, 1987); and others on sense of place.

2. See Dan Kemmis's chapter in this collection as well as his book, *The Good City and the Good Life* (New York: Houghton Mifflin, 1995).

3. Information on Libby's historical struggle can be found in Richard Waverly Poston's *Small Town Renaissance* (New York: Harper and Brothers, 1950); additional historical materials were provided by Mark White, archeologist for the U.S. Forest Service, Libby, Montana.

4. For more on forest use practices in Chamba, see Karen Gaul, "Negotiated Positions and Shifting Terrains: Apprehension of Forest Resources in the Western Himalaya" (Ph.D. diss., University of Massachusetts, Amherst, 1994).

5. For data on the Shimokawa case, we have drawn from the research of Cliff Montagne, Department of Soil Sciences, Montana State University, Bozeman.

6. Gary Meffe et al., *Principles of Conservation Biology* (Sunderland, MA: Sinauer Associates, 1994), p. 20.

7. See Ben Orlove, "Ecological Anthropology," *Annual Review of Anthropology* 9 (1980): 235–273.

8. See Scott Slovic's book, *Seeking Awareness in American Nature Writing* (Salt Lake City: University of Utah Press, 1992), as well as his chapter in this volume.

9. For discussions on ways we construct and interact with "wilderness," see William Cronon, ed., "The Trouble with Wilderness; or, Getting Back to the Wrong Nature," in Cronon, ed., *Uncommon Ground* (New York: W.W. Norton and Company, 1995, pp. 69–90); Roderick Nash, *Wilderness and the American Mind* (New Haven: Yale University Press, 1967); and Dan Flores, "The Great *Despoblado* and Other Fantasies of Wilderness," in Flores, ed., *Horizontal Yellow: Nature and History in the Near Southwest* (Albuquerque: University of New Mexico Press, 1999), pp. 1–35.

10. See Madhav Gadgil and Ramachandra Guha, *Ecology and Equity* (New York: Routledge, 1995), and *Fissured Land* (London: Oxford University Press, 1990).

Part I

Northwest Voices

In the midst of debates about "local" versus "global" scales of analyses of cultural and environmental change, we recognize the need to begin at our own doorstep: Missoula, Montana, in particular, and the Pacific Northwest more broadly. This is a landscape from which we can embark upon an exploration that shifts from a local scale across regional, national, and international boundaries, and transgresses traditional academic disciplines and fields.

Former Missoula Mayor Dan Kemmis opens with a discussion of the city we inhabit and its relationship with the surrounding environment. While cities have often been seen as intruders on the landscape, especially in the American West, he argues that the city of Missoula can—and does—function as a nucleus for the surrounding areas. The city ties areas of the countryside to itself and to each other, and offers opportunities for integration with more distant areas through the concentration of communication and transportation technologies within its structure. This symbiotic relationship between rural areas and urban ones offers new possibilities for understanding and practicing a sustainable relationship between human activity and the ecosystems that sustain it.

In his address, "The Instability of Stability," Jack Ward Thomas reflects on the contemporary difficulties of managing American national forests but asserts unequivocally that the solution to these complex predicaments is not "devolvement" of our public lands. His paper harkens back to the discussion of the residents of Libby, Montana, who also have a stake in the protection, use, and exploitation of national forests.

With some realistic acknowledgement of a contemporary West that is made up of much more than pristine mountain landscapes, these chapters offer a sense of the struggles and ongoing negotiation between divergent perspectives in some particularly western communities and surrounding landscapes.

1

Focusing the Countryside

Daniel Kemmis

A low haze hangs on the houses
—firewood smoke and mist—
Slanting far to the Kamo river
and the distant Uji hills.
Farmwomen lead down carts
loaded with long white radish;
I pack my bike with books—
all roads descend toward town

—Gary Snyder
"Work to Do Toward Town"

We like history to accommodate our sense of order and proportion by dividing itself into neatly identifiable centuries. While it rarely succeeds in placing its corner-turning events squarely on years ending with several zeroes, history does sometimes provide us with usable centuries roughly corresponding to our numerology. The nineteenth century, for example, as an historically meaningful era, is now generally said to have occupied the years and events between Napoleon's defeat at Waterloo in 1815 and the Archduke Ferdinand's assassination in Sarajevo in 1914.

By that accounting, the twentieth century may prove to be short in years, if not in tumult. If it began with the world's descent into a series of bloody global conflicts, it may well have ended in 1989 in Berlin, Prague, Gdansk, and Moscow with the almost eerily peaceful conclusion of the Cold War. But if we were to insist that history provide us with an event closer to the year 2000 to mark the turn of this century, we might well look to Hong Kong's long-planned departure from the British Empire in 1997. That event may teach us, as nothing else has yet done, of the power of cities and city economies to remake the world and its history.

Forced into the empire in 1842 at the height of the Opium War, Hong Kong had served as a strategic British outpost until its capture by the Japanese during World War II. Restored to the empire in 1945, the city soon assumed a new geopolitical significance when, with Mao Zedong's communist victory on mainland China, Hong Kong became, along with Taiwan, a refuge for those most intensely motivated to escape the communist regime. It was against the background of the Cold War's East-West struggle that Hong Kong's fate was most often viewed, especially after 1984, when Britain negotiated with Beijing an agreement to return Hong Kong to China in 1997. But in fact Hong Kong had prepared itself to play a very different role in history, a role having far less to do with the struggle between communism and capitalism than with the place of cities in the political order. If 1997 proves to be more than a blip on the chart of history, it will be because Hong Kong's transition marks, more strongly than any other single event, the end of the age of the nation-state and the refocusing of human affairs around an almost forgotten but in fact irrepressible alternative: the city-state.

In the era of the nation-state, we came to take for granted those maps of the world where every single bit of land mass (except Antarctica) was assigned a color corresponding to the nation claiming sovereignty over it. So, with Hong Kong, it was assumed that the new maps produced in 1997 would simply change the city's coloration from, say, the green of the commonwealth to the orange of the People's Republic of China. But in fact, long before 1997, Hong Kong had irretrievably redrawn the real, living map of its part of the world. It had done so simply by succeeding as a city. Its remarkable economic success had, like a powerful magnet, etched its lines of force into the surrounding countryside, as if oblivious to the fact that many of those surroundings were still part of the People's Republic. By 1990, Beijing had already granted to Guangzhou Province the right to operate as a "special economic zone," enabling this region to carry capitalism much further forward than any other part of the People's Republic. What this amounted to was simply a recognition by the Beijing government that it would be to everyone's advantage to allow Hong Kong to exercise its natural economic influence within its own region.

Once that influence had been acknowledged, there was little chance of a reversal. China's need for foreign currency would not be diminishing after 1997, and long before then it had become clear that Hong Kong could generate far more of that currency if its natural economic relationship to its surrounding region were given the freest possible rein. Reduced to its simplest terms, what all this meant was that the historical logic of the city-state had become more compelling than the logic of the nation-state. To understand the historical significance of 1997, then, we need to consider in more general terms why the predominance of the nation-state in the modern era has begun to give way to the postmodern rebirth of the city-state.

After decades of observing cities more closely than any other American journalist of his generation, Neal Peirce finally concluded that as the economy had become more global, nations had steadily lost their economic relevance. "Nation-states," Peirce wrote, "excel at war; they are proving increasingly limited and sometimes shockingly incompetent in the arena of economics."[1] But the very globalization of the economy that had weakened nationhood from without was at the same time strengthening another, internal challenge to nationhood. The new configuration of the global economy, Peirce wrote, "drives one to visualize our great cities, their suburbs, exurbs, and geographic realms of influence as *citistates*—entities that perform as critical actors, more on their own in the world economy than anyone would have dreamed since the birth of the nation-state in the sixteenth and seventeenth centuries."[2]

Peirce's book, *Citistates*, was written after the fall of communism had opened the door to a "new world order" that would see more challenges to established nationhood in five years than had been witnessed in the preceding fifty. But well before Berlin tore down the wall that had sundered its cityhood, Jane Jacobs had prophetically sounded the two themes that Peirce now made the basis of his city-state argument. Like Peirce, Jacobs had seen that the essence of nationhood had always had more to do with war and defense than with the creative, productive, entrepreneurial work of economies. Convinced that city regions alone produced prosperity, while nations pursued a very different mission, Jacobs foresaw that the outcome of the struggle between the Soviet and the American empires would center upon their mutual effort to force each other to spend (mainly through the arms race) into oblivion or submission. "Today," she wrote in 1984, "the Soviet Union and the

United States each predicts and anticipates the economic decline of the other. Neither will be disappointed."[3]

Having apparently won the Cold War, Americans may be tempted to say that the Soviet Union's capitulation reflects its economic decline and our ascendancy. But that viewpoint requires us to ignore the overwhelming national debt we incurred in the course of the war, both the domestic debt of government borrowing and the international debt brought about by years of radical imbalance between imports and exports. The huge backlog of social problems, ranging through crime and drug use, homelessness, welfare abuse, and lack of health care, is one more form of indebtedness incurred in our single-minded pursuit of national ascendancy. Now, with the Cold War behind us, our inclination is to attempt to address these issues with new national policies and programs. But if Peirce and Jacobs are right, the nation is likely to prove as clumsy, inefficient, and ineffective in this arena as it ever has.

To the extent that the solution of social problems depends upon the sustained and sustainable generation of prosperity, the time seems clearly to have arrived to acknowledge that the nation-state is bankrupt—literally broke in terms of its multiple and crushing debts, but also bankrupt in terms of its capacity either to generate or effectively to reinvest the prosperity required to address the problems it continues to treat as its obligation and domain. "But if national governments are losing their power to innovate, to reposture a society," Peirce asks, "who will? To us [Peirce and his researchers], the inescapable conclusion is that the citistates have the potential to tackle these challenges."[4]

Why might cities, or "city-states," prove to be more capable than nations of generating prosperity or of deploying that prosperity to address social problems? The answer is necessarily complex, but behind any extended argument for the economic or social efficacy of the city lies the simple fact that a city is by its nature organic—it bears to its surrounding region a natural, organic relationship that is the very essence of a successful economy.[5] Unless we understand the compelling power of these natural organisms, we will be repeatedly astounded by their ability to wear down and render irrelevant national and other artificial boundaries—and we will therefore fail to appreciate or constructively assist the transition from the age of the nation-state to the new global age of the city-state. But with or without our conscious assistance, city economies will continue, relentlessly, to remake the world.

Phrases like "a successful economy" or "a growing economy" roll so easily from our tongues, pens, or keyboards that we no longer pay much attention to what they really mean, or what it might take for them to mean anything at all. To speak of "an economy" implies that there must be more than one, and that each has an identity, a shape, and boundaries of its own. But our language soon betrays a remarkable mental laziness on this score. No day passes, for example, without some Montana official speaking about "the Montana economy." But who can seriously believe that something as vital and fluid as "an economy" could be contained or in any meaningful sense defined by a set of arbitrarily drawn straight lines across the landscape, lines crossing the Continental Divide, encompassing on one side of that divide millions of acres of arid grassland and on the other more millions of acres of timber and mountain valleys? The economic activity generated by such landscapes cannot possibly be improved or intensified or made to produce more sustained prosperity by imposing upon it artificial boundaries like those of state lines or artificial names like "the Montana economy." But the economic activity generated by such landscapes might indeed be intensified and turned to greater human good and purpose by attending closely to how such landscapes and such economic activity, between them, define in their own terms something that can meaningfully be called "economies." In every case, such real economies turn out to be nothing other than the organic relationship of cities and towns to their surroundings.

It is almost impossible to describe those relationships without sooner or later resorting to the image of a nucleus within a larger structure. Sometimes the larger structure looks like a living cell, sometimes more like an atom, but from either perspective, the city supplies the function of a nucleus for an organized set of entities and activities surrounding it. Like a cell or an atom, a city region is a distinct, meaningful, indeed indispensable structure of wholeness, without which (at least from the perspective of human beings) the world itself would lose all coherence. And like a cell or an atom, the city region depends for its own coherence upon its nucleus, without which it can neither exist nor function.

I always enjoy flying home to Missoula, beginning to recognize once again familiar landscape after traveling to places I have not seen before, anticipating the multitude of ways in which the city will soon again engage my attention and energy. But I also enjoy flying into Missoula, or any other city, because of the opportunity it provides to observe the steadily intensifying level of activity that appears as the plane nears the city. From scattered farmsteads and villages, the network of highways, rail lines, and powerlines begins to converge as the density of dwellings and other buildings steadily increases. Finally, if the city is a large one, the skyline of the central business district will appear, proclaiming dramatically that here activity is so intensified and concentrated that it cannot be contained at ground level but has been pushed into the sky itself.

Nothing is so fundamental to a city as this concentration of humans and human activity within a small compass. All the problems that we call urban problems derive from this compactness, but we remain willing to struggle with those problems because of some constellation of human goods that seems unattainable except by means of such concentration. In fact, from the earliest institution of the marketplace, the gathering of humans and human activity in one place has remained crucial to the functioning of economies. Here the image of the nucleus becomes more than a metaphor as we see how the city market, by concentrating in one spot a certain critical mass of human energy and activity, creates in a very nearly physical sense a gravitational field whose lines of force both expand the vitality of the center and at the same time reach into and organize the surrounding countryside. It is precisely the synergy created by this concentration of human activity that makes the city the fundamental engine of all economic growth and change. When such engines assume the proportions of a Hong Kong, they can affect events on a global scale. But very small towns can also help us understand how the creative synergy of concentration operates to make economies work.

For years, my favorite local example of such synergy has been provided by the small ranching community of Drummond, fifty miles upriver from Missoula, where Flint Creek, descending from the snow-capped Pintlar Range, flows into the Clark Fork River. The Flint Creek and Clark Fork valley bottoms provide excellent winter pastures and hay meadows, supplementing the higher summer pastures in the surrounding mountains and more or less guaranteeing that Drummond's economy would center around cattle ranching. But any observant visitor to the Drummond area will notice that the animals grazing these pastures are not just cattle in general; most of them are bulls, raised to be sold as breeding sires to ranches throughout the Northern Rockies. Raising bulls is a very specialized form of ranching, requiring everything from expert knowledge of feed grains and hay to exceptionally sturdy fences for containing the sometimes explosive energy of bovine masculinity. Because buying a good bull is such a crucial choice for any rancher, most buyers want to be able to inspect their choices carefully and to have a suitable range of sires to choose from. This adds up to a need for one single place in which a number of bulls can be shown and auctioned, and here again the heft and feistiness of these animals means that normal standards for sales ring or loading chute construction will not suffice. No single rancher could supply enough bulls or an adequate auction ring to make such a market work, but in Drummond, the combination of landscape, climate, and entrepreneurship created over several decades a synergy that gradually converted more and more of the surrounding ranches to this specialized purpose, and eventually turned Drummond into the center of the region's breeding bull market.

This little economy could not exist or be sustained without Drummond as its nucleus. The market itself—in this case the auction ring and adjoining railhead—is the cornerstone of the economy. Less obvious but probably no less crucial is the role of the Wagon Wheel Cafe in bringing a number of ranchers together for coffee, lies, and gossip every morning. No one morning's storytelling would be likely to stand out as a turning point in the industry, but there is little room for doubt that over the course of many such mornings, the minutiae of skills and wisdom peculiar to bull-raising have circulated, competed, triumphed, or been vanquished, and finally have woven themselves more tightly together into the synergy that has earned Drummond the title of "The Bullshippers' Capital of the World."

Meanwhile, downriver in Missoula, a different kind and level of synergy had been evolving. After decades of relying upon timber-cutting and sawmill production as the base and center of its economy, Missoula began to read the handwriting on the wall that was eventually to transform economic reality throughout the Northern Rockies and the Pacific Northwest, as a convergence of overcutting and heightened environmental awareness sharply curtailed the supply of timber to the region's sawmills. As a number of sawmills closed in and around Missoula in the 1970s and 1980s, local business leaders began looking for ways to shore up what appeared to be a shrinking if not disintegrating economic base. After an early round of clumsy, often painful and divisive efforts at industrial recruiting, the Missoula Economic Development Corporation began paying closer attention to what was actually happening within the Missoula economy, as a means of understanding how it might most effectively work to strengthen that economy.

The group gradually became aware that alongside the still very substantial lumber-producing industry, a number of pockets or "clusters" of other kinds of businesses had developed over the years. Missoula's two major hospitals, for example, along with the University of Montana, had begun serving as centers around which a number of biomedical research and development enterprises had clustered. The number of writers and artists living in and around Missoula had grown steadily over the years, and with that increase had come a growing number of galleries, small publishers, and organizations offering workshops and retreats for artists and writers from throughout the West. Missoula had established a reputation as a bicycle-friendly city, and related to this, partly as cause, partly as consequence, two national bicycle organizations, one devoted to bicycle touring and the other to bicycle safety, had located their headquarters in Missoula, employing between them several dozen people.

As the Missoula Economic Development Corporation gained a clearer understanding of the fact of this clustering and the role of its resulting synergy in the expansion of the Missoula economy, it began using this insight as a means of attracting more employers to Missoula. This was the argument we used, for example, when the Boone and Crockett Club, the exclusive trophy-hunting organization founded by Teddy Roosevelt, decided to move its national headquarters from the Washington, D.C., area to a western location. Once Missoula found itself on the club's short list of possible destinations, we began feeding the club's officers information about the growing number of similar activities already located in Missoula.

Boone and Crockett's decision to relocate arose in the context of its own redefinition of its mission, especially its growing understanding that its old function of maintaining careful records of prize trophies had been gradually overshadowed by its work on protection of habitat for the animals it had previously seen only as prey. If the club was going to devote itself increasingly to habitat preservation, it made sense for its central office to be somewhere near where such habitat existed. And it made sense (or so we argued) for its headquarters to be located in a city that was both surrounded by such habitat and increasingly busy with a variety of activities concerned with preservation and enhancement of that habitat.

The work of The University of Montana's School of Forestry on habitat issues had already led the Boone and Crockett Club to endow a chair in that field at the Forestry School. But were the club's officers aware that the Rocky Mountain Elk Foundation, devoted to the protection of elk habitat, had already relocated its national headquarters to Missoula or that Region One of the National Forest Service had long been headquartered in Missoula? We recounted how, every spring, the International Wildlife Film Festival brought wildlife filmmakers from all quarters of the globe to Missoula for juried showings of the best new films about wild animals. All this, we argued, created a fertile cluster of actors and activities within which the newly defined mission of the Boone and Crockett Club would be very much at home.

Although Missoula had made its way onto the club's short list of possible new homes, it was not alone on that list, and as the club's decision neared, the competition escalated. We began to hear of efforts by some of our competitors to raise doubts about Missoula's suitability as the organization's headquarters. "Yes, Missoula is home to all those groups and activities it brags about—but Boone and Crockett is still a hunting organization; hunting is becoming more controversial, and Missoula seems to thrive on and breed such controversy," one argument ran. "We've heard that Missoula is also home to a number of antihunting activists and groups. Do you really want to run the risk of their picketing your board of directors' meetings?"

The club's response to these cautionary arguments, as it was reported to me, confirmed my already growing conviction that the synergy of closely related activities lay somehow at the heart of economic vitality. "Yes," the club said, in effect, "we are a hunting organization, but that now means that we have to be a conservation organization. Conservation is challenging work; no one has all the answers about how best to do it, and we think sound and sustainable answers are more likely to come from vigorous debates among committed practitioners than from isolated efforts of people or organizations who think they already know the answers." And with that, the club called the mayor's office to say that it had decided to move its headquarters to Missoula.

By itself, this decision would not make or break the Missoula economy; it would probably not even have a statistically significant impact on it. But for me, the episode was most important because of what it enabled us to understand about how the city functions as an organic economy, and how that economy necessarily depends upon and shapes the equally organic relationship between Missoula and its surroundings.

If the Economic Development Corporation had been asked to give a name to its efforts to persuade the Boone and Crockett Club to move to

Missoula, it would probably have called it "business recruitment." As a nonprofit organization, though, the club does not fit into the category of what we usually call "businesses," and in fact there are those who have argued that only private, for-profit enterprises should count as instances of successful business recruitment. On the other hand, nonprofit organizations like the Rocky Mountain Elk Foundation or Bikecentennial can become major employers in the local economy, so it would seem short-sighted to exclude them from consideration for "business recruitment."

As more groups discover Missoula's synergistic clustering around issues of habitat and ecosystem, they have begun to examine more closely the relationship between Missoula and the 10,000 or so square mile region for which Missoula serves in so many ways as the hub or nucleus. Like the Boone and Crockett Club, other organizations have come to this new way of understanding what Missoula is all about in the course of re-examining their own role in a changing world. The Forest Service offers what for me has been an intriguing example of this interlocking evolution of the city and its major economic components.

Located in the heart of the timber-producing reaches of the Northern Rockies, Missoula was destined to be a timber town, and with the late-nineteenth-century addition of The University of Montana and especially its School of Forestry to the city, it perhaps became inevitable that not only would sawmills, plywood plants, and a paper mill be located in Missoula, but that the federal agency with responsibility for managing all those millions of acres of trees would also have a major presence here. When the Forest Service established its system of regions and regional headquarters around the country, Missoula became one of those headquarters, taking special pride, of course, in the fact that this was not just any region, but Region One. Both the Forest Service Smokejumper Center and the national fire research lab were also located in Missoula. All this Forest Service presence simply testifies to the extent to which Missoula's economy throughout most of this century had centered around trees, and especially around the cutting of trees.

That era has rather abruptly ended, not only in Missoula, but throughout the Pacific Northwest. Its final chapter coincided with the sobering retrenchment of the federal government that so characterized the Reagan-Bush era, continuing into the Clinton-Gore administration with the recognition that the time borrowed for so many decades with borrowed money has run out, that the federal government must learn to live in real time, on real money, and that there is no way to make that transition except by a substantial rethinking of the role of agencies like the Forest Service. So just as the sustainability of the northern forests has come under searing scrutiny, the Forest Service has had to turn that same scrutiny on its own mission and its own methods (also see Jack Ward Thomas, Chapter 2, this volume).

One major product of that re-examination has been a shift in the Forest Service's emphasis from commodity production to what the Service calls "ecosystem management." Having settled upon that phrase, the agency at once found itself embroiled in an internal debate about the scope of the term, and specifically about whether it applied only to the natural world or whether human activities and human communities would have to be factored into the work of managing ecosystems. One voice said, "Stick with what you know," which meant trees and streams and animals. The other voice said, "It doesn't make any sense to manage ecosystems as if humans aren't part of them, and furthermore, if we don't help timber-based communities evolve sustainable economies, they will put so much pressure on the forests that we'll never achieve sustainability there, either."

Without exactly being asked for my opinion, I found myself siding with the second voice in this debate, for reasons that had nothing to do with the mission of the Forest Service, but everything to do with what it meant to be Missoula in the 1990s. As sawmills closed down throughout the region, including several in Missoula itself, I became aware of how much more resilient to these dislocations Missoula appeared than many of the smaller towns in our vicinity. In fact, Missoula seemed to be thriving as many of our smaller neighbors hung on the ropes of extinction. But for some reason I found myself increasingly nervous about that state of affairs. Part of what had fueled the growth in Missoula's economy during this period had been the expansion of retail and other service industries in Missoula, much of that expansion coming at the expense of retail and service trade in the smaller towns. While the resulting boost in Missoula's prosperity certainly made my budgets easier to balance, I could see that we were at the same time building up a backlog of expensive social problems that were themselves in no small part a result of the decline of the economic and social fabric of the smaller towns. Sustainability, it seemed, could not be viewed only as an issue in the forests or the small timber-dependent communities: Missoula needed to be concerned about the sustainability of its own prosperity, and the harder we looked at that issue, the more obvious it became that Missoula's long-range welfare would be better served by supporting the viability of the smaller towns around us than by growing at their expense.

Before long, the Missoula Economic Development Corporation had renamed itself the Missoula Area Economic Development Corporation (MAEDC) to reflect its commitment to promoting prosperity throughout the region for which Missoula served as the nucleus. With MAEDC's help, the City of Missoula and The University of Montana began working on a project to map and model the economy of this region—to understand more clearly the mutually sustaining relationship between the nucleus and the rest of the cell. The Forest Service joined in, as its internal debate began to settle out on the side of acknowledging that "ecosystem management" was not going to succeed without accounting for the human role in the ecosystem. What made it easier for the Forest Service to contribute to this effort was the fact, increasingly evident, that the region for which Missoula served as nucleus corresponded very closely with the Clark Fork River drainage, and therefore with a naturally bounded ecosystem.

For too much of our history, the business of cities has been perceived as a threat to the maintenance of ecological integrity. But if city-states are re-emerging as primary forms of human organization at the same time that environmental awareness is assuming global dimensions, it may be because we are just now gaining a kind of species understanding that human inhabitation must become more organic if it is to conform to organic ecosystems. The adaptation of life forms to one another and to the limitations and possibilities of their surroundings is what evolution has always been about, and it is precisely such evolution and adaptation which drives the re-emergence of the city-state.

In fact, what we were experiencing here in Missoula was our local equivalent of the Hong Kong story. In two entirely different settings, national governments were beginning to acknowledge that their own capacity to generate and sustain prosperity had waned, if it had ever really existed, and that the organic relationship of a city to its surrounding region had at least to be enlisted as an ally if not in fact as the primary actor in that work. The magnitude of this shift in perspective can hardly be exaggerated. Nowhere in this country and almost nowhere in the world for centuries now have we recognized the natural, self-defining boundaries of city-regions. The closest we ever come in this country is the almost entirely arbitrary lumping of several counties together for various state and federal purposes. The failure to recognize the organic, and therefore primary character of city-regions, the tendency to treat them instead as stepchildren of the "important" political entities of state and nation, is evident in the very name we give these arbitrary regions. Rather than letting these city-regions define themselves on the map, we cluster counties into "substate planning regions," as unartfully named as they are clumsily drawn.

Our political language, however, goes far beyond this in blinding us to the natural relationships between cities and their surroundings. By referring time and again to imaginary places called, in our political discourse, "rural America," "urban America," and "suburban America," we create an image and a practice of separate urban, rural, and suburban polities, and we all but eliminate the possibility of acting upon a sound understanding of how city center, suburbs, and rural surroundings might together operate as an effective engine of economic prosperity.

A trip to Washington, D.C., near the end of my first term as mayor left me sadly wiser on this score. I was one of a dozen panelists from what the invitation had called "rural America" invited to brief the secretary of agriculture on the best means of stemming the economic decline of so many rural areas. As the event unfolded, I found myself deeply impressed by the wisdom and passion of my fellow panelists from "rural America." Their consistent urging to leverage scarce federal resources by using face-to-face local collaboration to tap the immeasurable reserves of local know-how and resourcefulness seemed to me the best advice the national government could receive about how to deploy the relatively few dollars it might be able to devote to rural programs.

It was here, however, that the conversation became disconcerting. I could not shake off the perception that we were in part being asked to help the Agriculture Department come up with reasons to continue to have national rural programs at all. After all, if the truly effective resources are regional or local, why strain so hard to find some "networking" or "clearinghouse" or "leadership training" role for the national government? "Because we have to do something," the very walls of the imperial auditorium seemed to whisper, "or else why would we need to be here?"

As I listened to my colleagues make their case, it occurred to me that there might be a different, vastly more efficient and effective mechanism for accomplishing all the laudable human-resource-mobilizing objectives the panelists were asking the secretary and his department to pursue.

Throughout history, the role of cities has been precisely to focus, organize, and multiply the resources of the surrounding regions to which they are organically connected. In the era of the nation-state, we had not only lost sight of this essential role of cities, but what is worse, national policy had misled both cities and their rural surroundings into believing that they could prosper independently of one another, especially if each of them could open a wide enough pipeline to Washington. It would be difficult to overstate the extent of the damage this well-intentioned national legacy has imposed upon the only sustainable economies capable in fact of addressing the long list of woes I heard from the rural panel that morning, or the equally long list of my fellow mayors, whenever they get a chance to plead for more federal dollars for "urban America."

So it was that I argued to the secretary that the best long-term favor he could do for rural America would be to admit that there is no such place, nor any such thing as the "rural economy," just as there is no such place as "urban America" nor such a thing as the "urban economy." But there are real places like Louisville, Kentucky, and the region surrounding it, or real economies like that of Missoula—not the city itself of roughly 60,000 urbanites, but the city and its two dozen or so surrounding small towns whose long-term prosperity depends upon our figuring out how to make the region operate as the natural economy it is capable of being.[6]

If this were true, then one of the best ways for the Agriculture Department to help its rural constituents would be to insist upon a rigorous review of the long list of national policies that have exploded the natural integrity of city-regions, deluding city centers, suburbs, and rural surroundings into ignoring their mutual dependency. The result has been a gigantic and acutely nearsighted disinvestment in both central cities and rural areas, to the short-term but unsustainable advantage of that other, ultimate nonplace, "suburban America."

David Rusk, the former mayor of Albuquerque and author of *Cities Without Suburbs* (1993), refers to "four decades of misguided policies that have favored suburban development over inner cities, fragmenting urban areas by race and class."[7] The nation-state response to this situation is to begin asking how new national programs can right the balance. But no currently conceivable amount of federal largess to either city centers or rural areas could begin to compare in magnitude or effectiveness with the re-investment that would naturally occur if the national government were to stop enabling the illusion of these places' independence from one another.

Rusk cites the example of Seattle, where a new regional strategy resulted in the rejection of plans for a new 4,500–home suburb twenty miles from Seattle—exactly the kind of sprawl-and-flight phenomenon that national policies have so successfully encouraged. Seattle has begun to understand that its long-term viability can only be secured by acting like a city-region or city-state, and therefore it has begun to knit together the destinies of city, suburbs, and surrounding countryside. By deciding not to build a new suburb, the city-state at one and the same time preserves surrounding forests and, in Rusk's words, "strengthens the plan of [former] Mayor Norm Rice to rebuild Seattle's declining neighborhoods, since it will keep demand for housing within the city higher."[8]

Rusk argues, as Neil Peirce does, that those cities that, one way or another, have maintained or recaptured the natural, organic relationship between central city and suburbs are, by a number of measures, more successful than those metropolitan areas that have fallen for the siren song of suburban independence. Income disparities between central cities and suburbs, for example, are far smaller in the more organic city-states. It is the dysfunctionally cut-off central cities that teeter on the brink of municipal bankruptcy; Rusk found that credit ratings for more organically integrated city-states averaged two full grades higher than those for isolated inner cities. Here we have a telling measure of the role of city-states in the larger economy: The global bond market is signaling in unmistakable terms the fact that organic city-states are economically far more viable than those cities whose suburbs have let national policy persuade them that they are independent of their central cites. Neal Peirce goes a step further, presenting an expanding body of research demonstrating that those suburbs showing the most durable economic strength are the ones ringing the most economically healthy central cities.

The expanding awareness of the mutual interdependence of city and suburb establishes a logical plumb line that leads inevitably to the recognition that not only must central cities and their suburbs acknowledge their combined wholeness if they are to thrive and prosper, but that they in turn must understand their organic relatedness to the surrounding countryside. So, for example, Mayor Jerry Abramson has insisted that Louisville begin exploring how the long-term viability of that city might depend upon the economic health of the hundreds of small towns for which Louisville serves as the hub. So Berlin has asked the German Bundestag formally to recognize and allow the city to pursue its natural connectedness to its surrounding region, as Beijing had recognized Hong Kong's relationship with Guangzhou. So every lesson I had ever learned as mayor led me to argue to the secretary of agriculture that the best favor he could do for "rural America" would be to meet with the secretary of housing and urban development and the secretary of transportation and agree to dismantle all the national programs that had made "rural America," "urban America," and "suburban America" think they could prosper in isolation from one another.

I knew, of course, that a message so outlandish (in the root sense of the word) could not be digested in a morning's briefing. But it was not until the end of the session that I fully understood how deeply entrenched in the very concrete of Washington's foundations is the resistance to such an argument. Looking back, I saw a hint of it the day before when I had told one of my own senators what I intended to say to the secretary. Senator Max Baucus's response, which I found commendably wistful, was that rural senators had no choice but to fight for rural programs just to keep the growing urban centers from getting all the money. So I should have been prepared for the secretary of agriculture's closing words to us: "We just want rural America to get the same treatment urban America gets—no more and no less." That, I thought, was a wish that might well come true, to the deepening dismay of both rural and urban America.

An outlander can never go to Washington without being moved once again by the palpable sense of history clinging to the place. As a farm boy who became a mayor, I am always drawn to Jefferson and his elegant memorial, always reminded of his distrust of cities, of his impossible dream that the frontier would allow us forever to create farmers faster than people piled up in cities. The secretary of agriculture's closing words were just another version of that forlorn Jeffersonian formula for parity between the false enemies of "rural America" and "urban America." But it was Jefferson too who warned us against ever getting caught in the dead doctrines of a bygone age—especially his own—and who called for a revolution every now and then to keep alive the human meaning behind his timeless revolutionary invocation of "the course of human events." The nation created by Mr. Jefferson's document has so commanded our attention that we can barely conceive that "the course of human events" has finally brought us to the end of the age of the nation-state, and to the renaissance of the city-state. We will not get on with the work of our own age until that realization strikes home.

Notes

1. Neal R. Peirce, *Citistates* (Washington, DC: Seven Locks Press, 1993), p. 1.
2. Ibid., p. x.
3. Jane Jacobs, *Cities and the Wealth of Nations* (New York: Vintage Books, 1984), p. 200.
4. Peirce, *Citistates*, p. 12.
5. The concept of the organic, as used here, does not lend itself to a precise definition but may be understood generally as meaning "of the nature of an organism," a complex structure whose shape, size, and internal relationships are determined by means of natural adaptation to surrounding conditions, rather than by a plan or design imposed from the outside. The earth itself is organic in these terms. So are continents, and so are the city regions described here.
6. No such city region is an island unto itself, of course, and no self-respecting city-state would expect to prosper without entering into relationships and agreements with others for the provision of such necessities as continental transportation systems or global communications systems. But recognizing organic city regions as primary political and economic structures, and building larger structures to meet these needs, is a vastly different approach from giving a national government the power to pursue rural and urban policies that ignore that organic wholeness.
7. David Rusk, "The Metropolitan Perplex: Suburban Renewal," *Nation Cities Weekly*, November 8, 1993, p. 4.
8. Ibid.

2

The Instability of Stability

Jack Ward Thomas

As my key staff and I suffered through the acrimonious congressional hearings of 1995, I was struck with how many times "stability" or "predictability" of timber supply as an absolute necessity was mentioned by committee members and witnesses. The issue is at the forefront of the discussion of how national forests should be managed. These continuing debates and changes shake the pillars of the temple of the faithful who chant many mantras with the same meaning—"nondeclining, even flow," "community stability," "annual sale quantity," "predictability." This refrain was apparent in hundreds of the responses that the Forest Service received to the proposed revised land use planning regulations published in the *Federal Register:* "Give us guaranteed results and assured stability."

Today, I can see that the goal of the "regulated forest" and the resulting predictable output of commodities that I learned in school is no more than a dream, a dream conjured up in very different times. The regulated forest was an attainable goal in a time when there was more cheap (easy to access and log) timber available over the next ridge and risks to the environment were either less appreciated or more palatable than at present. Further, it was assumed that good forestry was, as a matter of course, good wildlife management, good watershed management, and so on.

By now it is obvious that this dream was built on the pillars of the seemingly boundless virgin forest, an ethic of manifest destiny, and the hubris of thinking we could predict the response of nature and humans. Perhaps it is time to recognize that such stability is not attainable in any western region, except for relatively short periods of years or decades.

Why? Consider the variables that interact to affect long-term stability of timber supply. Each variable is subject, more or less independently, to considerable change over the longer term. Taken together, in terms of their interactions, these variables are guaranteed to produce different levels of uncertainty and make attainment of stability unlikely.

It is increasingly apparent that ecological processes are not as well understood nor as predictable as had been assumed by natural resource managers steeped in Clementsian ecological theory of orderly and predictable succession of plant communities from bare ground to a mature, steady state. Ecologists now understand that ecological responses to management actions may vary widely depending on the interactions of influences ranging from vagaries of climate to impacts from previously executed management activities.

Impacts of insects and disease in managed forests are unpredictable and no more than marginally or temporarily controllable. The levels of insect populations and diseases are influenced by the interactions of ecological processes and previous forest management actions, evident enough with native insects and pathogens. Given an adequate time frame, the continued exchange of forest pests and diseases between continents is certain. Consider the consequences of introductions that have already taken place, such as chestnut blight, white pine blister rust, gypsy moth, to name but a few. Methods of "control" are constantly evolving, but the feasibility of such treatments is dependent on a number of factors including environmental impact, cost effectiveness, public acceptability, and legality—all of which fluctuate. Only twenty-five years ago the pesticide DDT was widely applied in the forest environment, highly effective in suppressing some insect "outbreaks," and assumed to be benign to the environment. Times change; DDT is now banned from such use in the United States.

Fire seems less and less "controllable" or even manageable—at least not at the levels assumed in the past. Of course, fire is part and parcel of ecological processes. Debates now rage over appropriate policy toward fire control, the use of prescribed fire, and where, when, if, and how to suppress wildfire. The extent and severity of wildfires that occurred in the past decade would not have been considered likely one or several decades ago.

Drought comes periodically and is not highly predictable in terms of occurrence, duration, severity, or influence. The interactions of weather extremes with other variables that affect the forests can be dramatic. For example, consider the interaction of the spruce budworm outbreak and severe drought in the Blue Mountains of Oregon. If global warming and its effects on weather patterns predicted by some scientists materialize, there will be significant impacts on the ability of managers to forecast commodity production. Others question the entire hypothesis. Uncertainty abounds.

Management actions have a profound effect on future forest conditions; this, of course, is expected. Such management actions vary widely, however, and plans change quickly in the wake of better ecological understanding and shifting markets, public opinion, cost/benefit estimates, funding availability, and legality. Management actions often produce the anticipated results, but they take place with capabilities in risk assessment that are rudimentary at best.

Funding is the fuel that drives most land management activities. Funding for forest management—at least on federal lands—has never come close to programmed levels. Furthermore, it has proven to be neither stable in amount nor in designated purpose. The amounts and focus of funding change dramatically with surges of political tides, changes of persons in power, and the economic and social pressures of the moment. Perhaps the instability of natural resources management is one of the attributes of a vibrant democracy.

The best management plans can be effective only when executed by a qualified work force, one of adequate size, with appropriate skills, and experienced in working within particular ecotypes and cultures. A work force in a constant state of flux as the result of budgetary cuts, shifts in policy, changes in organizational structures, and fluctuations in size does not have the highest probability of producing predictable results. The last several years have been notable for serious changes in work force numbers and skill mix—with significant losses among the most experienced personnel.

Science continues an inexorable march toward "truth" or, at least, some better approximation thereof. Unfortunately, for the sake of predictability, in the course of this march, new knowledge, understanding, and hypotheses for management come even more rapidly to the fore. Inevitably, the results prove perennially unsettling to the status quo and cause adjustments, sometimes dramatic, in management approaches. Stability, it seems, can be maintained only in the absence of new knowledge and technology. In the longer term, achievement of some degree of stability will require a constant balancing act between new knowledge that increases yields and new knowledge that produces changes in or constraints on present practices. Unfortunately, this recognition has led some in political power to seek stability by means of limiting the acquisition, dissemination, or use of new knowledge.

Finally, land management officials must attend to the activities of markets for wood. Markets determine prices to be paid for commodities and, in turn, the feasibility and purpose of management for the production of wood fiber. They also influence the timing of the cutting of trees and the intensity of management. Markets then produce both short- and long-term effects on forest management that can have an unsettling effect on stability and form of supply. Local fluctuations in markets for wood products are becoming even less predictable as timber markets become increasingly worldwide in scope. Closely related to markets for wood are the effects of substitution of other products for wood. As the price of wood increases, more and more substitutes are developed and put on the market, which serve to constrain some wood prices at the margin.

Perhaps the most important variable influencing stability in forest management and resultant timber-cut levels is public opinion. Significant shifts in public opinion can be noted over the past fifty years, with notable fluctuations in the last two to three decades. More recently, public opinion has focused on appropriate forest management and, more specifically, "good management" of public lands. Many laws created during that time have direct influence on federal land management and thus reflect the shifts. Examples include the determined move by foresters to even-aged forest management in the period of 1960–1985 and the subsequent retreat from "clear-cutting" in the early 1990s.

These shifts in public opinions come to bear on land managers through politics. As the political pendulum has swung back and forth over the decades, associated effects on forest management and timber supply are obvious. Politics most obviously play a role in the enactment of laws that can and do dramatically affect forest management. The interactions of such laws as the Multiple-Use Sustained Yield Act, the National Forest Management Act, the Wilderness Act, the Wild and Scenic Rivers Act, the Clean Air Act, the Clean Water Act, the Endangered Species Act, and others, which geometrically increase those effects, have produced a situation where timber yield has become difficult to predict. This predictability is also shaken by administrative actions of regulatory agencies exercising their authorities under these laws. Note the reductions of 80 percent in timber yields from the public lands in the Pacific Northwest as the result of the decisions to list the northern spotted owl, the marbled murrelet, and various species of salmon as "threatened" under the Endangered Species Act. Such listings, of course, were the result of the recognition of more complex social and environmental problems.

Of equal significance is the increase in the number of court cases and appeals as a consequence of these laws and their interactions directed toward actions of federal land management agencies. New court decisions are, in turn, rendered at an ever-increasing rate. Each such court decision has potential to influence the predictability of timber supply and other multiple uses (grazing, fish and wildlife, recreation and water).

Added to this already fluid situation is the recent tendency of both the administration of President Bill Clinton and Congress to micromanage the activities of federal land management agencies through the budget process. Today, the longstanding struggle for power between the executive and legislative bodies over management of federal land is often played out in the form of more and more detailed budget direction to land management agencies. And it is becoming increasingly common for Congress to alter dramatically the effects of law and evolved case law by giving contrary direction in legislative budget action with the caveat, "all other laws notwithstanding." These "quick fixes," however, frequently cause more problems in federal land forest management over the long term than they "fix" in the short term. The increasing acrimony of the debate over the advisability of and approaches to carrying out the timber salvage and release of the "318 sales" mandated in the Rescission Bill of 1995 is such an example.[1]

In response to budget direction in compliance with the applicable laws that are constantly and independently subject to interpretation by courts, government agencies have developed increasingly complex processes that attempt to lay out a path, a yellow brick road to the Emerald City, guaranteeing a managerial decision that will stand up to judicial review. These complex processes, in turn, produce a veritable minefield of potential violations that resource managers must avoid in any attempt to produce commodities that conform with often-conflicting laws and regulations and political direction. Any violation of process, no matter how slight, may well result in a judicial injunction. These complex processes—which become more complex with each court loss—require more sophisticated technical assessments and additional time and money to execute. As a result, timber sales are more expensive to execute; "below-cost" timber sales become difficult to avoid. The spiral of increasing cost and difficulty in producing timber from federal lands with returns that are above costs needs careful examination. Are better, more environmentally sensitive timber sales the result?

Given the myriad of interacting variables, it is time for concerned citizens and our leaders to accept the reality that the dream of a stable timber supply and other "products" from public lands is an illusion. Certainly, this conclusion is inevitable if the status quo is maintained. If the stability or predictability of timber supply (or any other product) is deemed important, the picture painted here is a gloomy one. However, while stability seems likely to be considerably less certain than in the "good old days" when vast expanses of virgin forests and confident forest managers buttressed the myth of stability, commodity production from federal lands could be much more predictable than at present.

Through the interaction of laws, regulations, court cases, and expedient administrative direction, the overriding de facto policy for the management of federal lands has become the protection of biodiversity. This policy, I believe, is the crux of the raging debate over the levels of commodity production that can be expected from the federal lands. Such an important policy should be recognized and examined closely by the American people, the president, and Congress. If the protection of biodiversity is to be the guiding principle for the management of federal lands, it should be clearly stated, recognized openly, and the consequences accepted. A clear statement of policy regarding preservation of biodiversity is one key to the "stability" debate.

Other keys to the debate are a realistic assessment of what we can expect to know about ecosystems and a more conservative approach to forest management. Ecological processes are too complex for complete understanding. However, such understanding is being enhanced and can be accelerated with increased levels of research effort. The trend toward using ecosystem management concepts in carefully defined contexts holds promise for discouraging oscillations in forest management outputs. In the past, these fluctuations have been caused by managerial attempts to sustain biodiversity through "recovery," the practice of addressing one threatened or endangered species at a time.

Using past experience as a guide, outcomes of management actions can be conservatively estimated. Fluctuations in timber supply can be moderated by taking a conservative view of "annual sale quantity" projections as opposed to the tendency to make overly optimistic projections like those that resulted in the first forest planning efforts of a decade or so ago. Clearly, the optimistic projection was the trademark of the first generation of forest plans. Conservative approaches are more apt to produce predictable results, and if the results exceed those anticipated, it is easier to increase commodity yields than to deal with the social and political consequences of low outcomes.

Funding could be guaranteed over longer time frames. For example, steady funding for a five-year period with the ability to shift funds between budget line items at the discretion of the head of the land management agency would add considerable stability to programs. Likewise, work force numbers and composition could be predicated on work to be done and objectives achieved rather than on politically driven manipulations unrelated to necessary work. Or, conversely, the work to be done could be adjusted quickly to match funding and work force. Doing "more with less" can only stretch so far as the corollary situation of doing "less with less" quickly sets in.

We need to invest more time and money in research and synthesis of extensive information for use in guiding management. The search for new understanding through science may produce short-term instability in commodities such as timber supply as managers react to new information, but such efforts are essential to long-term stability if renewable natural resources are to be managed in a sustainable fashion. In the end, there can be no turning back from science—no matter how politically expedient that may seem in the short run. As the human population multiplies with escalating per capita demands on natural resources, it becomes a race between increasing knowledge to ensure the sustainability of renewable natural resources and ultimate disaster. While the cost of the acquisition of understanding through science may seem expensive, it is minuscule over the long term compared to the cost of ignorance.

The continued development of technology is likewise essential to make better and more environmentally benign use of available forested lands as well as improved uses for wood previously considered nonmerchantable. These developments and others can help maximize timber yields and thus offset constraints on wood supply that arise for other reasons. Efficiency in the harvest and processing of wood and in reuse (recycling) of wood fiber should be considered as valuable—or more valuable—than increased wood production. We must also seek out sustainable and aesthetically acceptable substitutions for wood and wood products.

Over the long term, wood substitutes too can influence the stability of "market share" for wood products.

The effects of shifts in markets for timber can be stabilized by allowing land management agencies more flexibility in when and how timber is marketed. Selling timber at a relatively continuous rate regardless of current price would seem irrational to any private landowner and might seem equally ill advised to land management agencies. Timber purchasers sometimes buy for speculative reasons the regular sales of federal timber, offered regardless of market conditions, and cut the timber at a more opportune time. Withholding federal timber from the market during periods of inordinately low prices should result in higher prices; selling when the price is relatively high should reduce prices. Over time, the market will see fewer fluctuations, which should, in turn, have a stabilizing influence. In this way, federal land managers could avoid "below-cost" timber sales, a strategy that would help to allay the political debate that surges around this complex issue. Timber sales could be offered at a relatively continuous rate and marketed at appropriate times in order to assure a steady work force and a mechanism to respond rapidly to market conditions.

The increased polarization of public opinion around the issue of federal land management could be balanced by bringing voices of moderation into the debate. In this way, the debate would include credible alternatives to the "spin doctors" that make a living through dissemination of propaganda and the creation and exacerbation of conflict. These gladiators get paid to win, not search out consensus. The Forest Service played the role of moderation in the past and could do so again given proper policy direction by the administration and Congress. So long as the land management agencies operate in an arena where national policy is unclear and federal land management agencies serve as "designated punching bags" for the gladiators, the melee will continue. If the Forest Service (among other agencies) were given portfolios and funding to take "the bully pulpit" for natural resources management, it could execute a clearly stated national policy in a sustainable manner and thus re-establish its historic role as a conservation leader.

Administrative findings of regulatory agencies concerning proposed management activities by land management agencies produce situations where equally or better qualified experts in management agencies are second guessed—an obviously disruptive, redundant, irritating, and expensive duplication of effort. For example, might it be preferable for regulatory agencies to produce or approve recovery plans for threatened or endangered species in cooperation with management agencies and then leave the responsibility for plan execution to the land management agencies? The current situation amounts to joint management of federal lands by management and regulatory agencies. Though this arrangement is working somewhat better over time, the situation should be re-evaluated with an eye to reduce redundancy, assure some increases in efficiency, and minimize the time of project execution.

It is time to acknowledge that the United States has come to a point where the interacting forces of the many laws and regulations that influence federal land management plus the constant upsets in balance that occur with decisions in court case after court case have produced a situation antithetical to predictability and stability of federal land management. The applicable laws should be evaluated in total and restructured to remove conflicts while radically simplifying management processes. Piecemeal changes in applicable laws could cause even more problems due to the upset in the balance of the myriad case law.

The laws might be changed to provide that the loser in a legal action pays the costs of the winner, particularly if the judge considers the plaintiff's case to be frivolous. In present circumstances, the government pays if it loses but the reverse is not true; the plaintiff does not pay costs if they lose. In fact, the government sometimes pays the plaintiff even when the government wins depending on the opinion of the presiding judge. This provides incentive to sue the government and no significant deterrent for such actions.

Complex processes that have evolved to deal with too much uncoordinated law and uncoordinated regulation and require too much interagency involvement should be simplified. Simplifying these processes, while maintaining the intent of the laws upon which they were built, will help channel the energies of natural resource management agencies away from process and toward the goal of achieving on-the-ground results that the public (or Congress and the administration) expects. The intent of any process should be to provide logical mechanisms for achievement of a defined objective. Agencies lose few lawsuits over the technical aspects of natural resource management. Lawsuits that produce losses for land management agencies most frequently focus on the details of adherence to process—with rules that change with the outcome of each lawsuit. The result has been the evolution of the "appeal-proof" or "suit-proof" process with detailed documentation covering every possible aspect of consideration. The aim of the National Forest Management Act and the Endangered Species Act was better land management, not "suit proofing." In my opinion, the original intent has been perverted. Risk aversion can be an expensive management style.

Perhaps it is time for a resurrection of the concept embodied in the Public Land Law Review Commission. The efforts of that commission, in the late 1960s, indicated important problems and solutions that were never significantly addressed by the political process. Most of the environmental laws that impact so extensively and disproportionately on the federal lands have been enacted since that time. It is not a time for timidity. The situation is producing more polarization among concerned citizens and conflicts in public land management, which leads to frustration in the body politic. The result could be poorly considered and sweeping changes in the responsibility for and/or methods of public land management.

So, while "stability" in timber supply (or any other supply) cannot be assured, improvements can be made. As natural resource managers, we stand on a slippery slope where we dare not stay. The evolving situation is politically, economically, and ecologically untenable. We must seek and find firmer ground. Frustrations associated with public land management have become so desperate that Congress is seriously considering transferring ownership of these lands or the "development" of their management to the states or other entities. This is a debate that could bear dramatically on stability.

In a 1995 hearing before a House budget committee, the chairman asked for my opinion as to the appropriateness of "devolving" the ownership or management of the National Forests. I asked, and was granted, his permission to answer that question from two perspectives, as chief of the Forest Service and as an individual citizen of the republic. Answering as chief, I spoke of the same ideas and concepts that were offered by Gifford Pinchot and the following twelve chiefs. Their rationale is a clear part of the conservation history of our country and need not be repeated here.

Instead, here I will elaborate on my individual answer. Perhaps you can think of what your answer would have been. And, while doing that, consider the factors that affect stable management of the public's lands—water, recreation, fish and wildlife, livestock grazing, mining, and so on. What is your personal stake in these questions?

I was born and raised in central Texas, a state with minimal amounts of public land. Hunting, fishing, and just wandering the woods was my passion, as it is today. But, any such endeavor required asking, begging permission, at times even sneaking, to go into the woods. I became highly adept at all three. Once grown, I went off to Texas A&M with the dream of being a wildlife biologist. Upon graduation, I found work with the Texas Game and Fish Commission and for ten years was instrumental in establishing and fostering wildlife management and its commercialization on private land. We were successful beyond our wildest dreams. But I never set foot on private property to hunt or fish without asking permission or paying a fee.

Eventually, I went to work for the Forest Service and for the first time in my life walked in a National Forest, land that belonged to me and to every other citizen of the United States. I thought I had encountered heaven on earth. The land was my land; no one and no sign said to me "Keep Out." The days of begging permission and paying to get past those signs were over.

What an incredible inheritance from our forebears! These lands are an inheritance like no other people in the world possess, unique in human experience and incredibly precious. I often think about that as I move closer to the end of my life. I think much about what we will leave behind for the people of the United States.

Yet, there are those who say our nation cannot afford to maintain that inheritance. My response is, how can we afford *not* to sustain that heritage? These lands are a part of America's culture—the only such lands that the vast majority of us will ever own. Ten percent of the American people control 90 percent of the national wealth. Is that not enough? Can we have nothing of our great inheritance for the American people at large? Can anyone seriously believe that devolvement of ownership or management of the nation's land will not bring the day closer when those "keep out" signs will spring up around the borders of what was once our land?

When the 191 million acres were placed in the National Forest system, they were lands of little value. Some of those lands, particularly east of the Mississippi, had been seriously mistreated. Over the next 100 years, these very same lands have become incredibly valuable, too valuable some believe, for the American people at large to own. If they have increased so much in value in 100 years, it is not too difficult to imagine how valuable those lands will be in another 100 years. By then, it is likely that our nation's population will have doubled and, perhaps, redoubled. If our public lands are worth gold today, they will be worth diamonds in another 100 years. But their monetary worth is not the issue. The issue revolves around ownership and control of these lands.

To say that we, as a people, cannot afford those lands is to say that we would devolve our heritage and our inheritance for a mess of potage. Speaking strictly for myself, I say that these are my lands, and my lands are not for sale, are not to be given away, and are not for devolvement. I have asked my sons, and they agree. My grandchildren are too young to talk much, but they will learn to know and appreciate their heritage if these lands are still theirs as citizens of the republic. Of course, my grandchildren and their children to be born in twenty-five or so years have no voice today. So I speak for them now, for I believe that they deserve a chance to make some choices, the same choices that today's citizens were given by our ancestors.

I ended by saying to the congressman, "Speaking for me, my children, my grandchildren, I object." The congressman asked, "Why do I think your answer as chief was 'No' and your personal answer is 'Hell no!'?"

So, while citizens consider questions of stability and of viable communities, it is necessary to ponder an even deeper question. What role do the National Forests and other public lands play in the culture of our nation and, perhaps more importantly, in the culture and economy of our regions and states? I cannot conceive of America without National Forests. The most destabilizing act I can visualize for good wildland natural resource management in America would be the devolvement of the National Forests and other public lands. But, perhaps, I am too steeped in Forest Service traditions and too emotionally and viscerally attached to these lands that I own in common with all Americans. Perhaps, but I do not think so. I certainly do not feel so.

Every American should consider the facts swirling around the issues of devolvement and have his or her response ready as the debate begins. It is time to realize that guaranteeing a completely stable supply of commodities from public lands is a goal that cannot be realized under present circumstances. The situation, however, can be improved by significant changes in the current management of public lands. Improvement is not only feasible, it is necessary.

Note

1. "318" sales originate from a "rider" (Section 318) of the 1990 Appropriations Bill that required a joint effort of industry and environmental groups to work with the Forest Service to put up old growth timber sales on each national forest in the Northwest, the goal of tiding over industry and providing some semblance of "stability" as the spotted owl crisis was addressed by the Interagency Scientific Committee. Senator Hatfield of Oregon and Senator Adams of Washington were cosponsors. Some of this timber was immediately sold and cut, and some sold and not cut. Those sales were resurrected by the "salvage rider," which required that they be released to the original buyers under the original conditions.

Part II

Historical Overviews

The essays in this section offer some broad-ranging historical and conceptual frames for the cases to follow. Although each is quite different, as a set they map out some basic geographical and conceptual markers of Asia and the Pacific Northwest, introducing some definitions for and understandings of landscapes across different cultures and times. Each interpretation presents new insights, reflecting possibilities for broad analyses of physical and ideational landscapes.

Rhoads Murphey's overview of land use and abuse in China, India, Japan, and Southeast Asia over the millenia brings into focus Asian realities. J. Baird Callicott and Karen G. Mumford trace the development of western ideas and concepts related to conservation, thus laying a foundation for a better understanding of the new concepts that promise to be useful in the Pacific Rim area and in the twenty-first century. Dan Flores asserts the primacy of mountain environments in human history and particularly in the environmental history of the American West.

———— 3 ————

Asian Perceptions of and Behavior Toward the Natural Environment

Rhoads Murphey

All Asian cultures in the areas east of Afghanistan and south of the former Soviet Union have long been noted for their admiring attitudes toward nature, comparable perhaps to those attributed to the pre-Columbian Indians of North America. For the literate Asians whose thoughts have come down to us, nature was seen as powerful but benevolent and nurturing, something to which people should adjust to rather than attempt to conquer. Such perceptions were doubtlessly influenced by the munificence of the environmental base of most of monsoon Asia, which offered the combination of warmth, moisture, and fertile lowlands conducive to the development of the world's most productive agricultural systems and consequent dense populations. Nature was seen as grander than comparatively puny humans within the whole cosmos, and also as offering a model for human behavior. Nature was observed as running by rules, and in the Asian view, society should also do so. Poets and painters, especially in East Asia, described nature through the eyes of a lover, not as an obstacle or opponent, and saw it as a place to escape the hurly-burly of everyday life and to restore a truer vision (see Yang, this volume). All of this is often contrasted with the Western view, inconsistent especially with the European Middle Ages, but as old as the Book of Genesis, where God says "let us make man in our image . . . and let

Note: The author has chosen to use the Wade-Giles system of romanization. At first mention of a Chinese word, the pinyin equivalent (if it differs) is included in parentheses.

him have dominion . . . over all the earth," an attitude acted on in spades
as modern technology has given people the means to alter drastically
the environment (see Flores, this volume).

The Asian record, however, makes clear that, despite the professed
values of the literate elite, people have altered or destroyed the Asian
environment for longer and on a greater scale than anywhere else in the
world, even in the twentieth-century West. Elites—officials, courtiers,
and landowners—were only about 2 percent of the population in all
Asian countries until modern times. Most of the population were peasants, whose struggle to maintain themselves, especially as a population,
continued to grow and obliged them to maximize short-term gain at the
expense of preservation of the environment. The biggest single cause of
environmental destruction has been the comparatively huge Asian population totals, half or more of world totals since the beginning of civilization. Han China alone held more people than the Roman Empire at its
height, and India's population remained about the same as it was during
the Maurya Dynasty in the fourth century B.C. until approximately the
eighth century A.D. The populations of Korea, Japan, and Southeast Asia
lagged behind but grew rapidly from the nineteenth century, while China
passed 1 billion by about 1980 and at present rates will be overtaken by
India at the end of the twentieth century. South Asia as a whole (undi-
vided India plus Sri Lanka and Nepal) has been close to the China total
for at least a decade.

The pressures that this mass of people exerted on their environments—
if only to clear land for the agriculture necessary to feed them—were
overwhelming. Asian farming has long been admired by uncritical Westerners as a model of careful resource use. Especially in the irrigated
areas, it achieved a long-term balance while at the same time growing
the same crop, predominantly rice, often two or even three crops per
year, in the same fields century after century without declining yields.
Irrigated rice is in fact a remarkably stable system, fed with large quantities of organic fertilizers (including human manure, or nightsoil, whose
supply, of course, increased as population grew). In the generally warm
and sunny climate of the rice-growing areas, the water in the paddies
supports a variety of aquatic life—small fish, snails, crabs—which can
be harvested or left to decompose when the paddy is drained and thus
enrich the soil. Sunlight and high temperatures, plus the high level of
organic fertilization, promote the growth of blue-green algae in the shal-
low water, which effectively fix nitrogen from the air, returning it to the

soil at harvest and thus maintaining the nitrogen balance on which nearly all food plants depend. A variety of nutrients also enters with the slowly moving irrigation water.

The clearing and leveling or terracing of land for wet rice, however, involved the progressive deforestation of China and India, a process now widespread also throughout Southeast Asia. Japan, having destroyed the Korean forests, has largely preserved its own tree cover, especially in the mountains where it is most needed to check erosion, but has fed its monstrous modern appetite for wood by ravaging the forests of Southeast Asia. The continued increases in population throughout monsoon Asia since early Neolithic times multiplied the assault on the forests and on the wealth of animal species that inhabited them. China is said to be or to have been the home of a greater abundance and variety of faunal and floral species than any other comparable area, given its wide range of climates and habitats. This may still be the case, but no one has counted the many species that have been extinguished. The most prominent animals were wiped out first, such as the elephant and rhinoceros by T'ang (Tang) times (eighth century A.D.). Although a few tigers survive along the Burmese border, it is clearly a threatened species, now confined also to parts of northeastern Manchuria. Tigers, elephants, and rhinoceros are also on the threatened list in India and now live mainly in protected reserves; as in China, many other species have become extinct in India. Tigers, elephants, and rhinoceros survive in dwindling numbers in Southeast Asia as their habitats are destroyed and human populations continue to swell. But these large and conspicuous mammals are only a tiny sample of the long list of species wiped out by human pressures.

Certainly the most serious and disruptive human impact has been the removal of most or parts of the original forest cover. This has resulted in disastrous consequences in the hillier and wetter areas, but has also long been a major problem in drier and flatter regions, most notoriously the Yellow River flood plain of north China.

The monsoonal climate is characterized by heavy rains concentrated in the high sun period; much of the affected area is in varying degrees of slope. Terracing can limit erosion but does not wholly prevent it and requires constant labor to maintain the terraces. As tree and even bush cover were progressively removed, rivers, streams, and irrigation works became choked with silt. Silt deposits built up in stream beds, blocking or restricting normal channels. As a result, the flooding became both more frequent and more destructive as peak flows could not be retained in the attenuated beds and spread over surrounding areas. The Yellow River is typical of most of the rivers of monsoon Asia, although it shows these problems to an extreme degree, as do its tributaries, which have drained an almost entirely deforested landscape deeply covered in soft, easily eroded loess soil. As deforestation has spread, there are virtually no streams now that are not heavily silt laden and increasingly prone to flooding. The Yangtze (Yangzi) River, especially above Wuhan, used to run in winter a beautiful jade green; now it is brown with mud all year round as the higher slopes in Szechuan (Sichuan) have been logged off. The Ganges has long been similar, like all the other rivers of South Asia, and the rivers of Southeast Asia now fit the same pattern.

Forests were cleared primarily to make way for agriculture, as ever-steeper slopes were pressed into use through terracing to feed the growing populations. But there was also rising demand for fuel, still acute but now involving distant day-long searches in most areas, and for grass and leaves to feed penned animals. Charcoal was produced *in situ* since it could then be transported so much more easily and cheaply to markets; charcoal burners cut huge swaths through the forests and often inadvertently started fires that destroyed large additional areas. Finally tree and even brush cover was cleared or burned to destroy the shelter it offered to wild animals and also to bandits—"men of greenwood." As populations throughout monsoon Asia rose, the consequent pressures on forests mounted. By the 1980s, although we have no precise data, China probably had only about 8 percent of its total area covered by forest, and India about the same, both dangerously inadequate to protect the soil (let alone endangered species) in a climate of heavy rains; ecologists recommend for both countries about 30 percent forest cover, a proportion not seen in either country since before the fifteenth, or even fourteenth, century. What few tree stands remain are concentrated understandably in the most remote and steepest mountain areas far from bulk transport lines, but even there the chainsaw and the logging truck are producing new inroads in areas where traditional technology made costs prohibitive.

It was remoteness, shortage of bulk transport, and steep slopes that preserved what forest remained in India and China after about the fifth century A.D. In the more accessible areas, both had already been heavily invaded in the search for timbers for the monumental capital cities of the Mauryas and Guptas at Pataliputra in the central Ganges valley, and for construction of the Ch'in (Qin) and Han capitals, near modern Sian

(Xian) and at Loyang (Luoyang), among other cities. Both cultures built primarily in wood; Pataliputra was also surrounded by an immense wooden wall. Indian demand for wood was also increased by the universal Hindu practice of burning the dead, each body requiring a very large pyre. What accounts we have suggest that all the accessible tree stands in the Himalayan foothills, especially those close to rivers, and most of the forests of central India had been cut by the end of the fifth century A.D.[1] In China, E.H. Shafer maintains that by the middle of the eighth century A.D. all accessible pines in Shantung, Shansi, and Shensi had been cut to burn for soot, which was the chief ingredient of Chinese ink, although building needs must surely have been at least as important.[2] In Japan, after the late start of literate city-building civilization, there were similar massive inroads on the forests accessible from the Kyoto area as both palaces and temples, all of wood, were built on a very large scale beginning in the eighth century A.D.

In every country, wooden construction (except for the stamped earth and brick walls around all Chinese cities) invited catastrophic fires, and most cities and temples burned repeatedly, to be rebuilt of wood each time. Fire was also probably the most important means of destroying forests to make way for agriculture, as it had been since Paleolithic times, and was also used as a weapon against wild animals. Into the contemporary period, as for centuries before, hillside forests and brush cover are often set alight in the dry months of autumn, especially in southwest China, partly to discourage or drive animals and in part to obtain with minimal effort fertilizer from the ash that the rains would wash down to cultivated land at lower levels. Shifting cultivation, which persists in parts of India and China as well as upland Southeast Asia, also involves burning off patches of forest in rotation to clear land for crops; in the course of the cycle, which is as long as twenty years, large areas are thus destroyed.

As in Europe and North America, the forest was often seen as an enemy or merely as something to get rid of. In China, where the written record is by far the most complete, a few voices were raised against this mindless destruction as early as Mencius (third century B.C.), to whom is attributed the pithy proverb "Mountains empty, rivers gorged." Mencius condemned the practice of clearing new land on slopes and the use of fire: "Yih set fire to and consumed the forests and vegetation on the mountains and in the marshes so that the birds and beasts fled away to hide themselves."[3] The text of the Huai Nan Tzu (second century B.C.)

includes comments on the burning of forests as fuel for smelting ores. The T'ang Dynasty (A.D. 618–897) saw a new spurt of population, and the continuation of migration southward, as the old northern areas had become less productive after some 2,000 years of soil use, deforestation, and consequent silting. The Cheng Kuo (Chengguo) Canal built during the Ch'in Dynasty is reported to have irrigated 4 million *mou* (one *mou* is approximately one-sixth of an acre) in the third century B.C. By the eighth century that had shrunk as a result of siltation from deforested slopes first to one and then to a half million *mou*.[4]

The move south turned new energies to the attack on southern forests, first in the Yangtze valley, then following its southern tributaries, and finally fanning out up the hills and mountainsides in the climate of heavy rains. Over time, the original southern landscape was transformed on a massive scale, including the terracing of even the steeper slopes (a process largely completed under the Ch'ing (Qing) as the population continued to increase. The result was unrecognizable either to earlier inhabitants or to those who followed the early waves of T'ang southward migration.

One crop, first used during the T'ang period, that made less destructive use of slopes in the south was tea, which replaced the original tree cover with a perennial bush cover; although this was less effective in checking erosion, the spreading roots of the tea bushes held the soil far better than cultivated fields. The tea plant flourished in the cool, wet climate at higher altitudes along the Yangtze–West River divide, including the Bohea Hills. Later, after the sixteenth century, New World crops entered Asia via the Spanish base in the Philippines. These included, most importantly, maize, a notoriously poor cover crop, which leaves much soil exposed and was grown on slopes all over Asia since it did not need irrigation. The spread of maize as a major food crop further accelerated the erosion of slopes and siltation of water sources everywhere it was grown. Maize helped to sustain the growing populations, which in turn meant new pressures for more cultivated land.

Our approximate figures for China are based on the official "censuses" but are really only guesses. For the Han Dynasty (212 B.C.–A.D. 220) we may estimate a total population of China as 60 million plus, for the T'ang period perhaps 75 million, and for its successor, the Sung (Song) period (A.D. 960–1279), probably over 100 million. This total may have reached 150 million during the Ming Dynasty (1368–1644) and then entered a period of very rapid growth during the Ch'ing period, doubling or tripling by the end of the dynasty in 1911 and laying the basis for another doubling from 1950 to 1981. Only Japan has reached stable population growth among Asian countries, and although growth rates for the rest are not as excessive as for most of Africa or Latin America, the totals are already so huge that adding even 2 percent per year (close to the Asian average outside Japan) represents an enormous number of new mouths to feed—and more pressures on the environment.

How did it happen that the clear love of untrammeled nature consistently reflected in the poetry and painting of the Asian elites was so totally ignored in practice? There is admittedly some beauty in the man-made landscape, a panorama of stepped or terraced fields climbing the slopes as well as valley bottoms, flashing like mirrors as they reflect the sun, constructed and maintained by many centuries of cumulative labor, and which retard but do not prevent erosion. But this is a very far cry from the original landscape of 1000 B.C. As from the beginning, the loss of the forests and their nonhuman occupants (the latter a serious loss by modern standards) does not seem to disturb most people. It must be noted that human concern for the preservation of other species is extremely recent in the rest of the world, and generally ineffective. How and why did Asians so completely ignore their own elite view of nature as something to be admired and protected? The simple answer of course is that the elite were few (in China estimated as less than 2 percent of the population, a figure that is probably similar in the rest of Asia), and that, however few, they were never the ones who did the work of society. It was nonliterate peasants who confronted nature, cleared the forests, created the terraces, exterminated wild animals, and provided the growing populations with wood for fuel and building, in response to market demands; it was peasants who struggled to survive droughts and floods and to grow enough food to feed themselves. These were demands that could not be denied or postponed in the interest of coming generations. That, in brief, is the story of human destruction of the environment in Asia, with a longer and more devastating history than in the less populous West.

In China, by far the best documented case but also the largest, shortages of timber, erosion of land, siltation of irrigation works and streambeds, and increased flooding were all apparent and commented on by the eighth century A.D. and multiplied during the Sung period, when in addition to new capital cities and palaces made of wood, there was now a large navy and merchant fleet. The palaces of the Southern Sung at

Hangchou (Hangzhou) were built in large part of Japanese pine suggesting that the Chinese had already cleared the more accessible slopes in the south and hence were obliged to import wood by cheap sea transport.[5] In the north, the conversion to coal as metallurgical coke came just in time to avoid a fuel crisis as charcoal supplies were exhausted. After the Mongol interlude, which wreaked its own destruction on wooded areas, the construction of massive new Ming capitals at Nanking (Nanjing) and Peking (Beijing), and the many large ships, including the fleets of Cheng Ho, which now traded throughout maritime Asia on a major scale, created further inroads on the remaining tree cover. The first Ming emperor, Hung-wu, started a reforestation program, but it yielded to the growing market pressures. It was aptly noted by the Jesuit Gabriel Magellan in his mid-seventeenth-century book, *History of China*, that "the wealthiest merchants of China are they that trade in salt and wood."[6]

Efforts by the great Ch'ing emperors Kang Hsi (Kangxi) and Ch'ien Lung (Qianlong) to try to restrict both building and access to forests met the same fate. As population began its major modern increase under the Ch'ing order, terracing spread onto ever-steeper slopes, and other marginal land was cleared for cultivation, including areas on the arid margins in the north and northwest where dust bowl conditions were soon created. This process was further accelerated during the late nineteenth century after railroads were extended out into the steppe borders, plus the increasing use of deep drilled wells and power-driven pumps. Millions of Chinese moved north and northeast from increasingly overcrowded and marginal north China, soon outnumbering the native inhabitants (primarily Mongols) and replacing their traditional nomadic grazing with settled agriculture. The consequences of the ploughing of the steppe, including the experience in North America, are well known. The Jesuit Father Gerbillon accompanied Kang Hsi on a tour of Ninghsia (Ningxia) in 1697, and his account notes the prosperity of the area and the ready availability of wood from the still existing but marginal forest of the northwestern mountains.[7] But by the time the American geologist William W. Rockhill visited Ninghsia in 1891 the forest had vanished and the area as a whole was impoverished.[8]

In China proper, a few forest stands remained after the Ming Dynasty, including those in the Han River highlands, which were settled, with inducements by the Ch'ing, in part to discourage banditry and rebellion. These "shed people," as the settlers were called, cleared most of the tree cover to plant crops, with the usual disastrous results in erosion, siltation, and flooding. Elsewhere, trees survived longest in the most remote and mountainous areas, including western Fukien (Fujian), western Yunnan and Szechuan, and the Manchurian borderlands. Nineteenth-century Western observers described most of China as already deforested, including the Hong Kong area and the coastal zone northward. By the turn of the century, followed by the warlord years and general immiseration (which nevertheless seems not to have prevented continued population growth), deforestation accelerated. By the 1930s, most of China was essentially stripped of its trees except along the far western and northeastern borders and a few pockets in other steep mountain areas. Few of the latter have survived the doubling of human population since 1950 and the coming of new technological assault weapons like chainsaws and logging trucks, but perhaps the greatest single engine of forest destruction is still the insatiable demands of a market serving over a billion people, the same engine that has been responsible for the deforestation of India. Our image of Asians as seeking a harmonious relationship with nature is contradicted by Asian behavior—including the behavior of those at the top of the elite group: emperors, with their megalomaniacal desire for huge palaces and capital cities, all built of wood. E.H. Shafer, the T'ang scholar, put it succinctly: "The idea of man as an agent of environmental change was as little noticed in the Far East as in the Far West."[9] The same point is made by Yi-Fu Tuan in his article, "Discrepancies Between Environmental Attitude and Behavior: Examples from Europe and China."[10] Peasants (and timber merchants less urgently) were driven to destroy their environment in order to stay alive in the immediate present and future and did not have the luxury of safeguarding their own or their descendants' future.

Since 1950, in addition to consuming most of the small remaining tree cover, the Chinese have built a massive industrial structure, in general using the "quick and dirty" approach, while India has done the same on almost as large a scale. Even Korea and Taiwan have joined the group of dangerously polluted countries, following the same path. China's main energy source is from its large deposits of coal, mainly soft coal with a high sulphur content, and most of its industrial plants, like those in India and elsewhere in Asia outside Japan, are heavily polluting. The Chinese call air pollution "yellow dragon," a graphic description since it can be seen as well as smelled and tasted. We have no reliable measures of Asian air pollution outside Japan, but it is clearly among the worst in the world. In India, to give only one example, air pollution (including acid rain) has so eaten away at buildings such as the Taj Mahal that there is serious talk of relocation. Water pollution in India, China, and Korea is as bad; most water supplies are loaded with industrial toxins, for example, the Hwangpu (Huangpu) River at Shanghai, which for many years has now been biologically dead. In each country there are regulations on the books, but they are not effectively enforced. In rural areas these problems are far from absent, since so many of those areas have new industrial plants. There the pollution is augmented by the indiscriminate use of pesticides; the dangers were sharply illustrated by the tragedy in a pesticide-producing Union Carbide plant at Bhopal in central India, where some 2,500 people died in 1984 following the accidental release of clouds of pesticide gases. Poor maintenance was blamed. The Chernobyl disaster is another example of the destructive potential of new industries. Bangkok is following in the path of Seoul and Taipei in creating some of the world's worst atmospheric pollution, although the levels reached there are probably still less than the levels in major Indian and mainland Chinese cities. A major contributor to air pollution in every country but China is the automobile, creating giant traffic jams in many cities.

China is currently pursuing economic growth at any cost through what are referred to as "market forces." The market is responsive only to profits and tends to have a devastating effect thus on the environment, a lesson that the West has been learning since at least the time of William Wordsworth. Agriculturally, the steppe borders of China continue to be ploughed, and overirrigation has begun to produce the familiar results long experienced under such conditions in India, Australia, central Asia, and North America: salinization and alkalinization of the soil which totally destroys its agricultural potential (the extreme case can be represented by the salt flats around Great Salt Lake). Every year both China and India are obliged to abandon farmland in areas where there is insufficient natural rain fall to flush away the salts and alkalines brought in by the irrigation water. It was at least in part for this reason that much of the cultivated area of the ancient Indus civilization was destroyed and that China saw its cultivated land decline after the sixth century A.D. in the north and northwest. But the insatiable demand for food and commercial crops by growing populations already over a billion in both China and South Asia as a whole continue to break all ecological rules and to further destroy the environment.

In both India and China the early destruction of the tree cover in the north was soon paralleled by attacks on the forests of the south. South

China, beyond the Yangtze, does at least get ample rain in most years, and thus some kind of cover, if only grass or bamboo, can remain or regenerate to hold the soil, although not as effectively as trees. On the other hand, the steep slopes characteristic of much of the south, and the heavy rainfall, tend to increase erosion. The original, unaltered nature of the forest cover of the south can be guessed at from what resulted when a large area was fenced and policed around the mausoleum of Sun Yat-sen on Purple Mountain outside Nanking in 1927–1928. In the following twenty years a heavy cover of mixed hardwood and coniferous forest grew up, regenerated from seeds, roots, and seedlings without any other human interference. Similar evidence is provided by the few and scattered temple groves that have been protected, although on a much smaller scale—perhaps providing a hint that elite values were not totally extinguished as population pressure drove most people to attack the environment rather than protecting it. But it appears that south China in general, if only it could have been left alone even briefly or partially, might have survived the massive human impact with greater protection against erosion, soil loss, siltation, and flooding, not to mention the loss of innumerable species.

One can very roughly guess at the worst and most obvious consequences of progressive deforestation in China by examining the frequency of floods and droughts in Chinese history. The two often go together, since trees act like a sponge on the land; their branches break the force of the rain, their roots not only hold the soil in place but absorb rainfall and transpire or release it gradually, keeping the water table high. With the trees gone (and in the arid north little or nothing to replace them, since grasses and brush cover regenerated only slowly and were continually cut in the search for fuel), floods and drought increased rapidly. Several scholars have attempted to measure the incidence of both since the Chou (Zhou) Dynasty (fourth century B.C.) on the basis of the fragmentary and often imprecise records that survive. They all find a large rise in both catastrophes beginning in the Han period, increasing more abruptly after the T'ang, and peaking during the Ch'ing (1644–1911).[11]

By the eighteenth century or earlier, wells in north China were running dry, and in the 1930s and 1940s the American engineer O.J. Todd measured the silt content of the Yellow River near Kaifeng at its flood peak as about 40 percent of total volume.[12] Sand and gravel along the river's bed are left there when the flood subsides, and together with the continual deposition of silt have left the river bed in many places higher than the surrounding ground. The inevitable breakout of pent-up flood-waters through breaches in the dykes repeatedly cost thousands of lives and often left behind infertile sand or gravel rather than the desirable silt. Siltation was primarily responsible for several disastrous Yellow River course changes as the old bed became blocked and the next flood forced its way into a new bed, alternately north and south of the Shantung peninsula.[13] The series of dams built in the 1960s according to what was called the Staircase Plan found their reservoirs filled with silt within a few years, and many had to be abandoned. This is also a worry for the huge Three Gorges Dam on the Yangtze. Tree planting schemes in the Yellow River watershed, the only long-term solution, had only partial success. Many of the saplings died from lack of water, which was often not available in this arid north China area on slopes far from water sources.[14] Those that survived were devastated by local peasant cutting in the urgent search for fuel. Given the pressures on local people in this especially poor area, it would have taken armed guards to preserve the trees. Throughout China, a common expression for "never" was "When the streams run clear," equivalent perhaps to our "When Hell freezes over."

South Asia

Massive deforestation began even earlier in India (as well as what is now Pakistan), including the cutting of trees in the Himalayan foothills to be used as fuel, floated down the Indus and its tributaries, for making the bricks of which Harappa and Mohenjo-Daro were built. As in China, but probably about two centuries or more earlier, the invention of iron tools meant a quantum leap in tree cutting, not only because it provided greatly superior tools. It was also accompanied by population surges based on food increases resulting from better tools for cultivation and irrigation.[15] As in China, forests were felled mainly to clear land for farming but also to provide wood for building and for fuel. In the Vedic age (c. 1000 B.C. to c. 500 B.C.) the Ganges valley was cleared and settled and by the time of the Mauryas (322–180 B.C.) had become the major area of population and production. The south, beyond the forested Vindhya range, kept its trees longer, but there too they yielded to the assaults of a growing population, especially after the first century A.D. with the rise of several south Indian kingdoms. Peninsular India, below the Vindhyas, is rimmed by mountains and much of the Deccan Plateau lies in a rain shadow cast by the Western Ghats behind Bombay. As in north China, this meant that once removed, tree cover could not regenerate and was replaced by far less effective grass or scrub, at best. The northwest, beyond Delhi, as far as Afghanistan and the Indian Ocean coast, is largely a desert or near-desert and probably never had any significant tree cover. India thus had far less extensive forested areas than China, in addition to their earlier depletion.

One way to measure their progressive disappearance was the diminishing number of elephants, important as a resource for warfare and hence commented on. It has been suggested that the shortage of elephants contributed to the collapse of the Delhi Sultanate in the fifteenth century.[16] By now both elephants and tigers are threatened species, surviving for the most part only in protected reserves. Colonial rule joined with princely states in regarding both species as supreme objects for *shikari* or hunting, shooting them in droves as late as the 1930s. The victorious hunters, such as the turn-of-the-century Viceroy Lord (George) Curzon, were usually photographed with a foot resting on their dead trophies. The coming of the railways—British India built a far larger network of lines than in China—brought new attacks on the forests, especially for trees suitable for railway ties or sleepers. Before the railways, Indian as well as Burmese and Thai teak was exported worldwide for ship-building and to feed the extensive shipyards in Bombay and Calcutta, since teak resists rotting and attacks by marine worms. Initially, railway fuel was, of course, wood, but it was soon replaced with coal.

Like the Ming and Ch'ing emperors, the British colonial government did try to check forest destruction and started plantations of the most desirable species as early as 1870, but as in China, such efforts failed to survive increasing demand for wood. The colonial rulers tended to think of forests as an obstacle to agriculture but protected large areas as a source of railway supplies. Peasants, traditionally dependent on gathering and cutting in their local areas, for their own needs and occasionally for sale, were the consistent losers. Beginning in the 1850s much of the original forest in previously inaccessible Assam and the Nilgiri Hills in south India was cleared for tea plantations, and efforts were made to prohibit shifting cultivation, on which many so-called tribal peoples depended. These various measures provoked repeated peasant revolts in which forest officials were killed, followed by brutal reprisals.[17] Like some of the Chinese elite, a few of the more farsighted of the colonial officials decried the spreading deforestation even in the first three decades of the nineteenth century. They correctly blamed it for the major increases in siltation and flooding in the Ganges and its tributaries (where steam navigation was begun, as on the Indus, in the 1850s) and in the largely unnavigable rivers of the south.

The often violent monsoonal climate, with torrential rains concentrated in the first month of summer, of course greatly aggravates the problem. It was estimated in the early 1970s that India was losing 6 billion tons of soil every year through erosion, while at the same time water tables fell below the level of many wells and irrigation systems became choked with silt.[18] The cut-to-growth ratio continued to show a dangerous imbalance between plantings and their maturation on the one hand and cutting on the other. A million hectares of forest are still destroyed yearly, and according to one scholar more than 60 percent of India's land area has become "degraded."[19]

Controversy continues to erupt over the proposal for dams on the Narbada River in central India, like the similar controversy over the Three Gorges Dam on the Yangtze. Both projects are unfortunately typical of the major efforts since 1950 in each country to increase the supply of power and secondarily to improve navigation and flood control. The effects of these projects have already been basically disruptive to both settlement and ecology and now threaten to move into higher gear. Large areas are now or will be flooded, displacing major population concentrations, which then require resettlement in already crowded alternative areas. Ecologists in both countries and abroad are deeply concerned also that several species will be endangered or exterminated by these projects. They argue that nearly equivalent amounts of power can be generated by smaller dams on tributaries, without the need for flooding such large areas, or any flooding at all, and without the damage to wildlife. But once again, burgeoning populations and market forces appear to have triumphed over all other considerations, including a more humane and environmentally conscious view of the future. Many Indians attach deep religious significance to the Narbada, but even that has so far not been enough to stem the tide of "progress."

As most of India was stripped of its trees, the desperate search for wood penetrated into the Himalayan foothills, from Kashmir through Nepal to northernmost Bengal. By the time of Indian independence in 1947, the difficulty of access to or from these steep slopes far from major roads or rail lines meant that they contained a large part of the country's remaining forest cover, critically important to hold the soil and retain water since they received the full force of the monsoonal rains. There had been earlier efforts to bring out timber, especially from the extensive stands of deodar and pine, desirable as railway ties, since the beginning of railway-building in the 1850s, but inaccessibility had protected most of the forested area. With the spread of motor roads and new technology, which aided the assault on previously untouched forests in the sub-Himalayan area, the Indian government adopted policies similar to its colonial predecessor: a combination of letting contracts for felling to commercial operators and reserving tracts for government and future commercial use, keeping out the traditional local peasant users. This produced a new wave of peasant protest known as the *chipko* movement (from Hindi *chipko*, to hug), in which organized peasants dramatized their protest by hugging or encircling trees marked for destruction. Others among the Indian "Greens" helped to further organize the movement and also reacted to the sharp increase in the flooding of all the Himalayan rivers, clearly the result of deforestation. From the inception of the *chipko* movement in 1973, organized demonstrators obstructed or prevented commercial tree felling in the reserved forests of sub-Himalaya. The movement soon spread to central and south India and included public readings from the *Bhagavad Gita*. The government response was to impose a short-term moratorium on tree felling in parts of the Himalayan area and elsewhere, but the long-term pressures will continue to mount.[20]

Nepal is a special case, heavily impacted by tourism, which has become the country's chief source of income. The Nepalese environment—steep slopes and heavy monsoonal rainfall—is especially fragile; erosion has increased uncontrollably. Thanks in part to public health efforts, the basic population of subsistence farmers has boomed and has thus greatly increased the cutting and collecting of wood. Wood was once available nearby but now, as in India, requires long daily journeys into the steeper mountains. Tourism means greatly increased numbers of visitors who live for the most part in expensive hotels and hire Nepalese (mainly Sherpa) guides for their walking tours, while consuming huge amounts of electric power, food, and fuel. The trails they use crisscross the landscape, and add measurably to the wear and tear on the easily damaged vegetation and soil. Nepal is one of the poorest countries in the world, measured (as always, unreliably) by economists' tools such as per capita income, a function of gross domestic product. It is difficult to create a useful gauge of welfare when so much of the economy rests on subsistence agriculture. But there is no denying the poverty of most Nepalese and the consequent attractions of working in some capacity in the tourist industry, which continues to draw ambitious young people to Katmandu and other towns but does very little for their or their country's long-term development.

Japan, Korea, and Taiwan

Steep, inaccessible slopes protected much of Japan's forest cover. Even now, only some 17 percent of the total land area is cultivated, and the population hugs the sea along the narrow coastal plains within, at most, about forty miles of tidewater. The early Japanese state was formed in the Kinai area, between what is now Osaka and Kyoto, including the first capital at Nara. Until very recently, the Japanese built entirely in wood; by the tenth century A.D., the construction and rebuilding after repeated fires of Nara and Heian later renamed (Kyoto), with their large attendant temples and monasteries, devastated the forests on the margins of Kinai, where trees could be extracted at bearable cost. In the Kamakura area (now a suburb of Tokyo) the construction of a new political center under the Kamakura shogunate (1185–1338) occasioned a similar devastation there and in the adjacent Izu Peninsula, where some timbers could be brought to Kamakura by sea. With the establishment of the Tokugawa in 1600 and the ensuing building boom in Edo (later renamed Tokyo), the shogun's capital, the same massive inroads—but on a larger scale—cleared most of the lowland forest of the Kanto plain and of the adjacent hills. Like all Japanese cities and buildings, Edo burned repeatedly and was rebuilt on an even grander scale.

By 1650 there were increasing notices of erosion, silting, and floods, especially serious given the amount of land in steep slope and the vital importance of the limited lowlands and their irrigation systems. In Japan, too, rainfall is often heavy, although spread more uniformly throughout the year than in India or China, and tree cover provides essential protection. By the end of the seventeenth century the Tokugawa government began to impose controls on tree cutting, which with characteristic Japanese efficiency and the absolute powers of the totalitarian shogunate, did preserve and probably increased much of the country's forested area that remained. Much of this careful preservation was lost with Japan's forced draught industrialization beginning in 1870, the tripling of its population by 1940, and the veritable orgy of building that resulted.[21]

An expansionist Japan took over Korea, de facto in 1895 and more firmly in 1910. In addition to mining minerals for export to Japan and robbing food crops to feed its own rapidly growing population, colonial rule led to a sharp decline in Korean living standards, which fell by about half. Japan largely deforested Korea to supply its own insatiable market for wood.

Like Japan, Korea is mountainous, and about the same proportion of its land surface is cultivated, suggesting, again, slopes too steep for agriculture. Japanese rule of Taiwan from 1895 and of Manchuria de facto from 1905 and as an integral part of Japan from 1931, cut similar inroads into the remaining Manchurian and Taiwanese forests. In Taiwan, extensive stands of camphor trees—now in demand in world markets— were seriously impacted. Both Korea and Taiwan were originally heavily forested, but the Japanese stripped them to feed home demand. In Japan itself, the strict Tokugawa closure and reforestation of most forests, admirable as a conservation measure, excluded traditional peasant collecting and cutting and fueled increasing peasant protests, part of the rash of peasant rebellions that marked the last century of the Tokugawa and the years from 1870 to 1940.

With the end of the Pacific War in 1945, the new government, even under the American occupation, recognized the need to protect forest areas and to pursue extensive replanting. Despite the hectic pace of new economic growth, efforts, especially in comparison with China or India, were probably more successful than at any time in the past. In contrast to these two mainland countries especially to Korea, the landscape of Japan today is not scraped bare of trees, especially in the mountains, where trees are badly needed. For the most part, Japan is covered with luxuriant tree growth, a rare sight elsewhere in Asia. Japan's mild, moist, maritime climate means rapid rates of regeneration. In addition, there has never been any large number of loose grazing animals, which have plagued efforts to regrow tree cover or even brush in India and especially China. The modern Japanese farmer, no longer so heavily dependent on wood or even charcoal as fuel, uses gas, electricity, or kerosene for both heating and cooking. Rural roofs are increasingly constructed of tile, a material more suitable to the wet climate, and while some wood is still needed for building and repair, most of it is now bought in the market. Nevertheless, it should be emphasized once again that modern Japan has protected its forests today by ravaging those of Southeast Asia—just as it had earlier destroyed the forests of Korea, Manchuria, and Taiwan.

Japan also exports pollution, toxic wastes, and heavily polluting industries, again mainly to Southeast Asia, so as to preserve the home islands. The chief challenge of modern Japan's industrial growth and the major environmental impact has been pollution, which began to loom as an urgent problem in the 1960s when Japanese industrialization reached full speed. The challenge, however, first presented itself with the initial spurt of major industrialization in the 1870s and the widespread poisoning of local people by effluents from the Asahi copper mine north of Tokyo. Japan suffers from the extreme concentration of its population and its industry, in the narrow coastal corridor already referred to, from Tokyo to Osaka, and more recently on to northern Kyushu. The introduction of the private car, earlier in affluent Japan than elsewhere in Asia, added enormously to urban air pollution. By 1960 Mount Fuji was no longer visible from Tokyo, and there were mounting cases of pollution-caused suffering and disease. The first incident to attract national and international publicity was mercury poisoning at Minamata, near Nagasaki, where a synthetic chemicals plant used mercury and dumped it into the bay. Fish died, and those who ate them suffered from mercury poisoning, soon dubbed "Minamata disease." The same tragedy took place at another chemical plant in Niigata. Then a nearby zinc refinery dumped cadmium into the adjacent river; cadmium destroys the calcium in human bodies. A large petrochemical complex at Yokkaichi poisoned both air and water and led to the condition termed "Yokkaichi asthma." These and other cases led to growing national awareness of the dangers of pollution and to the passing of strict controls by the national diet (parliament) in 1970, including controls on car emissions that made Japanese cars the cleanest burning in the world. By the end of the 1970s, Mount Fuji was again visible from Tokyo, and most pollutants, especially heavy metals, had been removed from most fresh-water supplies.

It was all done quickly, efficiently, and at surprisingly low cost— estimated by the Organization for Economic Cooperation and Development (OECD) at between 1 and 2 percent of total production costs. One may argue, however, that Japan by that time had the economic margin lacking in the rest of Asia, and had learned a harsh lesson on the menace of pollution. Unfortunately, controls imposed in 1970 have not kept pace with new industrial growth and burgeoning car ownership, and Japanese ecologists fear that pollution levels are building up again toward new disasters. The official line is that pollution has been "solved," and there is renewed urgency about maintaining, or restoring, economic growth. Japan also has invested heavily in nuclear energy, far more than the United States, a concerning development in this earthquake-prone zone. As already mentioned, part of the Japanese "solution" to pollution has been simply to export it, equivalent to sweeping it under the rug and hardly an acceptable answer.[22]

Southeast Asia

Before the end of the colonial period in the years following 1945, there had been only limited inroads into the heavy native forest cover in Southeast Asia, with the exception of Dutch-controlled Java. Java was, in effect, transformed in the course of the nineteenth century into a vast plantation producing both rice and sugar on the highly fertile volcanic soil. The British took over lower Burma in 1852 and cleared much of the dense monsoonal forest of the Irrawaddy Delta to permit commercial growing of rice, much of it for export. In 1886 upper Burma was added, with its extensive teak forests, like those in neighboring Thailand; both were exploited to satisfy world markets, although cutting was heavier in Burma until after 1945. Malaya remained relatively undeveloped until the growth of rubber plantations and tin mines to feed the monster of the automobile age after the turn of the century. The French completed their control of Vietnam about the same time as the British in Burma (1886) and increased the pace of deforestation especially in the south, but the central mountain spine in Vietnam retained most of its trees (where they were most needed to check erosion). The north had long been densely populated unlike the rest of Southeast Asia until recently. Except for its mountainous parts, much of the north was deforested long ago as a result of population pressure. As the Vietnamese moved their occupation and control southward after about the tenth century, these same pressures progressively removed most of the forests of the plains. The French replaced some of the remaining southern tree cover with rubber plantations, but major forest destruction awaited the all-out assault of the Americans from 1964 to 1974, including the use of agent orange to defoliate the forests, thus exposing the Viet Minh and their allies, leaving long-term poisons in the soil and severely affecting the lives of millions of people.

In Southeast Asia, as in India, many cutover areas have been replanted with eucalyptus; eucalyptus gives a quick timber harvest under warm conditions, but it crowds out other trees and lowers the local water table with its high water needs.

The part of Southeast Asia that has suffered most from exploitation of its forests and other resources is the Philippines, first under the Americans beginning in 1900. The Americans worked with Filipino partners to clear land for sugar and tobacco and to cut heavily into the forests in search of tropical hardwoods, notably what is called in the trade Philippine mahogany. Since the Pacific War, the archipelago, with its proximity to Japan and its compliant government willing to sell off Philippine resources as well as to receive Japan's toxic wastes and polluting industries, has suffered even greater depredations. It has become more completely deforested than any other part of Southeast Asia, but Filipino peasants have not benefited; it remains a country dominated by a few rich but inhabited mainly by poor peasants. The profits have gone to foreign entrepreneurs and their Philippine partners. In addition, sugar and tobacco are notably soil exhausting and leave the land less able to support basic food crops. It remains a sad story, an originally rich environment plundered for the benefit of a few, and with most of the harvest moving to markets abroad.[23]

In the Philippines, as in all of Southeast Asia, animal and plant species have been wiped out as their habitats have been destroyed, and local peasants have been disadvantaged, as in India, by finding many of the forested areas closed to their traditional use while contracts are issued for commercial cutting. Japan still builds in wood, but one of the biggest Japanese market demands is wood for chopsticks and *bento* (box lunches). Japanese still buy huge amounts of tortoise and turtle shells for ornamental use despite the widely acknowledged threat of extinction of many turtle species, especially the prized hawksbill. There have been peasant efforts similar to the *chipko* movement in India to obstruct logging crews and to build barricades across logging roads, as in Sarawak (see Peluso, this volume).[24] As more and more land is cleared for farming to feed the growing populations, chemical fertilizers and pesticides on a huge scale are further damaging the environment.

The tropical forests of Southeast Asia, like the fast-shrinking forests of Amazonia, are a major world resource and play an important role in stabilizing world climate. Complaisant governments everywhere have shown wholly inadequate concern to preserve this resource and have been all too quick to turn it into money for a quick profit from foreign exploiters rather than taking a longer-term and more conservationist point of view. This is the same mentality that accepts fees from Japanese seeking to dispose of toxic wastes. Poverty is certainly pressing and as always tends to focus on short-term gain, but in the longer term it seems clear that the people as a whole will suffer. A variety of estimates suggest that by the end of the present century only 15 to 30 percent of the forests standing as of 1990 will remain. The tropical forest contains a vast wealth of plant and animal species and has acted as a living gene bank. Plants are still being found with important healing qualities. No world body has the power to tell governments anywhere that they must preserve rather than squander their own resources, no matter how vital they are thought to be for the rest of the world. The chief targets of exploitation have been the Philippines and Indonesia, where notoriously corrupt governments have been all too cooperative with overseas corporations. But it is precisely in these countries that the most extensive and richest tropical forests lie.[25]

Conclusion

> If you were to ask me why I dwell among green mountains,
> I would laugh silently; my soul is serene.
> The peach blossom follows the moving water;
> There is another heaven and earth beyond the world of man.[26]

We have been misled by the appealing nature poetry, the exquisite paintings of nature left behind by the literate elite—and perhaps also by the nature-based philosophy of Taoism—into thinking that Asia was different from the West—"the acquisitive society" of Richard H. Tawney. We entertain misperceptions that Asia values and protects the environment, sees it as grander than human affairs, and that the human goal derived from this appreciation of the landscape is to reach a "harmony between man and nature." If one examines what has happened in Asia since the Paleolithic, one finds little or no support for such assumptions, while even in the West the poetry of Virgil in the *Georgics*, the religion of Druidism, and closer to our own time, the poetry of William Wordsworth and John Keats, to name only a few, suggest that at least some of the Western mind was sensitively attuned to nature. Unfortunately, in both East and West other more mundane considerations determined most behavior. The overriding factor in the East has been the sheer numbers of people pressing on the environment, complemented in more recent years by the advance of technology and the demands of industrialization. Just as voices were raised in the West against the destructive soulessness of industrialization, in every period from the third century B.C. in the East there were both warnings against the destruction of the environment and its consequences and celebrations of the beauty and peacefulness of nature. But the struggle for survival on the part of a continually growing population, and more recently short-sighted greed in the mad rush for economic development, have been far more powerful forces and have destroyed the environment on a huge scale. The consequences for human welfare, in every country, do not bear thinking about.

Notes

1. See Madhar Gadgil and Ramachandra Guha, *This Fissured Land: An Ecological History of India* (Berkeley: University of California Press, 1993).

2. "The Conservation of Nature Under the T'ang," *Journal of the Social and Economic History of the Orient* (1962): 280–301.

3. Mencius, Book 3, Part 1, Chap. J:7, in *The Four Books*, trans. James Legge (New York: Paragon Reprint, 1966), p. 628.

4. Chi Ch'ao-ting, *Key Economic Areas in Chinese History* (New York: Allen, 1936).

5. Paul Pelliot in *Toung Pao* 21 (1922): 436.

6. Quoted in S.A.M. Adshead, "An Energy Crisis in Early Modern China," *Ching Shih Wen Ti* 3 (1974): 20–28.

7. See William W. Rockhill, "Explorations in Mongolia and Tibet," Smithsonian Annual Report, Washington, DC, 1892.

8. Ibid.

9. *The Vermillion Bird: T'ang Images of the South* (Berkeley: University of California Press, 1967), p. 120.

10. *Canadian Geographer* 12 (1968): 176–191. See also Rhoads Murphey, "Man and Nature in China," *Modern Asian Studies* 1, no. 4 (1967): 313–333.

11. Yao Shan-yu, "The Geographical Distribution of Floods and Droughts in Chinese History," *Far Eastern Quarterly* 2 (1943): 357–378; Chang Chi-yun, "Climate and Man in China," *Annals of the Association of American Geographers* (March 1946): 44–73; Chu Ko-ching, "Climatic Pulsations During Historic Times in China," *Geographical Review* (June 1926): 274–282.

12. "The Yellow River Problem," *Proceedings* (American Society of Civil Engineers) (December 1938): 242–243. See also C. Greer, *Water Management in the Yellow River Basin of China* (Austin: University of Texas Press, 1979), and S. Eliassen, *Dragon Wang's River* (New York: J. Day Co., 1958).

13. For a tabular summary of Yellow River course changes in the past 2,000 years, see Joseph Needham, *Science and Civilization in China*, vol. 4, pp. 242–243.

14. See inter alia S.O. Richardson, *Forestry in Communist China* (Baltimore: Johns Hopkins University Press, 1966).

15. See D.D. Kosambi, "The Beginning of the Iron Age in India," *Journal of the Social and Economic History of the Orient* 6, part 3 (1963): 309–318.

16. Simon Digby, *War-horse and Elephant in the Delhi Sultanate* (Karachi: Oxford University Press, 1971).

17. See *inter alia* B. Ribbentrop, *Forestry in British India* (Calcutta: Office of the Superintendent of Government Printing, 1900); E.P. Stebbing, *The Forests of India* (London: J. Lane, 1922); Gadgil and Guha, *This Fissured Land*.

18. A. Rosencranz et al., *Environmental Law and Policy in India: Cases, Materials, and Statutes* (Bombay: N.M. Tripathi, 1991), p. 10ff.

19. Ibid.

20. On these issues in general, and on chipko in particular, see Ramchandra Guha, *The Unquiet Woods: Ecological Change and Peasant Resistance in the Himalaya* (Berkeley: University of California Press, 1989).

21. On all of the above, see Conrad Totman, *The Green Archipelago* (Berkeley: University of California Press, 1989).

22. For more details on pollution in Japan, see R. and E. Murphey, "The Japanese Experience with Pollution and Control," *Environmental Review* 8, no. 3 (1984): 284–294.

23. On all the above, see David Kummer, *Deforestation in the Postwar Philippines* (Chicago: University of Chicago Press, 1991), and R. Broad and J. Cavanagh, *Plundering Paradise* (Berkeley: University of California Press, 1993).

24. For a study focused on Java but relevant to the rest of Southeast Asia, see N.L. Peluso, *Rich Forests, Poor People* (Berkeley: University of California Press, 1992).

25. On all the above, see P.W. Richards, *The Tropical Rain Forest* (Cambridge: Cambridge University Press, 1952).

26. The T'ang poet Li Po, as translated by Robert Payne in *The White Pony* (New York: Mentor, 1960), p. 163.

—— 4 ——

The New Concepts
in Conservation

J. Baird Callicott and Karen G. Mumford

During the second half of the twentieth century, concern for the natural environment has become very nearly universal. Both the gravity and ubiquity of this concern were underscored by the unprecedented meeting of all the world's heads of state at the June 1992 United Nations conference on environment and development. In retrospect, the significance of this event seems to lie more in the realm of symbolism than in that of international law. In other words, the details of the treaties, whether they were endorsed by every country, and whether they will be implemented in good faith—all this will fade in importance. Of lasting importance will be the monumentality of the event itself. At the conference, held in Rio de Janeiro, virtually all the world's heads of state met for the first time—ever—not to create or dismantle military alliances, nor to discuss currency and banking reform, nor to set up rules of world trade, but to try to agree to care for the Earth. Meanwhile, responding to the same sense of crisis that precipitated the Earth Summit, a new "transdisciplinary" science of Earth care, called conservation biology, rapidly coalesced. One discipline included in conservation biology, along with such things as genetics and ecology, is philosophy—more particularly, conservation philosophy and ethics (Meffe and Carroll 1993).

Around the globe, the *practice* of nature conservation goes back in human experience beyond historical horizons. Let us not romanticize the past, however; not all "traditional" peoples lived lightly on the land

Research for this paper was partially funded by the Great Lakes Fishery Commission.

(Denevan 1992). On the other hand, there is ample ethnographic evidence for the practice of nature conservation among indigenous peoples in the Western Hemisphere before the European conquest (Martin 1978; Posey and Balee 1989), though often conservation—say of game species—might have been the unintended side effect of spiritual beliefs or religious rituals (Reichel-Dolmatoff 1976). And there is ample documentary evidence of the practice of deliberate nature conservation in premodern Europe and Asia—medieval British and Japanese forest—use laws, for example (Peterken 1981; Totman 1989). The practice of nature conservation is, in a word, immemorial, though it may not have been universal.

The *philosophy* of nature conservation, however, is recent and predominantly North American. That is precisely because the practice of nature conservation was interrupted in the Western Hemisphere for about 400 years after the European conquest. The European conquerors and colonists left a world of comparative scarcity and found a world of superabundance. The Old World regime of restrictions on the harvest of forest products and game animals was both harsh and undemocratic (Peterken 1981). Of the many freedoms to be enjoyed in the New World, free hunting, fishing, and tree-felling ranked right up there with the more abstract religious and political liberties. In the fledgling United States, until the end of the nineteenth century, in other words, nature conservation would have been believed to be about as counterrevolutionary and un-American as a state religion or a Yankee monarch—if anyone had seriously suggested mandating it. With the completion of the transcontinental railroad, the slaughter of the bison herds, and the subjugation of the Plains Indians—all in the last quarter of the nineteenth century—the North American frontier palpably closed and the need for nature conservation dawned on a few thoughtful Euro-Americans. But against the politically charged and ideologically colored background of colonial and republican laissez-faire exploitation of nature in North America, nature conservation had to be packaged and sold to a skeptical public. Thus did a philosophy of nature conservation emerge in North America about a century ago.

Two schools of thought then formed: the nature preservation school and the resource conservation school. And they have dominated nature conservation for most of the twentieth century, first in North America and then throughout the rest of the world. The former has its origin in the work of Ralph Waldo Emerson (1836) and Henry David Thoreau (1863) and was classically articulated by John Muir (1901). The latter has its origin in the prophetic work of George Perkins Marsh (1864) and was classically articulated by Gifford Pinchot (1947). With the emergence of a self-conscious conservation philosophy, conservation practice became more focused and deliberate. But with two distinct schools of thought guiding it, conservation practice was not always entirely consistent.

Unfortunately, these two schools of thought have been in a competitive, not complementary, relationship almost from the beginning. In the summer of 1897, in a Seattle hotel lobby, Muir confronted Pinchot with a newspaper article in which the latter, the first chief of the United States Forest Service, was reported to have endorsed a policy permitting ranchers to run sheep in the newly created national forests. According to the historian Roderick Nash:

> When Pinchot admitted that he had been correctly quoted, Muir shot back: "then . . . I don't want to have anything more to do with you. When we were in the Cascades last summer, you yourself stated that sheep did a great deal of harm." This personal break symbolized the conflict of values that was destroying the cohesiveness of the [embryonic] conservation movement (1967, p. 138).

After a century of conflict, we may hope that the philosophical schism in the conservation movement that was rent in that Seattle hotel lobby can be mended. The two new philosophies of conservation, emerging now at the present turn of the century, promise to be, though similarly dichotomous, more cooperative than competitive, more complementary than mutually exclusive. If more coherence and unity in conservation thought can be achieved, we may also hope that the conservation movement of the twenty-first century will become more internally coordinated than it was during the twentieth century.

Conservation Philosophies

At the core of the old resource conservation school of thought is the doctrine that nature's bounty should be exploited, but exploited efficiently, and the benefits of doing so distributed equitably. Its motto is "The greatest good of the greatest number for the longest time" (Pinchot 1947, pp. 235–236). Resourcism (as this school of thought may be dubbed for short) is anthropocentric and materialistic. It is informed principally by the modern mechanistic and reductive physical and social sciences.

In the United States and Canada it was institutionalized in federal and state conservation agencies, such as the Forest Service, the Fish and Wildlife Service, the Bureau of Land Management, and state and provincial departments of natural resources.

Preservationism is not so easy to nail down. Thoreau is less concerned with preserving wild nature for its own sake than for its tonic effects on the individual soul and the nascent American culture and civilization. Muir was the first person to our knowledge to intimate that nonhuman beings had rights too, but he states the preservationist case mostly in terms of the benefits to people afforded by the experience of nature in its primeval and pristine condition. To characterize Thoreau as a transcendentalist is problematic. Muir was clearly influenced by American transcendentalism—by Emerson as well as by Thoreau—but in the work of Muir, as in that of Thoreau, there runs a strong strain of Calvinist misanthropy. However obscure and uncertain its metaphysics and axiology, at the core of the preservationist school of thought is the doctrine that unspoiled nature is sacred. And if it must be regarded as a "resource," nature has higher uses than as merely raw material for agriculture and industry. Emerson, Thoreau, Muir, and more recent preservationists (such as David Brower) variously argue that contact with wild, undefiled nature invigorates and strengthens the body, delights the senses, inspires the imagination, energizes the mind, elevates the soul, and provides an occasion for transcending finite human consciousness and experiencing humility in the realm of the Other. The preservationist philosophy animated nongovernmental conservation organizations, such as the Sierra Club, the Wilderness Society, and the Nature Conservancy (Fox 1981). And when it did influence public conservation-agency policy—such as the policy designating wilderness areas in the national forests, parks, and other public domains—it came across in terms of "recreation": hiking, camping, hunting, fishing, and such. Though still very much alive in the public discourse, by the end of the twentieth century, both of these classic North American philosophies of conservation have become intellectually untenable.

Classic resourcism is wedded to a pre-ecological scientific paradigm. Various natural resources, that is, are conceived in isolation from the others and "managed" independently: forest resources independently of fish and wildlife, mineral resources independently of soil, water, and the biota. In reality, however, soil, water, plants, and animals are not independent of one another. Aldo Leopold was among the first recovering Resourcists to articulate the conundrum:

Ecology is a new fusion point for all the sciences. . . . The emergence of ecology has put the economic biologist in a peculiar dilemma: with one hand he points out the accumulated findings of his search for utility in this or that species; with the other he lifts the veil from a biota so complex, so conditioned by cooperations and competitions that no man can say where utility begins or ends (1939, p. 727).

Classic preservationism is largely uninformed by any scientific paradigm whatsoever. Areas were selected for preservation on the basis of such qualities as monumental, sublime, or picturesque scenery, or because they offered opportunities for outdoor recreation, or simply because they were so rugged and remote that they were not good for much else. They were not selected because they harbored endangered species, contained an extraordinary variety of species, quintessentially exemplified native biotic communities, or performed vital ecological services especially well. Exported to the rest of the world, preservationism proved to be, if anything, more pernicious than resourcism. In long-inhabited and densely settled regions of the world, such as the Indian subcontinent and equatorial Africa, American-style national parks were created by dispossessing and forcibly relocating the indigenous inhabitants who had been living sustainably for many generations in scenic hinterlands (Harmon 1987; Guha 1989; Shiva 1991a). For national parks and monuments such factors are still used but not for biodiversity reserves in which the main focus is species conservation.

The New Concepts in Conservation

Now, with the advent of conservation biology, some new conservation concepts have emerged. The most salient are biodiversity, ecological integrity, ecological restoration, ecological rehabilitation, ecological sustainability, sustainable development, ecosystem health, ecosystem management, and appropriate technology.

These new conservation concepts can be sorted out and defined in many ways. We think that they can be most generally and insightfully ordered by association with two new schools of conservation thought that are simultaneously taking shape. These schools are divided by a very deep difference of opinion about the correct answer to the age-old philosophical question, "What is 'man's' place in nature?" and, less profoundly, by allegiance to two different approaches to ecology.

On the one hand, is the segregationist school of thought. It stems from the old preservationist tradition running back through Muir to Thoreau and ultimately, we suspect, to the Puritans. Man is a case apart from nature; man and nature are not one, but two. What distinguishes man from nature is not the biblical image of God or its early modern philosophical equivalent, divine rationality, or even such contemporary empirical differentia as language and tool use. Rather, man's acquisition of culture, according to one leading contemporary segregationist, rockets humanity right out of nature's ambit (Rolston 1991). If you think that way about the man-nature relationship, you will be inclined to think that any human modification of nature is unnatural. And to the extent that residues of the Puritan belief in man's original sin still haunt your mind, you will also be inclined to think that any human modification of nature is a defilement of innocent nature by innately depraved man.

On the other hand is the integrationist school of thought. It does not stem from the old Resourcist tradition. Indeed, Pinchot himself explicitly drew a radical distinction between man and nature: "There are just two things on this material earth," he wrote, "people and natural resources" (1947, p. 325). Resourcism is, in all probability, also rooted in Puritanism and simply reverses the value polarity of the man-nature dichotomy characteristic of preservationism—such that man brings sweet salvation and beneficent domestication to a demonic and brutal wilderness "wasteland." Integrationism stems rather from the Darwinian perspective of man as a precocious primate, a naked ape, and is reinforced among some leading contemporary integrationists by the integrative doctrines and practices of Asian religions, especially Buddhism and Taoism (Snyder 1990, 1995; Sylvan and Bennett 1988).

The segregationists seem to perceive the world through the lens of community ecology—a bottom-up, biological approach to ecology that begins with organisms, aggregated into populations, which interact in biotic communities. The integrationists seem to perceive the world through the lens of ecosystem ecology—a top-down thermodynamical approach to ecology that begins with solar energy coursing through the biota, which is organized, ultimately by the energy flux itself, into primary producers; first-, second-, and third-order consumers; and decomposers—all quite indifferently to species identity. The connection between a segregationist view of the man-nature relationship and community ecology seems to be this: Human beings in general, and agricultural and industrial human beings more especially, tend to modify profoundly the biota to suit themselves. Inevitably, then, the mix of species in biotic communities is altered, and so, from this perspective, man appears to be an external—and destructive—force of change. Such changes in the biota as man imposes, however, do not necessarily affect the ecological processes that comprise ecosystems, as, shortly, we shall more fully explain and illustrate. Since, from the perspective of ecosystem ecology, some human changes in the biota do not adversely affect ecosystem processes, then man may appear to live in harmony with nature.

Now, by means of the distinction between the new segregationist and integrationist philosophies of the man-nature relationship and their associated ecologies, perhaps we can get a grip on the new concepts in conservation. The first three are more at home in the segregationist glossary.

The *summum bonum* (or greatest good) of conservation biology is the preservation of biological diversity or biodiversity (Soulé 1985). At first, preserving biodiversity was simply understood to mean preserving species. But a species can be preserved—for a while at any rate—in a zoo or lab. So now, preserving biodiversity is understood to mean preserving the diversity of genes within populations, diverse populations and "metapopulations" of species, diverse assemblages of interacting species populations (or biotic communities), and diverse assemblages of biotic communities (or landscapes). From the point of view of biology in general and community ecology more particularly, organisms, distinguished according to species, are ontologically primitive. Modern, mechanized human culture is fast destroying this fundamental biological reality. Proud of their links to classic preservationism, the leading champions of biodiversity advocate setting aside "big wilderness" areas—not for recreational, aesthetic, or spiritual enjoyment by human pilgrims—but as habitat for nonhuman species populations (Noss 1990; Foreman 1995).

Ecological integrity is a closely related conservation desideratum. A biotic community has integrity if all its "native" component species populations are present in historic numbers interacting in "natural" ways. Some argue that ecological integrity is a better *summum bonum* for conservation biology than biodiversity, because the biodiversity of a community can be artificially increased by introducing exotic species into vacant or underexploited niches (Angermeier and Karr 1994).

If a biotic community is disturbed by some "natural" force, such as a lightening-caused fire storm or a hurricane, its integrity will not have been compromised, from the segregationist point of view. But should a biotic community be humanly disturbed, by, say, logging or plowing, resulting in the loss of native species and/or the invasion by alien species, its integrity would have been compromised and may be more or less completely restored by getting rid of the exotic species and reintroducing the native species.

The inherent dynamism of nature (Botkin 1990) and the recognition in contemporary ecology that biotic communities are routinely disturbed by natural as well as by human forces (Pickett and White 1985) makes contemporary conservation philosophy more complex for both segregationists and integrationists than it was for either preservationists or resourcists. Conservation must aim at a moving target, or put a different way, conservation is a four-dimensional problem.

Ecological rehabilitation, ecological sustainability, sustainable development, ecosystem health, ecosystem management, and appropriate technology are more at home in the integrationist glossary (see Figure 4.1 and Table 4.1).

Biotic communities are composed of species populations. Ecosystems are composed of integrated ecological processes—such as primary production of biomass and nutrient recruitment, retention, and cycling (O'Neill et al. 1986). Ecosystems are healthy when the integrated ecological processes that compose them go on normally (Costanza et al. 1992). The species populations that function in ecological processes—the tree species, for example, that extract minerals from the subsoil, that photosynthesize and produce biomass, that hold the topsoil, and modulate the flow of surface water—may be interchangeable, within limits. A recent ecology textbook provides a good illustration:

> The community structure of forests in the southeastern United States was radically altered by the blight that removed the American chestnut as a critical component of the canopy of the eastern deciduous biome. . . . Meanwhile the contemporary record at the end of the last century gives no indication that ecosystem function in those same places altered one jot, even at the height of the epidemic. The chestnut, as indicated by simulation studies, seems to have been merely one workable alternative for primary production and energy capture (Allen and Hoekstra 1992, p. 92).

From the point of view of community ecology, the chestnut blight was an ecological disaster. From the point of view of ecosystem ecology, it was of little or no significance. The demise of the American chestnut and its replacement by other hardwoods was accidental. But what

Figure 4.1 **Associations between "Man"–Nature Relationships, Conservation Philosophies, "Ecologies," and Conservation Concepts**

"Man"-Nature Relationship	Humans separate from and defile or destroy innocent Nature		Humans part of and embedded within Nature	Humans separate from and control wild nature
Nature Conservation Philosophies	Preservationism	Segregationism	Integrationism	Resourcism
"Ecologies"	Non-ecological approach	Community ecology i.e. bottom-up biological approach-natural systems organized around organisms, populations, and interacting biotic communities	Ecosystem ecology i.e. top-down thermodynamic approach- natural systems organized around energy or nutrient flows, etc.	Pre-ecological, reductive, mechanistic, scientific approach
Conservation Concepts		Preservation of biological diversity and ecological integrity Ecological restoration	Ecosystem health Ecological rehabilitation Sustainable development Ecological management	

Table 4.1

Characteristics of Traditional Resource Conservation and Nature Preservation

Characteristic	Resource conservation	Nature preservation
Doctrine	Nature's bounty should be exploited efficiently and benefits distributed equitably	Unspoiled nature is sacred and has higher uses than merely as raw materials
Values toward nature	Anthropocentric Materialistic	Anthropocentric Nonmaterialistic
Early supporters	George Perkins Marsh Gifford Pinchot	Ralph Waldo Emerson Henry David Thoreau John Muir
Basis for decisions	Pre-ecological scientific paradigm: modern mechanist and reductive physical and social sciences; resources managed in isolation for yield	Nonscientific qualities of natural area: aesthetics, picturesque scenery, recreation, rugged, remote, etc.
Type of supporting	Federal, state, and Provincial natural resource Agencies in the United States and Canada (e.g., U.S. Forest Service, Bureau of Land Management)	Nongovernmental conservation organizations (e.g., Sierra Club, Wilderness Society)

happened suggests that resource managers can deliberately replace some of the species that happen to be functioning in a hitherto unmanaged ecosystem by others that are of greater economic interest to human beings without significantly compromising the health of the biome (though certainly this sort of substitution would compromise its integrity).

An ecosystem that has been ravaged by, say, strip mining, and is in a dysfunctional condition (barren of photosynthesizing vegetation, losing topsoil, subject to flash flooding followed by desiccation, etc.) may be rehabilitated. One way to rehabilitate it would be to restore the native biotic community. But another way would be to establish a wholly different community, the component species of which function harmoniously in a healthy new ecosystem. A good example is the creation of Schmeekle Reserve near Stevens Point, Wisconsin. A wetland there was mined for sand and gravel. Afterward, the hole and surrounding acreage was taken over by the University of Wisconsin-Stevens Point College of Natural Resources. Groundwater filled the hole making a lake. The naked shore was planted with trees, shrubs, sedges, and grasses, and the lake was stocked with aquatic organisms. After twenty years, the area has been ecologically rehabilitated—the shore does not erode, the lake is habitat to naturally reproducing populations of fish, and so on. But it was not restored.

Sustainable development is the most problematic and controversial new concept in conservation. It has a decided Resourcist ring, since maximum sustained yield was the Holy Grail of reductive resource management. Sustainable development achieved global currency with the 1987 Brundtland Report (as *Our Common Future* is commonly called), and since then various constituencies have tried to define it self-servingly. Developers would like the public to think that the term means sustaining development or, more cynically still, sustaining economic growth. In the Brundtland Report, sustainable development was defined thusly: meeting "the needs of the present without compromising the ability of future generations to meet their own needs" (World Commission on Environment and Development 1987). The substitutability axiom of neoclassical economics allows this definition to be interpreted antithetically to nature conservation. When a given natural resource becomes scarce, its price increases—which encourages entrepreneurs to find or invent a cheaper substitute (Barnett and Morse 1963). According to this way of thinking, then, there are no irreplaceable natural resources, and the needs of the present can be met by rapidly exploiting current organic natural resources to commercial (if not to biological) extinction and bequeathing a legacy of wealth and technology and a culture of business and inventiveness to future generations—by means of which they can meet their own needs. The substitutability axiom in neoclassical economics is technological optimism by another name, an optimism that we do not endorse and, indeed, that appears risky at best and cavalier at worst.

A more conservation-friendly gloss of sustainable development can be fashioned in tandem with the concepts of ecological sustainability and ecosystem health. In the modern past, any proposed development project has, in theory at least, been judged by an economic criterion. To be sound, its benefits, measured in dollars, must exceed its costs. For a proposed development project to be deemed "sustainable," it should meet an analogous ecological criterion. It should be ecologically sustainable as well as economically sound. And what is an ecologically sustainable development project? One that does not compromise ecosystem health. Amazonian hydroelectric impoundments, such as the Tucuruí Dam in Brazil, that flood and destroy many square miles of rainforest may be economically sound—though that too is questionable—but they are certainly not ecologically sustainable (Lutzenberger 1996). Agroforestry projects in the same region, however, that carefully increase the frequency of economically exploitable plant species, such as rubber or Brazil nut trees, in standing forests without altering the forests' structure are both economically sound and ecologically sustainable (Peters et al. 1989).

Appropriate technologies are those that are adapted to ecological exigencies. Conversely, inappropriate technologies are those that attempt to adapt ecosystems to technological exigencies. Broad-spectrum chemical pesticides are examples of inappropriate technologies, while sonically interfering with the mating behavior of a particular pest species is an example of an appropriate technology.

Ecosystem management came onto the nature conservation scene in a policy directive from the U.S. Department of Agriculture Forest Service chief, Dale F. Robertson (1992). If ecosystem management is to be a real alternative to the old, failed Forest Service policy called "multiple-use resource management," then it must mean managing ecosystems with the primary goal of maintaining their health—with commodity extraction as a secondary and subordinate goal.

That man and nature are two is, as noted, a doctrine common to resourcism and preservationism. But these two approaches were mutually exclusive in application, not complementary, because the good-guy/bad-guy hats were switched around. In preservationism, nature is good, innocent, sacred, and although originally sinful man may fall short of being evil, at least his presence and cultural artifacts profane and sully nature. In resourcism, man alone is intrinsically valuable, and nature is, if not evil, a value-free material larder. In resourcism, conservation means efficient use of natural resources, together with fair distribution of the spoils; in preservationism, it means fencing off as much pristine nature as possible and excluding all consumptive or extractive human exploitation. From the point of view of preservationists, efficient forestry on the publicly owned national forests—clear-cutting followed by single-species, even-aged tree plantations—was thoroughly destructive. From the point of view of resourcists, preservationists were hellbent on locking up valuable natural resources. Reconciliation was not possible.

The global legacy of the struggle between resourcists and preservationists is a zoned biosphere. The urban-industrial zone is altogether beyond the pale of conservation. So is much of the intensive agricultural zone. In such industrialized regions, nature has been profaned and natural resources have been exploited inefficiently and inequitably. Some lands and waters, resourcists believe, are still capable of producing a maximum sustained yield of one or another commodity—grain, beef, timber, fish—if properly managed. Here and there, in out-of-the-way areas, are scattered a few scenic national parks and designated wilderness recreation areas, thanks to the hard work of dedicated preservationists. Taken altogether, however, this is not a landscape of hope or promise.

Toward a Complementary Philosophy of Conservation

The new philosophies of conservation offer a more sanguine prospect. Although their positions on man's place in nature are diametrically opposed, the segregationist's and integrationist's preferred approaches to ecology—community ecology and ecosystem ecology, respectively—are complementary. A whole and complete science of ecology requires both perspectives. This theoretical complementarity suggests a corresponding complementarity in application.

The segregationist emphasis on the preservation of biodiversity or biological integrity and ecologically restoring areas that have been adversely, but not irredeemably, impacted by industrial forestry or agriculture is appropriate for actual and potential designated wilderness areas, wildlife refuges, national and state parks, world heritage sites, the core areas of international biosphere reserves, and the like. National parks and designated wilderness areas are, accordingly, being redefined as biodiversity reservoirs, the primary function of which is to provide living room for interacting and mutually dependent nonhuman species populations (Noss 1990). Thus reconceived, they might be expanded and multiplied to realize the goal of preserving biodiversity and ecological integrity. This is the segregationist ideal. Basically, it deanthropocentrizes and ecologizes the classic preservationist program.

The integrationist emphasis on ecosystem health, ecological rehabilitation, ecosystem management, ecological sustainability, sustainable development, and appropriate technology is a philosophy of conservation more suited for the proportionately much greater part of the world that is inhabited and economically exploited by human beings. The really innovative idea in contemporary conservation is the integrationist ideal. Instead of disparate, single-resource management for the greatest economic good of the greatest number for the longest time, it conceives of human economies as embedded in the larger and more enduring economy of nature. Its goal is to adapt human economies to ecological exigencies, through the development and adoption of appropriate technologies, thus to achieve a mutually sustaining relationship between human economies and the ecosystems in which they are embedded.

The integrationist ideal of adaptive human economies employing appropriate technologies should mix in well with the struggle of non-Western peoples for economic independence and cultural autonomy. Traditional human economies were ecologically adaptive, by necessity, and those that survived for countless generations were, by definition, ecologically sustainable. The evanescence of the rapacious industrial/consumer economy is obvious to any reflective and unbiased observer. Sustainable development might consist in re-establishing traditional economies that have been swept aside in the headlong rush toward Westernization; or more progressively, in re-establishing traditional economies, not as an end point, but as a basis upon which to innovate. Traditional paddy rice cultivation is an example. Green Revolution rice cultivation increased yields but the costs of improvement included dependence on imported inputs of fertilizers, pesticides, herbicides, and irrigation equipment, and thus on the vagaries of international commodity and currency markets; concentration of landholdings, and thus dispossession and unemployment among rural populations; and disuse of a wide variety of seed stocks selected for local conditions and tastes (Shiva 1991b). But for all of its exquisite integration of culture and landscape, who is to say that traditional paddy rice cultivation could not be improved by, say, genetic engineering, or some other nontraditional technologies?

The new complementary philosophies of nature conservation should be especially welcome in densely populated and long-settled regions of the world, such as Asia. Some of our fellow voyagers in the odyssey of evolution need—now more than ever—extensive and continuous habitat, in which human residence and economic activity are prohibited or severely restricted. But if such reserves are conceived and designed as reservoirs of biodiversity, rather than as outdoor recreation facilities for foreigners and the privileged class, their value might be more readily appreciated. And people everywhere need to have a secure and reliable livelihood. The classic, originally North American, resourcist and nature preservationist philosophies present a zero-sum choice between efficient but, more often than not, destructive resource development on the one hand and elitist nature preservation on the other. The new, ecologically grounded philosophies of nature conservation, by contrast, envision scientifically selected and managed reservoirs of biological diversity integrated into locally adapted, technologically sophisticated, sustainable human economies embedded in healthy ecosystems.

Examples of conservation projects that successfully integrate preservation of biodiversity with ecologically sustainable development in an Asian setting are the Khao Yai National Park in Thailand and the Dumoga Bone National Park in Indonesia (Gradwohl and Greenberg 1988). The former provides habitat for wild Asian elephants and, for its human residents, employment, health services, income from limited tourism, and economic and agricultural assistance. The latter protects a highly endemic flora and fauna and a steep forested watershed, the health of which is vital to lowland paddy rice farmers who otherwise might suffer catastrophic floods. In exchange for their cooperation in endangered species and watershed protection, residents have been provided with state-of-the-art irrigation works.

Bibliography

Allen, T.F.H., and T.W. Hoekstra. 1992. *Toward a Unified Ecology.* New York: Columbia University Press.

Angermeier, P.L., and J.R. Karr. 1994. "Biological Integrity Versus Biological Diversity as Policy Directives." *Bioscience* 44: 690–697.

Barnett, J., and C. Morse. 1963. *Scarcity and Growth: The Economics of Natural Resource Availability.* Baltimore, MD: Johns Hopkins University Press.

Botkin, D.B. 1990. *Discordant Harmonies: A New Ecology for the Twenty-first Century.* New York: Oxford University Press.

Costanza R., B.G. Norton, and B.D. Haskell. 1992. *Ecosystem Health: New Goals for Environmental Management.* Washington, DC: Island Press.

Denevan, W.M. 1992. "The Pristine Myth: The Landscape of the Americas in 1492." *Annals of the Association of American Geographers* 82: 369–385.

Emerson, Ralph Waldo. 1836. *Nature.* Boston: James Monroe.

Foreman, D. 1995. "Wilderness: From Scenery to Nature." *Wild Earth* 8 (4): 8–15.

Fox, S. 1991. *John Muir and His Legacy: The American Conservation Movement.* Boston: Little, Brown, and Company.

Gradwohl, J., and R. Greenberg. 1988. *Saving the Tropical Forests.* Washington, DC: Island Press.

Guha, R. 1989. "Radical American Environmentalism and Wilderness Preservation: A Third World Critique." *Environmental Ethics* 11: 71–83.

Harmon, D. 1987. "Cultural Diversity, Human Subsistence, and the National Park Ideal." *Environmental Ethics* 9: 147–158.

Keystones, R., et al. 1992. *Ecosystem Health: New Goals for Environmental Management.* Washington, DC: Island Press.

Leopold, A. 1939. "A Biotic View of Land." *Journal of Forestry* 37: 727–730.

Lutzenberger, J. 1996. "Science, Technology, Economics, Ethics, and Environment." In *Earth Summit Ethics: Toward a Reconstructive Postmodern Philosophy of Environmental Education*, ed. J. Baird Callicott and F.J.R. da Rocha. Albany: State University of New York Press.

Marsh, George Perkins. 1864. *Man and Nature: Or Physical Geography as Modified by Human Action.* New York: Charles Scribner.

Martin, C. 1978. *Keepers of the Game: Indian-Animal Relationships and the Fur-Trade.* Berkeley: University of California Press.

Meffe, G., and R. Carroll. 1993. *Principles of Conservation Biology.* Sunderland, MA: Sinauer Associates.

Muir, John 1901. *Our National Parks.* Boston: Houghton Mifflin.

Nash, Roderick. 1967. *Wilderness and the American Mind.* New Haven, CT: Yale University Press.

Noss, R. 1990. "What Can Big Wilderness Do for Biodiversity?" In *Preparing to Manage Wilderness in the Twenty-First Century*, ed. P.C. Reed, 49–61. Ashville, NC: USDA Forest Service.

O'Neill, R.V., et al. 1986. *A Hierarchical Concept of Ecosystems.* Princeton, NJ: Princeton University Press.

Peterken, G.F. 1981. *Woodland Conservation and Management.* London: Chapman and Hall.

Peters, C.M., et al. 1989. "Valuation of an Amazonian Rainforest." *Nature* 339: 656–657.

Pickett, S.T.A., and P.S. White. 1985. *The Ecology of Natural Disturbance and Patch Dynamics.* New York: Academic Press.

Pinchot, Gifford. 1947. *Breaking New Ground.* New York: Harcourt Brace.

Posey, D., and W. Balee, eds. 1989. *Resource Management in Amazonia: Indigenous and Folk Strategies.* New York: New York Botanical Garden.

Reichel-Dolmatoff, G. 1976. "Cosmology as Ecological Analysis: A View from the Rain Forest." *Man*, n.s., 12: 307–318.

Robertson, D.F. 1992. "Ecosystem Management of the National Forests and Grasslands." Memorandum to regional foresters and station directors.

Rolston, H. 1991. "The Wilderness Idea Reaffirmed." *Environmental Professional* 13: 370–377.

Shiva, V. 1991a. *Staying Alive: Women, Ecology, and Development.* London: Zed Books.

———. 1991b. *The Violence of the Green Revolution: Third World Agriculture, Ecology, and Politics.* London: Zed Books.

Snyder, G. 1990. *The Practice of the Wild.* San Francisco: North Point Press.

———. 1995. *A Place in Space: Ethics, Aesthetics, and Watershed.* Washington, DC: Counterpoint Press.

Soulé, M. 1985. "What Is Conservation Biology?" *Bioscience* 35: 727–734.

Sylvan, R., and D. Bennett. 1988. "Taoism and Deep Ecology." *The Ecologist* 18: 148–152.

Thoreau, Henry David. 1863. *Excursions*. Boston: Tichnor and Fields.

Totman, C. 1989. *The Green Archipelago: Forestry in Preindustrial Japan*. Berkeley: University of California Press.

World Commission on Environment and Development. 1987. *Our Common Future*. Oxford, UK: Oxford University Press.

World Resources Institute. 1992. *World Resources 1992–93*. Oxford, UK: Oxford University Press.

——— 5 ———

Mountain Islands, Desert Seas: Mountains in Environmental History

Dan Flores

In *The Great Plains: A Study in Institutions and the Environment*, now regarded by historians of the American West as the most influential work ever written about aridity and the region, the Texas historian Walter Prescott Webb penned a pair of lines that ought to startle all of us who inhabit mountainous country: "So far as civilization is concerned," Webb assured his readers, "the mountains are negligible. Unless they contain minerals they are of relatively little importance in the development of human society."[1]

Now, I admire Webb's work and the clarity of his writing. But I have read those dismissive lines more than once and wondered what on earth a historian so attuned to environmental influences could have possibly meant by them—or whether they were merely the equivalent of a literary migraine, the result of some sweltering day on his ranch in the Texas Hill Country that momentarily addled a sensible man's judgment.

I have come to think that Webb meant what he said, and that he not only believed it, but subtly influenced two generations of American historians since. Certainly modern environmental historians have internalized Webb's assertion that regional distinctiveness in the American West was less the result of a historical *process* (as in Frederick Jackson Turner's famous "frontier" hypothesis) but was more accurately the end product of environmental uniqueness that made the West different from everywhere else in North America. The most important of these western ecological truths, according to Webb, was the overwhelming influence of aridity across the region.

Western aridity was already a full-blown idea when Webb articulated and popularized it, thanks largely to the legacy of the nineteenth-century West's most important federal bureaucrat, John Wesley Powell.[2] The first map that tens of thousands of readers saw upon opening Webb's *The Great Plains* was a Powell-adapted map of western America with a series of concentric circles drawn around it to illustrate the tightening grip dryness had on the region. From Powell to Webb, and through him, that imagery absolutely colored yet another highly influential twentieth-century book about the West, Wallace Stegner's *Beyond the Hundredth Meridian*, a biography of Powell that even used the aridlands concept in its title.[3] Right up until his death in 1992, Stegner continued to articulate the aridlands theme, as in this passage from *The American West as Living Space*:

> Aridity, and aridity alone, makes the various Wests one. The distinctive Western plants and animals, the hard clarity . . . of the Western air, the look and location of Western towns, the empty spaces that separate them . . . the pervasive presence of the federal government as land owner and land manager, the even more noticeable federal presence as dam builder and water broker, the snarling states'-rights and antifederal feelings, whose burden Bernard DeVoto once characterized in a sentence—"Get out and give us more money"—those are all consequences, and by no means all the consequences, of aridity.[4]

Potent pictures conveyed in potent words. Reading them or hearing them, you can literally smell the sagebrush, feel your lips crack, taste dry dust in your mouth. Yet, as with much truly powerful writing, there is reductionism going on here. Stegner and Webb, both champions of discarding myth and seeing reality, are themselves engaging in a bit of myth-making.

Because the truth is, the American West is not a uniformly arid province at all. It does possess deserts, and slickrock canyons, and much vast and open shrubland of greasewood and sagebrush. And the Great Plains, at least west of about the ninety-eighth meridian, in places still present badlands and great grassy sweeps that rivaled trans-Ural Asia as the premier dry grasslands province of the world. But not all of the West is desert influenced. The Pacific Northwest in some respects replicates the environmental conditions of Western Europe; the southern Cascades, for example, produce more annual runoff than most of New England.[5] More directly relevant here, the interior West also includes a convoluted set of mountain chains rising like emerald islands from the lowland sea of encircling plain, sagebrush steppe, and cactus desert. As a consequence of Mountain West complexity, because the mountains do not present an unbroken face throughout and because of peculiar difficulties they have presented to human settlement, this Mountain West has been more difficult for academics to characterize—oddly enough given their imposing visual presence—or rather more difficult to see than simpler landscapes like the deserts or plains.

But neither in world history nor in American history have mountains been "negligible" in human civilization. And in the American West, the fact of mountain ecology—mountains as fountains of moisture, as the sources of the West's surging rivers, as homes to alpine-adapted lifeforms very different from those of the dry lowlands, mountains belted by dense evergreen forests that grade into scrubby forms both low down and high up—all this gives the lie to aridity as the sole shaping influence in the American West. Indeed, a good many of the western characteristics that Stegner attributed to aridity in *The American West as Living Space* (1987) are actually a consequence of the mountain presence, and of course the author of *The Big Rock Candy Mountain* (1943) and *The Sound of Mountain Water* (1969) knew that. My intent here, then, is to revisit the basis of western environmental uniqueness, and to assert the primacy of mountain environments in human, and particularly western American, environmental history.

As a special issue of the journal *Human Ecology* demonstrated a quarter-century ago, worldwide, mountains have always been formidable landscapes for human societies, with a set of complex environmental problems that amount in some ways to a reversal of those encountered in arid flatlands.[6] The fundamental, organizing principle for biological life in most mountain ranges is not aridity, but slope. Just as *dry* has far-reaching consequences on biological life, *slope* does as well. In mountains big enough, slope means complex topography, stratified life zones, a complicated mosaic of ecological opportunities, hence biological diversity. In big ranges, slope produces elevations that stress life to its limits; some mountains, including Asian ranges such as the Himalayas and American ranges such as the Andes and even parts of the Rockies, present difficulties of inhabitation that humans have not evolved to handle. While we evolved as exploiters of diverse edge habitats, our ecological history is that of a lowland species. Humans are naturally savannah, not mountain, apes.

Slope and elevation are not the only significant physiological characteristics of mountain country. Latitude combines with them to give mountain ranges like those in the American West a variety of different looks.
In the Northern Hemisphere, mountain ranges near the equator and north
of about thirty-five degrees are considerably cloudier and receive heavier
precipitation than ranges that lie between about twenty and thirty-five
degrees—accounting for visible differences in aspect between a range
like the Bitterroots in Montana and the Sandias in New Mexico. And
like vast plains, where radiating heat can generate anvil-head thunder-
storms and even tornadoes, mountains that are big and bulky enough are
able to create their own weather systems, including effects like chinooks
and inversions, which are significant in human affairs.[7]

They are also able to fashion their own individual ecologies. The
southern Rockies, for example, are high enough to act as settings for
relict ecologies from latitudes far to the north. And ranges like those in
the Great Basin, where the moist peaks are separated from each other by
thirty to fifty miles of searing desert, in the twentieth century have become laboratories for the study of island biogeography and specially
evolved endemics. Consider mountain biogeography anywhere around
the world and you cannot help becoming convinced, as Stephen Trimble
has said, that "the patterns of life repeatedly show how fragile and fleeting is any one incarnation of reality."[8] During the late Wisconsin glacials,
for example, when the Pleistocene lakes, Missoula and Bonneville, were
etching the shorelines visible on the slopes of the mountains above
Missoula and Salt Lake, there were no pinons or junipers in the southern
Rockies, and no ponderosa pines in the northern. During these glacial
episodes of only 140 centuries ago, alpine tundra and boreal forest spread
two-thirds of the distance to the equator along the spine of the Rockies;
relicts of those life communities remain there still. Now the trend of
floristic migrations is reversed, with desert-evolved species like pinon
pines steadily advancing northward into present Wyoming and Idaho.

These might seem like random and irrelevant factoids until one faces
their consequences in human economy. More so than the biological life
of the arid grasslands or the deserts, that of the mountains is remarkably
diverse from foothills to mountaintops, tends toward endemism, and
also changes dramatically under both climatic and human influences.
As one example, unlike the vegetation of the Great Plains, neither the
boreal meadows nor the southwestern shrublands that are chasing one
another up and down the length of the Rockies evolved in conjunction

with large herds of grazing species. With the introduction of Eurasian grazers into western mountains over the past 400 years, the western mountains have been more susceptible to exotic plant invasions under grazing than any other western ecoregions. At its most fundamental, the Mountain West has not presented a changeless face to human inhabitation throughout time, but has been a moving target, evolving independently from the human presence, but also as a result of it.

It should be no stretch of our imaginations to accept that the elevated mountains—with their verticality, their lifeforms, and their moisture—by all logic ought to stand alongside aridlands as the yin and yang of defining influences in western ecology and history. Yet historical tradition has not seen the West that way. Outside William Wyckoff and Larry Dilsaver's geographical compilation, *The Mountainous West: Explorations in Historical Geography*, most western scholars have followed Webb and Stegner's lead in emphasizing the aridlands as the key to the West. Beyond the historical geographers who contributed to *The Mountainous West*, social sciences and humanities scholars have not conceptualized the Rockies, Cascades, and Sierra Nevadas as asserting a primary environmental influence in western history. In part, perhaps, because the mountains of western America have been settled by such diverse ethnic and cultural groups as the Pueblo and Flathead Indians, New Mexican Hispanos and Mormons, scholars have experienced difficulty recognizing the Mountain West as a unified subregion. Two examples make this point. Despite mounting archeological evidence for some long-term inhabitations by Native American cultures with specially adapted mountain cultures, cultural anthropologists examining historic-era western tribes still have not recognized a "mountain culture area" in the American West, apparently because so many mountain-based groups (like the Utes and Flatheads) adopted Plains bison-hunting traits once the horse was available.[9] And as recently as 1993, a new journal dedicated to place and environmental writing served up a similar omission, associating Mountain West writers with the Great Plains, the Pacific Northwest, or the Desert Southwest rather than acknowledging a regional category of mountain-based writers.[10]

Unquestionably we need a new mountain-based perspective and appreciation in the American West. To achieve that requires perhaps some general grasp of mountains in world history. Understanding the proper and primary role of the Mountain West in American environmental history seems to call for an acknowledgment of the function and role of mountain landscapes in human history, the separate perceptions of mountains in the East versus in the West, some knowledge of the evolving image of mountains during the past 700 years in Western culture, and the use of mountains—mostly European and Asian ranges—as apotheoses of human-caused environmental disasters during the critical late-nineteenth-century period of American conservation. Finally, following the recent lead of the historical geographers, a few things need to be said about the significant environmental influence mountains have had in the history of Western civilization.

The number of world civilizations that have regarded mountain homelands as their cradles is probably impossible to calculate accurately. But despite the difficulties that great elevation and steep slope have presented to humans, few mountain ranges anywhere in the temperate latitudes have gone unoccupied. According to the geographer Yi-Fu Tuan, while steep mountain ranges may have been the last of the major habitat types that Paleolithic hunters exploited, nonetheless, 10,000 years ago it was mountain valleys that became the setting of the great agricultural, or Neolithic, revolution. Perhaps, Tuan suggests, that is why a mountain valley with a river coiling through it seems to function as a kind of ideal habitat, an Eden, in the human imagination. The earliest landscape representations in human art are mountain valleys coursed by rivers. These scenes, Tuan argues, are a mirror of gender dualism. The watered valley symbolizes an enveloping and fertile femininity. The surrounding mountains represent the masculine, and particularly in the Eastern tradition they act as ladders of transcendence to the spiritual.[11]

In the East, the reaction to the great mountains of interior Asia for a very long time seems to have been one of awe and spiritual sublimation. A mountain, as Lao Tzu describes one in the *Tao Te Ching*, is "a thing confusedly formed, born before heaven and earth, silent and void."[12] Yin and yang originally referred to the shady and sunny sides of a mountain—the opposites that replace one another in a natural moebius loop.[13] In his recent *Landscape and Memory*, Simon Schama characterizes the Taoist tradition with respect to mountains this way: The universe was anchored by four mountains with a fifth at its center, whose peaks were the "abode" of immortals who had successfully sought the way of the Tao. So the Taoist tradition invested mountains with a sacredness. Great mountains, while their iconic pyramidal forms might be symbolized in incense burners or other replications, were not profane landscapes of work and inhabitation the way valleys and plains were. Their heights were not absolutely off limits, but they could only be ascended, and lived in, by shamans or monks, for their peaks were guarded by dragons that feasted on the unworthy.[14] Indeed, even with modern developments like the Maoist and Cultural Revolutions, this kind of special regard for high mountains has not entirely been erased. It was not until 1986, for instance—and then primarily because westerners threatened to do it first—that Chinese explorers finally traversed the upper stretch of China's longest river, the Yangtze, from its sources on the Tibetan Plateau.[15]

By contrast, the way mountains are viewed in the Western tradition has undergone a striking evolution, more so than any other type of land-form. Of all the earthly configurations of soil and design, mountains have been problematic in the West for at least the last 2,000 years. The salient reason for this is that nowhere in the Judeo-Christian account of the Creation are mountains ever mentioned once! To many students of Genesis and Biblical scripture in the Middle Ages and beyond, this strange absence appeared to offer proof that mountains somehow were not part of the divine plan. The mountain's major role in the Christian tradition, in fact, occurs as the setting for the diabolical temptation of Christ in Matthew 4:8. So it ought to be no surprise that a landform that does not appear in Genesis, and is Satan's favorite haunt in the New Testament, might encounter something of a spin problem as Western history un-folded. As late as 1681, in his book, *Telluris Theoria Sacra* (Sacred Theory of the Earth), theologian Thomas Burnet asserted that there was good reason mountains did not appear in Genesis: They were, in fact, the chaotic residue of the Great Flood and should not be considered a part of the *original* and harmonious divine plan. Rather, Burnet compiled a list of favorite similes: mountains as warts, postules, and carbuncles.[16] The mind recoils at how this kind of sensibility would have viewed a soaring eruption of needled peaks like the Tetons. But, to borrow from the title of Marjorie Nicolson's book tracing the intellectual history of mountains in the traditions of Western civilization, somehow we modern folk see as "glory" what our near ancestors saw as gloom. That requires explanation.

The solution to fashioning a less repulsive attitude toward mountains in Western culture was experiential immersion. Inevitably this happened as population grew in Europe, and it took the form of the Benedictine monasteries in ranges like the Pyrenees where—in the tradition of Saint Jerome—acolytes could renounce participation in the worldly, as Jesus had done when tempted on the mountaintop. It also took the form of mountain ascents and mountain observations by Europeans who lived in the proximity of great mountains, ascents that were first intellectual and religious and then became gradually more aesthetic and spiritual as the dragons and hobgoblins retreated farther around the corners of the European imagination.[17]

Consider one of the great mountain-climbing stories of Western traditions. While Petrarch's famous ascent of Mont Ventoux in 1336 could still plunge the scholar, primarily interested in resolving an academic debate, into a soliloquy on the sensuous temptations of earthly scenery, Petrarch's debate with himself about scenery viewed from great heights set a new progression in motion. By the dawn of the romantic movement in Europe, the Western mind had effected a transformation with regard to mountains. The European landscape painters Salvator Rosa, Claude Lorrain, F.M.W. Turner, and eventually John Ruskin were converting European ranges like the Alps into, as Ruskin put it, "the beginning and the end of all natural scenery."[18] Edmund Burke's 1757 *Philosophical Inquiry into the Origin of Our Ideas of the Sublime and Beautiful*, with its classically romantic fascination with chaos, mystery, and wildness as the template of the sublime—and of great mountains as the form of that template—completed the evolution. It was an intellectual odyssey that quite literally prepared nineteenth-century American romantics to regard their mountains, complexly, but potently, as the freshest representatives of God's handiwork, even the seat of America's moral superiority over Europe. As Thoreau put it—shrieked it, really, with the wind in his hair atop Maine's Mount Ktaadn in August 1846—there was an American mountain refrain in the nineteenth century:

> What is this Titan that has possession of me? Talk of mysteries! Think of our life in nature,—daily to be shown matter, to come into contact with it,—rocks, trees, wind on our cheeks! the solid earth! the *actual* world! the *common sense! Contact! Contact!*[19]

Thus there was a message in nineteenth-century American high culture's take on mountains: altitude equals beatitude. This became more an operative force in American life from the moment Thomas Cole's Catskill Mountain paintings initiated the Hudson River school's canonization of mountain scenery. And it reached a kind of ecstatic frenzy when American romantic culture encountered the Far West. The noisy, large, operatic paintings of Sierra Nevada and Rocky Mountain sublime, executed by artist-adventurers Albert Bierstadt and Thomas Moran of the Rocky Mountain school, tilled the soil of the American mind for the national parks and federally legislated wilderness areas that are a principal American cultural contribution to modern world history.[20] For several decades, actually until the 1930s in the case of the national parks, American parks were synonymous with the Western mountains. Wilderness, for the most part, still is.[21]

The mountain ranges of western America have not been interpreted through the lens of romanticism solely. As a historical experience like that of Montana exemplifies, the resources of the western mountains were targeted by the global market as early as the fur trade of the 1820s. The two ways of seeing the American West—that of the romantic aesthete (the poster boy of which, John Muir, became a champion of mountain preservation) and that of the agents of economism, such as Marcus Daly, whose interests were in resource extraction—have clashed spectacularly for a century now. The story of that confrontation, so loudly a part of modern western history, offers another reason why Webb and Stegner's aridity hypothesis does not explain western history very well. In the modern history of the American West, the land use debate has centered around the public lands. And the largest slice of the arid West, the largely privatized Great Plains, has experienced relatively little of it.

The public lands are today the most visible institution that differentiates the Mountain West from the rest of the United States. It might be helpful in recognizing the important role of the mountains in western history to remember that in the 1890s when the U.S. government began to withdraw large parts of the public domain from privatization and for federal management, until the 1930s, public retention was aimed specifically at the mountains, not the arid deserts or plains. It was George Perkins Marsh, in his remarkably modern *Man and Nature: Or the Earth as Modified by Human Action* who set America's Western mountains in a historical continuum of mountain land abuse in Europe and Asia, and who had first offered a rationale for public retention and management of America's western mountains as federal commons. As Marsh told Americans:

> There are parts of Asia Minor, of Northern Africa, of Greece, and even of Alpine Europe, where the operation of causes set in action by man has brought the face of the earth to a desolation almost as complete as that of the moon.[22]

Marsh fashioned the first compelling linkages between forest cover and streamflow and was able to demonstrate that in the kind of mountainous country that Americans were then encountering in the West there were dangers in market forces and privatization. Although his book mentions examples of land collapse in the Orient, Marsh's primary example of a mountainscape that had suffered ecological collapse through logging and grazing was the French Alps. Marsh quoted a French observer:

> The Alps of Provence present a terrible aspect. . . . One can form no conception of those parched mountain gorges where not even a bush can be found to shelter a bird, . . . where all the springs are dried up, and where a dead silence, hardly broken by even the hum of an insect, prevails. . . . Man at least retires from the fearful desert, and I have, the present season, found not a living soul in districts where I remember to have enjoyed hospitality thirty years ago.[23]

The examples extended to both the southern and northern flanks of the Alps, as well as the entire Pyrenees chain. America's mountains would experience the same disasters if the country did not act. But how to act? In passages that scientists of the time did not miss, but historians such as Walter Webb apparently did, Marsh asserted flatly that "it is, perhaps, a misfortune to the American Union that the State Governments so generally disposed of their original domain to private citizens." Marsh continued, "It is desirable that some large and easily accessible region of American soil should remain, as far as possible, in its primitive condition."[24]

This was the inception of what history must consider the most significant event in the fashioning of the West as a region, one with far more long-term resonance than Lewis and Clark, or the Little Big Horn, or the respective impacts of Cody, Remington, the Homestead Act, even dam-building. The original creation of a permanent Western public domain in the form of forest reserves was intended to satisfy Marsh's call to recognize the ecological—and economic—reality of sloped and elevated country. As the water fountains for their surrounding aridlands, the mountains made the dry West wet; they made inhabitation possible for hundreds of miles downstream by protecting the headwater forests of western America's mountain lands. Other uses—logging, grazing, human recreation, protection of habitat for the western wildlife that was consolidating in the mountain fastness—came later. But far more than their mining history, their logging history, or their status as sublime landforms or recreational destinations, the Mountain West's salient contribution to western American history are the public lands that today quite literally define the region.[25]

As environmental history and historical geography conceptualize the American Mountain West today, that critical step—the communal ownership and regulated use of the high mountain zones by an American culture whose nineteenth-century arc, after all, was a blend of entrepreneurship and laissez-faire—stands as something of a startler. I think it is the most important in a list of characteristics that describes a central and highly significant role for mountains in western American history. These characteristics include the function of mountains as barriers to movement; their sporadic spacing of resources useful to human enterprise; the ecological complexity created by elevation, exposure, and latitude; and their precious snowpacks, which through a problematic but classic irrigation and diversion technology have made the rest of the West inhabitable—just as the Grand Canals, the Southern Waters North project, and the Three Gorges Dam have spread the waters of the Yangtze across arid China.[26] Finally, there is the end result of that slow-cooked western appreciation for mountains as aesthetically and spiritually inspiring places. In the American West, unique creations such as Yellowstone, Glacier, and Rocky Mountain national parks are one result. And since it was mountain settings that Aldo Leopold and Bob Marshall most closely associated with the American frontier experience, such places as the Bob Marshall Wilderness are also a part of the legacy of Rosa, Thoreau, and Bierstadt.

Woven like a natural geometry of design into the rug of this modern Mountain West are the public lands. They spill the mountain waters, harbor the last of the West's large and charismatic wildlife, serve—with all their carbuncles, warts, and postules now transformed into spires, faces, and talus—a democracy of recreators that would send Petrarch hurtling downslope in confusion and terror. Because of their marginality as inhabitable places for humans, mountains worldwide have tended to be set up as commons, and thus to have served as a training ground for human cooperation, management strategies, and settlement patterns.

In any true appreciation of the American West, this kind of mountain history ought to be front and center, particularly as the pattern is so obvious, and so old. By concentrating private lands in the valleys, public ownership in the form of the *ejidos* commons of New Mexico, the mountain "concessionaire zones" of the Mormons, and the national forests of the twentieth-century United States has served to create what historian Thomas Alexander has called the "oasis civilization" of the interior American West.[27] Our modern highland commons—national forests, parks, and wildernesses—now preserve most of the unsettled country and the aesthetic views, which have been so central in converting the Mountain West—in our time of satellite communication and air travel—from rural backwater to "last best place" in late twentieth-century American demographics.[28] Overcoming the antimountain religious forces of Western civilization, the mountain ranges of the modern American West thus have become a kind of sacred space for a secular society. Not an exact emulation of Asian traditions, but close.

So because of the peculiar arc of our history, we western Americans are not really mountain people; we are mostly valley people, which has meant that we have indeed lived mostly where the ground is more bare, the air dry and translucent, close in with the smell of sagebrush. Unlike Tibetan monks or the Benedictine hermits of the High Middle Ages, we westerners may not live in the alpine mists where, as the saying goes, "The state is shattered; Mountains and rivers remain." But we do live with mountains on our horizons, the sound of mountain water in our ears, and mountains and their significance burrowed deeply into our consciousness. And right there with aridity, Professors Webb and Stegner, there are mountains very much in our history.

Notes

1. Walter Prescott Webb, *The Great Plains: A Study in Institutions and the Environment* (Boston: Ginn and Company, 1931), p. 33.

2. Donald Worster, "The Legacy of John Wesley Powell," in *An Unsettled Country: Changing Landscapes of the American West* (Albuquerque: University of New Mexico Press, 1994), pp. 1–30.

3. Wallace Stegner, *Beyond the Hundredth Meridian: John Wesley Powell and the Second Opening of the West* (Boston: Houghton Mifflin, 1954; rep., Lincoln: University of Nebraska Press, 1982).

4. Wallace Stegner, "Living Dry," in *The American West as Living Space* (Ann Arbor: University of Michigan Press, 1987), pp. 8–9.

5. Larry Price, *Mountains and Man: A Study of Process and Environment* (Berkeley: University of California Press, 1981), p. 62; Thomas Vale, "Mountains and Moisture in the West," in *The Mountainous West: Explorations in Historical Geography*, ed. William Wyckoff and Larry Dilsaver (Lincoln: University of Nebraska Press, 1995), pp. 141–165.

6. See the special issue of *Human Ecology* edited by Stephen Brush on mountain cultures worldwide (volume 4 ([April 1976]), along with his "Introduction: Cultural Adaptations to Mountain Ecosystems," pp. 125–133.

7. Price, *Mountains and Man*, pp. 57–125; Melvyn Goldstein and Donald Messerschmidt, "The Significance of Latitudinality in Himalayan Mountain Ecosystems," *Human Ecology* 8 (1980): 117–134.

8. Stephen Trimble, *The Sagebrush Ocean: A Natural History of the Great Basin* (Reno and Las Vegas: University of Nevada Press, 1989), p. 51. See also Rexford Daubenmire, "Vegetational Zonation in the Rocky Mountains," *Botanical Review* 9 (June 1943): 325–393.

9. See Alan Osburn, "Ecological Aspects of Equestrian Adaptations in Aboriginal North America," *American Anthropologist* 85 (September 1983): 563–591. Paleolithic and Archaic mountain traditions are a special focus of *Ice-Age Hunters of the Rockies*, ed. Dennis Stanford and Jane Day (Niwot, CO: University Press of Colorado, 1992). See, particularly, George Frison, "The Foothills-Mountains and the Open Plains: The Dichotomy in Paleoindian Subsistence Strategies Between Two Ecosystems," pp. 323–342; James Benedict, "Along the Great Divide: Paleoindian Subsistence Strategies Between Two Ecosystems," pp. 349–359; and James Benedict, "Along the Great Divide: Paleoindian Archeology of the High Colorado Front Range," pp. 359–373. See also Wilfred Husted, "Prehistoric Occupation of the Alpine Zone in the Rocky Mountains," in *Arctic and Alpine Environments*, ed. Jack D. Ives and Roger G. Barry (London: Metheum, 1974).

10. Clark Wissler prepared the first Native American "culture area" maps for North America (1912). Since Alfred Kroeber reworked them in the 1930s, they have undergone very little revision. See Alfred Kroeber, *Cultural and Natural Areas of Native North America* (Berkeley: University of California Press, 1939). Also Raymond Gastil, *Culture Regions of the United States* (Seattle: University of Washington Press, 1975), which locates three culture areas within the modern Rockies: Southwestern, Mormon, and Rocky Mountain. Joel Garreau's *The Nine Nations of North America* (Boston: Houghton Mifflin, 1981) is of little help, referring to the Mountain West as the "Empty Quarter." For evidence that scholars fail to recognize a Rocky Mountain regional literature, see Bill Howarth, "Literature of Place, Environmental Writers," *Isle: Interdisciplinary Studies in Literature and Environment* 1 (Spring 1993): 167–173.

11. On valley importance, see Yi-Fu Tuan, *Topophilia: A Study of Environmental Perception, Attitudes, and Values* (Englewood Cliffs: Prentice-Hall, 1974), p. 122.

12. Lao Tzu, *Tao Te Ching*, trans. D. C. Lau (New York: Dutton, 1963), p. 82.

13. Fritjof Capra, *The Tao of Physics* (Boulder: Shambhala Press, 1975), p. 106.

14. Simon Schama, *Landscape and Memory* (New York: Alfred Knopf, 1995), pp. 407–408.

15. Lyman Van Slyke, *Yangtze: Nature, History, and the River* (Stanford: Stanford Alumni Association, 1988), pp. 176–180.

16. The major work on this subject is Majorie Hope Nicolson's *Mountain Gloom and Mountain Glory: The Development of the Aesthetics of the Infinite* (Ithaca, NY: Cornell University Press, 1959). But see also, Roderick Nash, *Wilderness and the American Mind*, 3d ed. (New Haven: Yale University Press, 1982), p. 45.

17. I am generally here following Schama's interpretation in *Landscape and Memory*, Chapters 7 and 8, and Nicolson's in *Mountain Gloom and Mountain Glory.*

18. John Ruskin, *Modern Painters*, (vol. 4; New York: John W. Lovell, 1873), p. 427.

19. Thoreau's passages atop Mount Ktaadn as quoted in Max Oelschlaeger, *The*

Idea of Wilderness: From Prehistory to the Age of Ecology (New Haven: Yale University Press, 1991), pp. 148–149.

20. See Barbara Novak, *Nature and Culture: American Landscape and Painting, 1825–1875* (New York: Oxford University Press, 1980), and Patricia Trenton and Peter Hassrick, *The Rocky Mountains: A Vision for Artists in the Nineteenth Century* (Norman: University of Oklahoma Press, 1983).

21. See Alfred Runte, *National Parks: The American Experience*, 2d ed. (Lincoln: University of Nebraska Press, 1987).

22. George Perkins Marsh, *The Earth as Modified by Human Action: A New Edition of Man and Nature* (1874; rep., New York: Arno and the New York Times), p. 43.

23. Ibid., p. 254.

24. Ibid., pp. 263, 326–327.

25. See Dan Flores, review of Wyckoff and Dilsaver, *The Mountainous West*, in *The Environmental Review* (forthcoming).

26. See Wyckoff and Dilsaver's introduction, "Defining the Mountainous West," pp. 1–59, in *The Mountainous West* for their particular list of Mountain West characteristics. I do not entirely agree with it and here offer my own version. See also Van Slyke, *Yangtze*, pp. 65–80, 184–190.

27. See Thomas Alexander, "Toward a Synthetic Interpretation of the Mountain West: Diversity, Isolation, and Cooperation," *Utah Historical Quarterly* 39 (Summer 1971): 202–206; Dan Flores, "The Rocky Mountain West: Fragile Space, Diverse Place," *Montana: The Magazine of Western History* 45 (Winter 1995): 46–56.

28. Such is the conclusion of the special issue on mountain adaptations in *Human Ecology* (vol. 4 [April 1976]). See, for example, Stephen Brush, "Introduction: Cultural Adaptations to Mountain Ecosystems," pp. 130–131; Robert Netting, "What Alpine Peasants Have in Common: Observations on Communal Tenure in a Swiss Village," pp. 140–141; Donald Messerschmidt, "Ecological Change and Adaptation Among the Gurungs of the Nepal Himalaya," p. 177; and Stephen Brush, "Man's Use of an Andean Ecosystem," pp. 143–149.

High mountain zones join swamplands and high altitude grasslands as the trio of landforms most often left as commons around the world because their resources are either diffuse or low in yield. See Bonnie McKay and James Acheson, "Human Ecology of the Commons," in *The Question of the Commons: The Culture and Ecology of Human Resources*, ed. Bonnie McKay and James Acheson (Tucson: University of Arizona Press, 1987), pp. 1–34.

Part III

Living a Landscape: Historical and Contemporary Cases

The cases of Libby, Montana; Chamba, India; and Shimokawa, Japan offer glimpses of focal points, or examples "on the ground" that are connected with larger interactions on a global scale, and attendant relationships of interdependence and integration. Dependence on timber and other forest products associates each of these towns with one another, as they are linked to many reaches of the globe.

The third section includes essays that highlight the ways particular understandings of and interactions with landscapes change over time. Some essays in this section explore the disturbing environmental and cultural repercussions generated by the forces of an extending global economy, such as Nancy Peluso's chapter on overexploitation of timber in Indonesia. Each essay addresses several common themes: lifestyles bound to landscapes in deeply symbolic ways, "wild nature" as indivisible from aesthetic and spiritual practices, ways that politics of power help to shape these symbolic and spiritual interactions, and the resultant changing conceptions of environments and interactions with them through particular historical and cultural shifts.

Xiaoshan Yang explores changing notions of nature in early medieval China as reflected in poetry and anchored in contexts of political and economic events. Allan Grapard shows how the creation of the modern nation-state has had drastic consequences for traditional landscape conceptualizations and representation after the dissociation of Shinto and Buddhist objects of cult in all religious sites of Japan in 1868. William Lang describes "western" and "native" perceptions of the Columbia River in the 1800s and the continuing legacies of these different "ways of seeing" in the 1990s. Vaclav Smil discusses myths of afforestation programs and food consumption trends in China, challenging many assumptions about Chinese natural resource use.

6

Idealizing Wilderness in Medieval Chinese Poetry

Xiaoshan Yang

The medieval era in China (approximately from the third to the sixth centuries) witnessed the rise and maturity of landscape poetry. This essay offers a few samples to demonstrate the change in Chinese attitudes toward nature as seen in the poetry of the period. Briefly stated, this change involves a process whereby wilderness is philosophically, religiously, and socially idealized. An inquiry into this process will not only deepen our understanding of the traditional Chinese conception of nature but also provide a culturally illuminating perspective from which to explore remedies for some of the serious abuses of the environment resulting from China's economic development in the recent past. I will focus on three distinctly different, though closely related, genres of poetry in which descriptions of nature occupy a prominent position. The Chinese have traditionally termed these genres respectively as the poetry of seclusion (*yinyi shi*), the poetry of mountains and waters (*shanshui shi*), and the poetry of fields and gardens (*tianyuan shi*).

The emergence of extensive descriptions of nature in medieval Chinese poetry was prompted by a complex of historical factors. Two may be mentioned here: the changes in Chinese intellectual thought as a result of the political realities of the time, and the move of the central court in the fourth century from the barren landscape of the north to the luxuriant scenery of the south.

Note: This chapter uses pinyin romanization, while some of the notes may use the Wade-Giles system of romanization, depending upon the author cited.

The consequences of the changes in the intellectual realm can be gauged from the opening observation in the seventeenth of the "Inner Chapters" of *The Master Who Keeps to Simplicity*, written by Ge Hong (283–343). The chapter begins as follows: "All those cultivating the divine process or preparing medicines, as well as all those fleeing political disorders or living as hermits, go to the mountains."[1] This classification of the mountain dwellers gives us a good idea of the political and intellectual causes for the literati's retreat to the mountainous wilderness. The collapse of the Han Dynasty at the end of the second century brought with it the downfall of Confucianism as its state ideology. The credibility of Confucianism was seriously undermined as it proved increasingly powerless in deterring the deterioration of the old imperial political order. Consequently, the Confucian ideal of actively engaging in civil service for the betterment of the people and the state lost much of its moral weight with the literati. Furthermore, Confucianism itself endorsed the notion that the gentleman may live in seclusion when the world falls into such disorder that public service is no longer possible. On numerous occasions Confucius expressed his admiration for people who retreated from the chaotic world in order to preserve their moral integrity. In other words, Confucianism provided justification for both political engagement and disengagement. Also worthy of mention here is that Confucius himself established an analogy between man and nature when he observed, "The wise find joy in water; the benevolent find joy in mountains."[2] Landscape (i.e., mountains and waters), therefore, has figured as a source of moral enlightenment in the Confucian tradition.

At the same time Confucianism was dethroned, the religious doctrines of Daoism, with their promise of immortality or (at least longevity) through life-prolonging herbs, elixirs, and yogic exercises, began to attract a sizable following among the literati hoping to achieve the liberation from the physical body (*shijie*) and thereby to become an immortal (*xian*). In Daoist lore, mountains constantly appeared as the abode of nature deities and immortal spirits. No wonder that "All those cultivating the divine process or preparing medicines . . . go to the mountains."[3] In a sense, the obsession with immortality was a direct response to the dangers of politics characterized by ruthless factional strife, involvement in which had cost a large number of literati their precious lives. As the literati retreated to the mountains, descriptions of mountainous scenery figured conspicuously in their poetry describing their life in retirement. References to Daoist classics were frequently woven into the descriptive fabric of Chinese landscape poetry.

Another intellectual impetus for the rise of nature poetry, which Ge Hong did not mention, was the widespread influence of Buddhism at this time. For many Buddhists, contemplation of landscape was a means to spiritual enlightenment. Mountains had always been held in awe and considered sacred in China. With the introduction of Buddhism to China, the sanctity of the mountains where Buddhist monasteries were founded assumed a new dimension.

The second cause contributing to the development of landscape poetry in medieval China was the move of the central court to the south. The beautiful mountains of Zhejiang and the lower Yangtze Valley proved fascinating to many literati. One hastens to add, however, that the aesthetic appeal of the southern landscape alone would not have been a sufficient factor. Beauty lies in the eye of the beholder. The Chinese poetic beholder was informed with Daoist and Buddhist ideas. What he saw in nature was to a large extent what Daoism and Buddhism taught him to see there. Those religious thoughts provided a deeper and more permanent significance beneath or above the surface of the natural landscape. As a great many literati at the time believed in, or at least had a penchant for, Daoism and Buddhism, their perception of the exotic landscape of the south was conditioned and guided by their religious beliefs.

Nature in Ancient Chinese Poetry

In themselves poetic descriptions of natural scenes and objects were by no means an invention of the medieval period. Indeed, they were as old as Chinese poetry itself. In order to appreciate the distinct features of medieval poetry in its representation of nature, it is helpful to contrast it with the poetry of previous times. As a general survey of "ancient" (i.e., "premedieval") Chinese poetry is neither possible nor desirable here, I will simply touch on three of the most important poetic milestones: *The Classic of Poetry* (*Shijing*), which is generally believed to have been put together in its present form around the sixth century B.C., though many of its poems may date back to much earlier times; *The Songs of the South* (*Chuci*) which was compiled in the first century of our era but most of its poems are attributed to Qu Yuan (c. 340–278 B.C.), and the rhapsody (*fu*) of the Han Dynasty.

In *The Classic of Poetry*, a great many poems begin with images drawn from nature to form either a parallel or a contrast with the human feelings and activities depicted in the succeeding lines. Traditional Chinese exegesis classifies the functions of these images in three rhetorical devices in *The Classic of Poetry*: straightforward presentation (*fu*), metaphorical imagery (*bi*), and evocative imagery (*xing*). Nature images seldom possess any inherent interest as objective descriptions of nature; instead, they are considered a vehicle for the delivery of certain moral and emotional messages. In other words, natural descriptions serve as a foil and never dominate in the poem. Furthermore, the formulaic structure of many of the poems in this anthology tends to make nature imagery appear somewhat arbitrary and sometimes even mechanical. Whereas the moralistic interpretation of nature images in specific poems of *The Classic of Poetry* often has been open to dispute, the representation of nature in *The Songs of the South* shows a unequivocally allegorical tendency. The names of plants are often explicit and implicit metaphors for certain moral qualities. Worthy of special notice in this collection are the three poems, "Summoning the Soul," "Great Summons," and "Summoning the Recluse," in which, as we shall see in a moment, the emphasis on the horrific aspects of wilderness compares meaningfully with the poetry of seclusion in the medieval period. Finally, the rhapsodies of the Han (206 B.C.–A.D. 220) on capital cities and royal palaces and parks were interspersed with descriptions of natural scenes and objects. Those descriptions, however, have a distinct stamp of artificiality, since they are often more visionary rather than visual. Instead of representing the poet's actual perceptual experience, the exhaustive enumeration of flora and fauna in these pieces is often part of an imperial ideological construction, which presents the royal dwelling place as a microcosm for the whole universe.

Zuo Si: The Poetry of Seclusion

Of the three genres of medieval Chinese poetry to be discussed, the poetry of seclusion has the most ancient genealogy, since antecedents can be found as early as *The Classic of Poetry*. Furthermore, it shows most dramatically the evolving attitude toward nature in Chinese poetry. For the purpose of comparison, we may take a look at the poem "Summoning the Recluse" in *The Songs of the South*, generally believed to be composed in the second century B.C. The poem starts with a frightening picture of the wilderness:

The cassia trees grow thick
In the mountain's recesses,
Twisting and snaking,
Their branches interlacing.
The mountain mists are high,
The rocks are steep.
In the sheer ravines
The waters' waves run deep.
Monkeys in chorus cry;
Tigers and leopard roar.[4]

For reasons not clearly explained in the poem, we are told that a prince went wandering in the dreadful wild mountains and would not return. The poem goes on to elaborate upon the frightfulness of this treacherous landscape dominated by wild animals and plants before it ends with a plea for the prince to return, because "in the mountains you cannot stay long." Here one finds a clear-cut antithesis between the city and wild nature, with the latter presented as a highly undesirable place.

There is probably a link between poetry that purports to summon the recluse and the shamanistic poetry for summoning back the soul that has left the body.[5] The two poems titled "Summoning the Soul" and "Great Summons" in *The Songs of the South* undoubtedly belong to the latter category. Here the contraposition between the city and the wilderness is stated in even more drastic terms. These two poems show a similar pattern. They start with a threat: Beyond the human realm there is nothing but horror. In the shamanistic incantations, the horrors of wilderness are enumerated in a deafening bombast. In "Summoning the Soul," for example, we are told that in the south and the east there are man-eating giants, ten metal-melting and stone-dissolving suns, semibeastly barbarians that sacrifice the flesh of men and pound their bones for meat paste, venomous cobras and swift-moving foxes, and the great nine-headed serpents that swallow men as a sweet dish. The dangers and hardships awaiting the lost soul in the north, west, above, and below, are no less horrendous. In contrast, the city to which the soul is summoned is full of delights that the human world can afford: lavish residences to live in, delicate fabric to wear, pleasing music to listen to, and gourmet food to eat.[6] As in the case of "Summoning the Recluse," wilderness is cast in negative light in its antithesis to human civilization.

The medieval poetry of seclusion shows a dramatic contrast with its precedent in terms of the representation of wilderness. This is most clearly seen in poems that bear the title "Summoning the Recluse." Whereas previously the recluse had been asked to return *from* wilderness, now the plea is for him to return *to* it in order to live the eremitic life. What we witness here is a transformation from demonization to idealization of wilderness. Zuo Si's (c. 250–c. 305) "Summoning the Recluse" is generally considered to be the most representative piece of this genre:

> Walking on the staff, I summon the recluse
> To the untrodden path that has lay here since antiquity.
> Though the cragged caves have no fancy structure
> In the hills there is the sound of zither.   4
> White clouds stay over shaded peaks,
> Red flowers shine in the sunlit woods.
> Rocks are washed by the stream like jade;
> Delicate scales of the fish bob up and down.   8
> Why must one have strings and flutes?—
> Mountains and waters have clear notes of their own.
> Why practice the whistling songs?—
> Bushes produce moving sound of their own.   12
> Autumn chrysanthemums suffice for food,
> Hidden orchids can be worn on the front of one's garment.
> Wandering around in the world makes my feet tired;
> I would rather just throw away the cap clasp.[7]   16

The poet is by no means unaware of the attractions of the human realm with its music of strings and flutes, but the music of nature—the sound of rustling trees and murmuring streams—supersedes and surpasses the music of artificial instruments. The description of the sounds of nature versus those of humans also harks back to the Daoist idea of the superiority of "cosmic music" over human music as found in the Daoist classic *Zhuangzi*.[8] The "whistling" in line 11 is a common Daoist practice believed to be conducive to a mystic kind of resonance in the universe.

In *The Songs of the South*, both chrysanthemum and the orchid flowers had been described as a replacement food for the individual wandering in wilderness; there had also been references to the latter as being worn on one's garment, hence the imagery in Zuo Si's poem here. In Zuo Si's time, consumption of chrysanthemum flowers was a dietary practice of achieving longevity among religious Daoists. Just how seriously the poet takes such a belief is immaterial; rather the point here, as in the eremitic poetry in general, is that wilderness is not only a place of spiritual liberation from the hustle and bustle of the mundane world but also one of material sufficiency. In the last line of the poem throwing away the clasp that holds the cap of an official is an unmistakable gesture of abandoning the life of officialdom and suggests an unburdened spiritual freedom. The retreat to the mountains, therefore, carries with it at least an implicit form of political protest against society at large.

Representative of the poetry of seclusion, Zuo Si's poem exemplifies a new poetic configuration of the mountains from a place of horror to a desirable alternative to the human world. The intellectual underpinning of this transformation for nature poets is a combination of Confucian ethics and Daoist religion that replaces the old primitive shamanism reflected in *The Songs of the South*.[9] In passing we may note that, in a similar manner, the rise of descriptive poetry in eighteenth-century England was brought about in part by changes in the intellectual fields of theology, science, and philosophy. The old disparagement of mountains as "moles and warts" of nature gave way to the new conception of the mountains as the epitome of the natural sublime.[10]

Xie Lingyun: The Poetry of Mountains and Waters

The second genre of Chinese medieval poetry, the poetry of mountains and waters, is generally considered to have culminated in, and perhaps initiated by, Xie Lingyun (385–433). With this poet, nature is more than just a place for retreat. Contemplation of nature provides religious and moral enlightenment as well as aesthetic enjoyment. One of the most illustrative examples of Xie Lingyun's conception of nature is his poem "The Prospect as I Cross the Lake on My Way from South Mountain to North Mountain":

> At dawn I set out from the sunlit cliffs,
> At dusk I rest by the shaded peaks.
> Leaving the boat, I look afar at the circular islets;
> Putting down the staff, I lean against the luxuriant pine.　　4
> The sideways are narrow and hidden;
> The islet-loops are like rings.
> I gaze at the twigs on top of tall trees;

I listen to the torrents in the deep ravine.   8
Rocks stretching, the water is divided in its flow
Woods dense, the trails lose their tracks.
How does one feel nature's discharge and procreation?—
All things are burgeoning and growing.   12
Fresh bamboo shoots are wrapped in green sheaths;
New rushes are coated with purple down.
Seagulls play by the springtime banks,
Pheasants sport in the gentle breeze.   16
Embracing transformations, my mind never gets tired,
Contemplating nature, my love increasingly deepens.
I do not lament that the departed are long gone,
I only regret that no one keeps me company here.   20
What I sigh over is not just traveling alone—
Without the appreciative companion, with whom shall I
communicate about Nature's principle?[11]

Xie Lingyun's landscape descriptions consistently employ parallel couplets.[12] With him, the use of parallelism is not just a mechanical device for poetic ornamentation; rather it correlates the underlying symmetry and order of nature itself and reflects the longstanding Chinese conception of the universe in terms of complementary pairs (e.g., the very idea of "universe" or "world" is comprehended in the pair of characters *qian* and *kun*, the two primary hexagrams in *The Book of Changes*). The very conception of "landscape" is expressed in the term *shanshui*, composed of the two characters that literally mean "mountain" and "water." Here Xie Lingyun's perceptual experience of landscape is precisely organized through the alternation between mountain scenes and water scenes: Thus line 3 describes a water scene, line 4 a mountain scene, line 5 a mountain scene, line 6 a water scene, line 7 a mountain scene, line 8 a water scene, line 9 a water scene, and line 10 a mountain scene.[13] Traditional Chinese literary criticism has long since recognized the correlation between verbal parallelism and cosmological complementarity, as can be seen in this well-known passage by the sixth-century critic Liu Xie: "Nature, creating living beings, endows them with limbs in pairs. The divine reason operates in such a way that nothing stands alone. The mind creates literary language, and in doing this it organizes and shapes one hundred different thoughts, making what is high supplement what is low, and spontaneously producing linguistic parallelism."[14]

The complementary structure of the landscape leads the poet to marvel at and ponder about the work of nature (lines 11–12). As the seventh-century commentator Li Shan observed, the terms "discharge" and "procreation" are a reference to the *The Book of Changes*, which describes how things burst into growth following the release of the cosmic force of nature: "In the discharge of heaven and earth, thunder and rain are procreated; in the procreation of thunder and storm, the seed pods of all fruits, plants, and trees break open."[15] The description in lines 13 through 16 vividly manifest this cosmic principle by focusing on the minor forms of nature and balancing them with nature's grandeur in the previous descriptive part. This poetic representation of nature is rooted in the philosophical idea that the cosmic Way (Dao) embodies itself in all forms of existence, great or small. Thus, on the aesthetic level, Xie Lingyun's description of nature achieves a balance, to borrow two terms popular in eighteenth-century Western aesthetics, between the sublime and the beautiful (or graceful). Xie Lingyun's poetry makes it clear that nature is not only an object of aesthetic contemplation but also a textbook from which important philosophical lessons can and should be learned. The specific message provided by nature may vary from poem to poem, but it is always there for the enlightened or "enlightenable" observer.

Xie Lingyun has been considered the true founder of Chinese landscape poetry for good reasons. His perception and representation of nature is constantly buttressed with the informing philosophy of Daoism and Buddhism. At the same time, his descriptions are based on his lived experience of the scenery and therefore display a kind of immediacy to the extent unprecedented in Chinese poetry. In the poems of *The Songs of the South,* wilderness is demonized in an exaggerated way and shrouded in shamanistic hues; in Zuo Si's poem, nature is approached from a "generic" perspective in that nature is presented as an ideal place in accordance with the attitude typical of the theme of "summoning the recluse" in general. Despite Zuo Si's descriptive details, nature in his poem still lacks true individuality that would come from the poet's immediate perceptual experience. Xie Lingyun's description, on the other hand, clearly demonstrates personal experience with nature. His landscape is one observed by the individual at a particular place within a particular time frame. The very titles of Xie Lingyun's typical landscape poetry often indicate such specificity, and in Xie Lingyun's intellectual framework, it is precisely the individuality of the poet's experience that opens the path to spiritual enlightenment. Behind his frequent lament that his appreciation of landscape is difficult to share with others is the idea that nature reveals its innermost secrets and significance only to the sensitive and perceptive observer. A collateral notion is that the most inaccessible parts of nature would yield the highest degree of aesthetical satisfaction. That is why in poem after poem Xie Lingyun presents himself as consciously seeking out scenery hitherto unexplored.

Xie Lingyun's landscape poetry sets up a pattern for the poetic description of excursions into nature. Lin Wenyue has described this pattern as basically a tripartite structure: the beginning lines that record the occasion of the excursion, the middle part that describes landscape (dominated by the use of parallelism), and the ending with its lyrical expression or philosophical reflection.[16]

Tao Qian: The Poetry of Fields and Gardens

If Xie Lingyun's description focuses on the wilder aspects of nature such as the unpeopled mountains and waters, then the poetic lenses of Tao Qian (365–427) zoom onto rural fields and gardens. Whereas Xie Lingyun presents himself as constantly and consciously seeking the unusual views, Tao Qian finds himself in perfect harmony with nature as it appears in his immediate and daily surroundings. Despite his efforts at effacing the gap between himself as the perceiver and the landscape as the perceived, Xie Lingyun's poetic record of his excursions in nature still reveals a clear dichotomy between the subject and the object with the former consciously trying to understand and appreciate the latter. For Tao Qian, nature is no longer an alien object to be intellectually explored; the return to external nature is the return to his true internal self. "Returning to Live in My Gardens and Fields" typifies the theme of "returning" in Tao Qian's poetry:

> Since youth I have been out of tune with the vulgar world,
> By nature I loved hills and mountains.
> By error I fell into the dusty net,
> And was away from home for thirteen years running.   4
> The bird in the cage longs for its native woods,
> The fish in the pond misses its former depths.
> At the edge of the southern fields, I opened the waste land;
> To keep to my simplicity, I returned to my gardens and fields.   8

Around my residence there is a couple of acres of land;
In my thatched cottage there are four or five rooms.
Elms and willows shade over the rear beams;
Peach and plum line up in front of the hall.   12
The village looms hazy in the distance
Where smoke hovers over the hamlet.
Dogs are barking in the deep lanes,
Cocks are crowing atop the mulberry trees.   16
In my courtyard there is no dust;
In my empty rooms there is leisure.
Long a prisoner in a cage,
I have now returned to nature.[17]   20

The very beginning lines of the poem establish an alliance between the "I" and the natural world of "hills and mountains" in opposition to "the vulgar world." The poet's erstwhile entanglements in the latter are recognized as a mistake in betraying his true nature. The "nature" to which Tao Qian claims to have returned at the end of the poem is therefore both the external nature in the form of a rural community and the poet's own internal nature. The inner self and the outer nature are fused in the act of returning.

Of course, Tao Qian's nature is different from Xie Lingyun's: One is the rural area; the other is the wilder aspects of nature. More important is the difference between each poet's relationship with his surroundings. As a wealthy aristocrat, Xie Lingyun could afford to roam around without ever worrying about the basic necessities of life. In fact, he himself was the one to remind us of the difference between the aristocratic and the common mountaineers: "The woodcutter and the recluse both live in the mountains, / Yet their reasons for doing so are quite different." Whereas the woodcutter goes to the mountains for his basic livelihood, a recluse like himself stays there "in the hope of achieving the subtlety where I am one with things."[18] As a gentleman-farmer, Tao Qian literally lived among and participated in the life of the rustics. As a result, agricultural activities are an integral part of his description of nature. Though it excludes the "vulgar world," Tao Qian's vision of nature integrates an idealized rural human community. Tao Qian's idealization of the rural area moves in two opposite but complementary directions. On the one hand, he identifies with the rustics of the village, where "when we meet each other, we talk about nothing idle, / But about how the hemp and mulberry are growing."[19]

On the other hand, the villagers are not mere "noble savages" as one finds in much of eighteenth-century European literature. They are elevated in their literacy as they come to the poet's house to form a poetry reading group: "We share our appreciation of extraordinary writings; / We join in analyzing ambiguous lines."[20]

Life in the agricultural community as presented in "Returning to Live in My Gardens and Fields," where the gap between a literatus and his neighbor farmers is bridged, not only embodies the moral and spiritual loftiness of Tao Qian as an individual but also points to his dearly cherished social model. Lines 15 and 16 are lifted almost verbatim from a folk song of the Han Dynasty, but they also echo a well-known passage in the Daoist classic *Laozi* (more commonly known as the *Dao de jing*), which presents a utopian society characterized by ultimate material and spiritual simplicity: "Though adjoining states are within sight of one another, and the sound of dogs barking and cocks crowing in one state can be heard in another, yet the people of one state will grow old and die without having had any dealings with those of another."[21] In place of Xie Lingyun's isolated individual seeking spiritual enlightenment in landscape, Tao Qian's poetry offers an isolated rural community as a model of social organization.

The philosophical Daoist concept of ultimate simplicity as the foundation for the ideal form of human organization is perhaps best thematized in Tao Qian's "Peach Blossom Spring," which has become the *locus classicus* in Chinese poetry of idealizing rustic life as an embodiment of a utopian society. In the famous preface to the poem, Tao Qian gives a prose account of how a fisherman during the Taiyuan period (376–397) of the Jin Dynasty, while rowing upstream, accidentally comes to a grove of peach trees in bloom along the banks of the stream. The grove extends to the foot of a mountain that is the fountainhead of the stream, where a small opening in the mountain is found, which barely admitted the body of the fisherman. A few dozen steps leads him to a broad and level plain where he finds a rural community separated from the outside world.

The poem itself is basically a versification of the prose account, but that does not detract from its value. The following translation omits the last eight lines of the poem:

When the clan of Ying broke the mandate of Heaven,[22]
Good men fled from the world.
As Huang and Qi went to Mount Shang,[23]

These people too escaped.
Gradually their route of retreat was obscured.
The path to their place was overgrown.
Helping each other they tilled the land;
At sunset they returned to their rest.
Mulberry and bamboo provided plenty of shade;
Beans and millet were planted in season.
Long silk thread was gathered from spring silkworm;
There was no king's tax at autumn harvest.
On the overgrown roads there was little traffic;
Roosters and dogs echoed each other in crowing and barking.
Their rituals still followed the ancient methods;
Their clothes had no new design.
Carefree, children sang ditties;
Joyous, the hoary heads visited each other.
When grasses grew, they knew the season was warm;
When the trees decayed, they knew the wind was fierce.
Though there was calendar;
The four seasons formed the year naturally.
Contented were they in their ample joy;
What need did they have for belaboring their intelligence?[24]

Tao Qian's utopia is apart from the contemporary world both spatially and temporally. Its hidden narrow entrance marks a spatial boundary. The separation is also temporal in that life here represents a stasis that had been maintained for 500 years. More important, this utopia is separated from the outside world in its societal organization and in its way of life. The residents live in perfect harmony with nature: Instead of being dictated by the artificial calendars, the rhythm of the agricultural activities accord with the seasonal cycles of nature, and their customs of living are those of ancient times. The harmony with nature also translates itself into the harmony in their daily life: The old and young are spared hard labor, and the farmers are spared tax.

One scholar on Tao Qian pointed out, and others agree, that the happy land described in the poem "differs in nearly every detail from the world of Tao Qian's own experience."[25] As the increasingly weakened central court was unable to restrict the expansion of private lands owned by the powerful large families of the aristocracy, the real farmers in Tao Qian's time suffered dislocation from their farmland and became the dependents of those large families.[26] Tao Qian's representation of farm life, therefore, tends to be idealized. On the other hand, the idealization is not merely a poetic fantasy. There is evidence to suggest that Tao Qian's utopian world as described in "Peach Blossom Spring" may have been based on contemporary reports of some secluded settlements for farmers to escape from the turmoil of the time.[27] Such reports certainly do not affect the artistic integrity of Tao Qian's poem, but we should be careful about hastily dismissing it as "not really relevant."[28] For the existence of such enclaves demonstrates that Tao Qian's poetic construction of a utopian society is not only a protest against the grievous reality of Qian's time but is also inspired by the actual practice of some farmers. In any case, Tao Qian vision of the simple agricultural community is a response to the actual human relations at the time.

Conclusion

From Zuo Si to Xie Lingyun to Tao Qian, wilderness (whether in the form of desolate mountains or faraway rural areas) transformed from a political sanctuary to a place for the individual's philosophical and religious enlightenment and finally to an ideal site for human society. The idealization of wilderness in medieval Chinese poetry ultimately signaled dissatisfaction with the human situation. The return to nature was propelled by the poet's sense of alienation from social conditions of the time. His perception of the brutal strife in the human world motivates his quest for harmony with the natural world.

It is clear, therefore, that man's perception and conception of nature is ultimately conditioned by his understanding of human relationships. This realization may help to explain the abrupt break with the traditional attitude toward nature in post-1949 China. Whereas harmony has been the goal of Confucianism, which has dominated in Chinese political thought for over 2,000 years, Communist China, as Rhoads Murphey has pointed out in the edited collection *The Chinese: Adapting the Past, Building the Future,* has adopted the dialectic ideology of class struggle as the motivating force of history. Political strife was considered not only a necessary but also a positive factor for the process of human society.[29] Chairman Mao Zedong unequivocally declared that "the philosophy of the Communists is the philosophy of struggle." This ideology became the official line not only in the political realm where class struggle was the perennial drama. It also manifested itself in the idea of combating and conquering the environment. It was believed that the adherence to the dialectic theory not only guaranteed the momentum of the revolutionary spirit that had put the Communists in power in the first place but also called for pressing nature to yield its maximum material benefits. In the 1950s, 1960s, and 1970s numerous verses were composed around the theme of conquering nature. One of the songs, attributed to an anonymous peasant in the late 1950s, proudly epitomized the combatant attitude toward nature:

> Let the mountains bow,
> Let the rivers make way—
> Here I come!

We should also mention at this point that the traditional Chinese attitude toward nature was never a monolithic emphasis on reverence for or harmony with the environment but has always had its inner tensions. Again, as Murphey has observed, the glorious achievements of the legendary emperors of early Chinese civilization all involved transforming and even conquering nature: the discovery of igniting fire, the evolution of agriculture, animal husbandry, irrigation, and flood control.[30] The legends of these cultural heroes suggest an ancient vision of the natural environment as hostile to and threatening the very livelihood of man. A theory of manipulating the environment for the material benefit of man was developed as early as the third century B.C. by Xun Zi, and it was no coincidence in this context that Xun Zi was found to be a positive ideological source in Communist China.[31]

The third factor to be taken into consideration is that, in China as elsewhere in the world, economic pressure has always played an important role in terms of man's actual approach to the environment. Environmental abuse is not just a modern issue, though our consciousness of it is certainly more acute than ever before. As early as the fourth century B.C., Mencius (370–300 B.C.), though speaking in a different context, offered us an example of deforestation. Mencius mentioned an Ox Mountain, which, because of its vicinity to a great metropolis, became barren after its trees were lopped by axes and sheep and cattle grazed upon it.[32] In fact, the gap between religious, philosophical, and aesthetic ideals and economic reality is a universal phenomenon. The theory of dialectic, however, seemed to bridge the gap for a while in Communist China in that economic activities, where environmental abuse took place, were justified and driven by the official ideology.

With the demise of the ideology of class struggle as the political guideline, China has witnessed a gradual restoration of some traditional cultural values in the last two decades or so. In the process of this restoration, environmental issues have also come to the forefront. We may expect or at least hope that the idealized wilderness of medieval landscape poetry will eventually help to inspire a more thoughtful approach to the environment as China strides forward in her economic development.

Notes

1. James R. Ware, trans., *Alchemy, Medicine, Religion in the China of A.D. 320: The Nei P'ien of Ko Hung (Pao-p'u tzu)* (Cambridge, MA: MIT Press, 1966), p. 279.

2. D.C. Lau, trans., *The Analects* (New York: Penguin Books, 1979), p. 84.

3. It is interesting to note here that, etymologically, as Paul Demiéville has observed, the two Chinese characters for the Daoist "immortal" (*xian*) and "mountain" (*shan*) are cognates. See his article "La Montagne dans l'art littéraire chinois," *France-Asie* 183 (1965): 10.

4. David Hawkes, trans., *The Songs of the South* (Harmondsworth, UK: Penguin Books, 1985), p. 244.

5. The people in the region of the ancient Chu kingdom (where *The Songs of the South* originated) had a shamanistic culture. See the description of this culture described by the first-century historian Ban Gu, as translated in Hawkes, *The Songs of the South*, p. 18.

6. The two pieces are translated in their entirety in Hawkes, *The Songs of the South*, pp. 223–230, 233–238.

7. Lu Qinli, ed., *Xian Qin Han Wei Jin Nanbeichao shi* (Poetry of Pre-Qin, Han, Jin and the Southern and Northern Dynasties) (Beijing: Zhonghua shuju, 1983), p. 734 (translations by Xiaoshan Yang).

8. See A.C. Graham, trans., *Chuang-tzu: The Inner Chapters* (London: George Allen & Unwin, 1981), pp. 48–49.

9. In Confucian ethics, the gentleman hides away from the world when it falls into disorder.

10. A detailed study of this subject can be found in Marjorie Hope Nicolson's *Mountain Gloom and Mountain Glory: The Development of the Aesthetics of the Infinite* (Ithaca, NY: Cornell University Press, 1959). For an illuminating comparative study, see J.D. Frodsham, "Landscape Poetry in China and Europe," *Comparative Literature*, no. 3, 193–215.

11. In Lu Qinli, *Xian Qin Han Wei Jin Nanbeichao Shi*, pp. 1172–1173 (translation by Xiaoshan Yang).

12. In a parallel couplet, the words in the first line correspond syntactically with the words in the same positions in the next line. The parallel structure can be seen even in the English translation here in lines 7 and 8.

13. Discussions of the use of parallelism in this particular poem by Xie Lingyun can be found in Lin Wenyue, "Zhongguo shanshui shi de tezhi" (Characteristics of Chinese Landscape Poetry), in his *Shanshui yu gudian* (Landscape and Classics) (Taibei: Chunwenxue chubanshe, 1976), pp. 23–62; Francis Westbrook, "Landscape

Transformation in the Poetry of Hsieh Ling-yün," *Journal of American Oriental Society* 100 (1980); 239–241; and Kang-i Sun Chang, *Six Dynasties Poetry* (Princeton: Princeton University Press, 1986), pp. 52–54. For treatment of the parallel structure in Chinese poetry in connection with the Chinese cosmogony, see Stephen Owen, *Traditional Chinese Poetry and Poetics: Omen of the World* (Madison: University of Wisconsin Press, 1985), pp. 78–107.

14. Liu Hsieh (Liu Xie), *The Literary Mind and the Carving of Dragons*, trans. Vincent Yu-chung Shih (New York: Columbia University Press, 1959), p. 190.

15. Xiao Tong, ed., *Wenxuan* (Anthology of Fine Literature), annotated by Li Shan (Shanghai: Shanghai guji chubanshe, 1986), p. 1047.

16. Lin Wenyue, "Zhongguo shanshui shi de tezhi," pp. 23–62.

17. In Lu Qinli, *Xian Qin Han Wei Jin Nanbeichao Shi*, p. 991.

18. Ibid., p. 1172.

19. Ibid., pp. 991–992.

20. Ibid., p. 994.

21. D.C. Lau, trans., *Tao Te ching* (Harmondsworth, UK: Penguin Books, 1963), p. 142.

22. "The Clan of Ying" refers to the ruling house of the first emperor of Qin, whose tyranny forced worthy men into hiding.

23. Huang and Qi were two of the four legendary "Hoary Heads" who fled from the rule of Qin to Mount Shang. Two poems (Lu Qinli, *Xian Qin Han Wei Jin Nanbeichao Shi*, pp. 90–91) on the theme of living in seclusion were attributed to them.

24. In Lu Qinli, *Xian Qin Han Wei Jin Nanbeichao Shi*, p. 986.

25. James Hightower, trans., *The Poetry of T'ao Ch'ien* (Oxford: Clarendon Press, 1970), p. 256.

26. See Kang-i Sun Chang, *Six Dynasties Poetry*, pp. 19–20.

27. See Chen Yinke, *Chen Yinke xiansheng wenshi ji* (Collected Works by Chen Yinke on Literature and History), vol. 1 (Hong Kong: Wen Wen Publications, 1973), pp. 205–218.

28. Hightower, *The Poetry of T'ao Ch'ien*, p. 256.

29. See Rhoads Murphey, "Man and Nature in China," in *The Chinese: Adapting the Past, Facing the Future*, ed. Robert Dernberger et al. (Ann Arbor: University of Michigan, Center for Chinese Studies, 1986), pp. 108–113.

30. Ibid., p. 105.

31. See Xiong Gongzhe, *Xun Zi jinzhu jinyi*, (Annotation and Translation of Xun Zi), 2d ed. (Taipei: Shangwu yinshuguan, 1977), pp. 325–329.

32. D.C. Lau, trans., *Men-tzu* (Harmondsworth, UK: Penguin Books, 1970), p. 164.

—— 7 ——

The State Remains, but Mountains and Rivers Are Destroyed

Allan G. Grapard

Historians of mountain religion divide Japan into three regions, each symbolized by a massif: to the west, Mount Hiko in Kyushu; at the center, the Ōmine Mountains and the Kumano area; and to the north, the Dewa Mountains. The term "mountain religion" is used to refer to what the Japanese call Shugendō, loosely meaning the "way of practices leading to supernatural powers." Its practitioners, known as *yamabushi*, became famous around the country not only for their ascetic exercises and claims to supernatural powers but also for their healing skills related to their knowledge of medicinal plants, for their remarkable knowledge of the land, and for their charisma.[1] Their main occupation, though, was to engage in arduous austerities in mountains around the country and to ritually course through entire mountain ranges at various times of the year in order to gain those supernatural powers. It is impossible to know how many mountain ascetics there were at any given time in the past, but there were several hundred sacred mountains in the three main islands in which the ascetics were active (Honshu, Kyushu, and Shikoku; Hokkaido was out of government control).

The present analysis will focus on Mount Hiko in order to suggest that the mountain was a social space—the community that occupied it for centuries could not and would not separate itself from thinking of its landscape in a complex manner. I hope that in the course of this chapter

I owe the title of this chapter to Gary Snyder.

one might gain a better understanding of what the terms "landscape" and "community" might have meant in Japan during the early modern period (1615–1868) and of how Mount Hiko's landscape, community, and their variegated meanings were radically altered a century ago, as a consequence of which the Japanese sense of nature and landscape, not to mention community, was torn asunder. I believe that studies of contemporary Japanese culture that do not include the past and its almost complete destruction in 1868 do nothing but lead to mischaracterization and misplaced optimism.

Mount Hiko's Early History

Mount Hiko appears in documents for the first time in the eleventh century, when it is noted that its Buddhist confraternities organized in 1094 at Dazaifu, and a violent protest ensued. As a result, the governor, Fujiwara Nagafusa, resigned and subsequently fled Kyushu Island and returned to Kyoto. This series of events indicate that the Buddhist community on the mountain during the Heian period (794–1185) had achieved political consciousness and military might in such manner that it could not be ignored anymore; there is, therefore, every reason to believe that it might have been in existence for some time before those events.

There is no indication of how the Buddhist community in question might have conceived of Mount Hiko at the earliest stages of its history; to all outward appearances, however, the first model that was used to conceptualize and represent the mountain was an understanding according to which Mount Hiko was the palatial residence of the Buddha of the Future (*Maitreya*). Classical Buddhist scriptures describe that residence as consisting of an outer realm extending down to this world and an inner palatial residence located in a transcendental space. These scriptures also state that the latter consisted of forty-nine chambers, and this architectural detail served as a template for Mount Hiko's transformation from a simple mountain into the physical embodiment of Buddhist cosmographic principles related to the belief in the Buddha of the Future. At some point during the Heian period, forty-nine caves located on or near Mount Hiko, connected by paths and used either for temporary seclusion or permanent residence, were associated with the forty-nine chambers of the inner residence where the Buddha of the Future was said to be awaiting the dawn on which he would initiate a new cosmic era. The conception of Mount Hiko, the residence of the Buddha of the

Future was, therefore, related to notions of cosmic renewal and of political and economic utopia.

Mount Hiko's Sacred Perimeter

During the eleventh century, pilgrimages to sacred mountains on the part of the imperial court reached their apex. Retired Emperor Shirakawa's first visit to the centrally located Kumano sacred region occurred in 1090. His spiritual mentor and actual guide at the time was a certain Zōyo, who became the general abbot of Kumano and was also given the abbacy of the Shōgo-in Temple, which had been created for the purpose of protecting the body of the state symbolized by that of the emperor. In 1160, Emperor Go-Shirakawa invoked the Kumano deities in Kyoto and built the Ima-Kumano Shrine to entice the deities to remain as protectors of the Shōgo-in Temple. Twenty-one years later Emperor Go-Shirakawa established economic support for that shrine by granting it twenty-eight domains scattered all over Japan; these domains were exempt from corvées and levies at the provincial and national levels. Listed among these twenty-eight domains was Mount Hiko. From then on apparently, the mountain was recognized as a tax-free space defined by specific boundaries that could not be crossed by governmental authorities. Four years later, in 1185, Minamoto Yoritomo, the Kamakura shogun, set up land stewards in each province of the country and Ōtomo Yoshinao became the first protector of Buzen Province, where Mount Hiko is located; in 1197 he ascended the mountain and offered a statue of the Buddha Amida. Mount Hiko then came to be known as the "Avatars of the Three Sites," and its three rounded peaks were conceived of as natural embodiments of three divine native entities associated with three Buddhist deities.

In 1213, *Hiko-san ruki*, the main medieval document concerning the history of the mountain, was compiled.[2] In that document we learn that in addition to its main temple there were more than 200 meditation halls, that the ecclesiastic population of the mountain consisted of 110 monks and 205 mountain ascetics, and that Mount Hiko was characterized by its forty-nine caves; the text lists each cave by name and narrates stories and legends associated with each, as well as the names of the main deities and their guardians enshrined therein. Most pointedly, however, this text mentions the *kekkai* (sacred perimeter) granted in 1181. I translate *kekkai* as sacred perimeter because its Indian equivalent signified the demarcation of an area in which deities were invoked, and by extension, the establishment of a consecrated zone for the arrangement of mandalas and the construction of temples.[3] *Kekkai* referred to those two phenomena, but it was also used at least since the ninth century to refer to entire geographical areas set aside and donated exclusively to Shinto-Buddhist institutions, which meant that the government waived its rights to control, inspect, and impose taxes and corvées on the land and people.

The boundaries within which Mount Hiko rose were not formed exclusively by an enclosure, a perimeter defined by imperial law in the twelfth century and retraced time and again by ritualized peregrinations on the part of various classes of mountain ascetics. A far more elaborate type of modeling of spatial experience, Mount Hiko was treated as the geographical embodiment of a Buddhist doctrine known as the "Four Lands Perimeter" in which the mountain was considered to consist of four superimposed layers marked by shrine gates and in which life was subjected to constraints growing in severity as one reached higher altitudes through each of those gates: At the foot of the mountain were the villages where both laymen and religious figures could live; on the second layer were located the villages of the mountain ascetics themselves; on the third layer were the caves in which these people engaged in their ascetic practices; and the fourth layer was a zone of undisturbed wilderness.[4] This model of spatial, religious, and social experience may have been established in the late twelfth or early thirteenth century, perhaps even earlier; its origins and meaning warrant a brief presentation, for that model was the result of the concrete application of ritualized meditations connected to the ritual known as the "Lotus Blossom Ritual," the analysis of which indicates the very site where "subjective" and "objective" spaces intersected to constitute Mount Hiko's true landscape.

The Lotus Blossom Ritual

As it was performed in Japan, the Lotus Blossom Ritual was a set of ritualized meditations leading to the imaginary participation in the Buddha Śākyamuni's preaching of the Lotus Sūtra. The ritual emphasized the eleventh chapter of that scripture in which another Buddha, named Prabhūtaratna, praises Śākyamuni and validates the contents of the Lotus Sūtra by making a jeweled stupa-shaped reliquary emerge from the ground and float in the air, and invites Śākyamuni to share his seat. The object of the Lotus Blossom Ritual was, primarily, a re-enactment of the vision outlined above, and its emphasis was on the vision of the two buddhas and on the subsequent vision of the multitudinous assembly of devotees levitating in open space.

The first step in the preparations of the Lotus Blossom Ritual involved setting up and decorating the all-important *dōjō* (site of practice), which was a square platform facing east; the *dōjō* should be underscored, for it refers not only to the organized space within which the platform was built but also to the mental space achieved by the ritualists. That mental space is that of the *subjective* "space" of the Buddha at the time of his awakening as well as at the time of his preaching the Lotus Sūtra, and it was symbolized by the *objective* "space" of the Bo-tree under which the historical Buddha is said to have had his ultimate experience.

Various mystic hand gestures, chants, and recitations of relevant segments of the Lotus Sūtra were performed as preliminary steps leading to the core of the ritual, which entailed a complex meditation on the term *dōjō* and consisted in visualizing the *dōjō* (and the meditation process) as consisting of "four lands," each representing a different modality of space and ontological status whose experience would gradually lead not only to the mystic state achieved when envisioning the two Buddhas seated in the stupa but to nirvana itself.[5]

It is probable that the ritual outlined above served as the doctrinal and ritual anchor for the particular and radical form of sacralization of Mount Hiko's space.The names of the four lands stipulated in ritual texts were applied to four superimposed layers encompassing the height of the mountain within the perimeter established in 1181. These four "lands" or zones were then subjected to separate regulations determining types of religious experience and modalities of social life prescribed at a given altitude in each zone. Mount Hiko was not merely visualized as though it were a *dōjō* in some kind of abstract way, however; it was transformed into one, which means that it was lived as a space that could be enacted (produced) only by means of ritual practices increasing in difficulty. Each zone was given the name of the four steps of the Lotus Blossom Ritual meditation.

Altitude and Altered States of Mind

The boundaries of the four lands of Mount Hiko were marked by some of the forty-nine caves mentioned earlier on, and by various shrines, inscribed stones, and the like, and were further marked by shrine gates set at various elevations to be reached, not just through the physical effort of ascent but through meditative exercises, the completion of specific rites of penance and their associated vision-inducing mystic body-mind states, and the observance of a number of purificatory practices. Life was strictly controlled in each of the four zones until the 1850s and was subjected to taboos and various legal restraints briefly outlined below.

The lowest zone was called the "Land of Cohabitation of Anchorites and Common People," and included hamlets located within the limits of the perimeter established in 1181. It was prohibited to cultivate the five grains or kill any form of life in that zone. The cultivation of tea and vegetables was allowed, however, and several houses specialized in midwifery, since giving birth was outlawed in the upper zones. *Hiko-san ruki* states that in the lowest zone the inhabitants "had no fields and survived on a diet of dew and herbs." Rice cultivation was legalized for the first time in 1858.

The entrance to the second zone, the "Land of Expedient Means Characterized by Remaining Worldly Attachments," was marked by a shrine gate made of bronze and situated at 500 meters altitude; its upper limit was marked by a gate made of stone and located at 700 meters. The four hamlets forming the religious community of Mount Hiko were located in the second zone. In 1868, most were abandoned and only a few buildings of the main hamlet remain. The bronze gate is today located at a lower altitude than it used to be in the past; it was moved at the end of the Edo period (1600–1868), when the main hamlet grew in size partly as a result of the Tokugawa shogunate policies lifting travel restrictions to encourage trade. The mountain ascetics were then allowed to transform their temple-like residences into inns, where they lodged and educated a growing number of travelers and pilgrims on whose generosity they increasingly came to depend, since they were losing direct economic access to land domains they once controlled. Grain cultivation was also forbidden in that zone. So was the delivery of children; pregnant women were required to move down to one of the villages situated below the bronze gate.

The third zone, the "Adorned Land of True Retribution Devoid of Obstacles," extended from the stone gate located in front of the main sanctuary to the wooden gate located in front of the practitioners' hall of the upper sanctuary. Since the third zone consists mainly of steep rocky escarpments that are not easy to reach, there are no halls of residence, but most of the caves in which the mountain ascetics practiced their austerities in total seclusion are found there. It was regarded as a realm inhabited by bodhisattvas, and therefore as an ideal place for the performance of visualizations and meditation. In the second zone there were many paths used for the transportation of foodstuff by bulls; in this zone, however, no horses or bulls were allowed. All possible precautions against pollution, particularly concerning death, were taken. Preservation efforts have continued to this day to keep the flora and fauna intact.

The fourth and uppermost zone, the "Land of Permanent Quiescent Radiance," extended upward from the wooden gate to the three summits of Mount Hiko at 1,200 meters altitude, which were regarded by the mountain ascetics as the actual embodiment of combined native and Buddhist deities, the Avatars of the Three Sites. Any release of sperm, excrements, urine, saliva, phlegm, or mucous from the nose, was prohibited in that zone. This was regarded as an ideal space to be left untouched, where the pure land of the buddhas and the world of humans were marked by the absence of difference.

The four zones of the mountain were metaphors for the prescription of social practice, in the sense that they represented the embodiment of a mental map of social hierarchy, itself based on an opposition between purity and pollution.

Through their ritual practices on Mount Hiko the mountain ascetics transformed a natural mountain in such a way that it appeared as transcendent and sacred, and the mountain accordingly became a reference point for larger understandings about the nature of the world, inasmuch as it became a symbol for relations of order. That is, the fundamental opposition between purity and pollution transcoded an opposition between nature and culture and was inscribed in the material used to build the gates, which was graded according to the amount of human work (culture) necessitated: melted bronze for the lowest gate, sculpted stone for the middle gate, and roughly hewn wood for the upper gate. That distinction between culture at the bottom and nature at the top in terms of the complexity of manufacture of the materials for the gates was explicitly stated and its import resides in the quasi-immanent character of its purpose: at Mount Hiko, nature or wilderness was the mark of transcendence. At the same time, the four Buddhist lands or zones functioned to reinforce an older, pre-Buddhist social prescription (social hierarchy grounded in opposition between purity and pollution), in the sense that they represented the embodiment of a mental map of social hierarchy, itself grounded in the opposition between purity and pollution. In that oppositional schema, pollution was at the bottom and purity at the top. Purity came to be associated with the highest domains of mystical experience accompanied by restraints on behavior, while pollution was associated with realms conceived of as "external paths" and "lower worlds." That opposition indicates that Mount Hiko's space is not to be interpreted solely along Buddhist doctrinal or ritual lines; it was also the site of manifestation of native deities, and native views concerning purity and pollution were also in effect, so that various notions and practices related to dirt, blood, disease, and biological functions came to be combined with the Buddhist order of things. Transcendence was quiescent and radiant, marked by immobility and the total absence of work; the lower and further away one went from it, however, the more "busy" one became, the closer one came to the world of work and to the dark and smelly realm of gutters and garbage flowing downstream. The mountain ascetics thus mapped out onto the mountain's topography a social topography in which they established strict correlations between altitude, cleanliness, morality and desire, and salvation. It would be wrong, as a consequence, to regard them as marginal groups in the overall medieval representation of social order, for they were at the very core of that representation: While some scholars have considered them to have been "marginal" figures in Japanese history, the mountain ascetics were actually playing a crucial role in maintaining vertical hierarchies at opposite ends of which the emperor and the outcastes were situated.

The Medieval Golden Age

Indeed, starting in the fourteenth century, the abbacy of Mount Hiko became an imperial institution, in the sense that the position was to be filled exclusively by members of the imperial house. The first instance occurred in 1333 when Utsunomiya Nobukatsu, the land steward of the Shiroi district of Buzen, placed as abbot of Mount Hiko the imperial prince Annin (renamed Jōyū Hō-shinn) after his ordination); that imperial prince was a son of Emperor Go-Fushimi. Thereafter, the abbacy was inherited, for the prince was married. This fundamentally Japanese social exception to the monastic principle of celibacy, however, also implied that the abbot could not reside in the monastery on the mountain, and the abbacy offices were then established at Kurokawa, south of the mountain. Due to the imperial house's hold on its abbacy, Mount Hiko's power grew in the fourteenth century, and its population became ever more involved with surrounding areas: The abbacy maintained close links with those toiling in their land estates, where they established subshrines of Mount Hiko, and encouraged those people to engage in pilgrimage and to travel through the country in order to attract believers and thus enhance their own economic relations.

A list of ritual assemblies of the Hiko multiplex dated 1445 provides some information on the social organization of the mountain community, which was divided into three groups whose members specialized in the preparation and performance of separate ritual functions. The first group, consisting of *Gyōja-gata* (mountain ascetics), organized the ritualized courses through the mountains in spring, summer, and fall. The second group, *Shito-gata*, emphasized Buddhist rites. The third group, *Sō-gata*, emphasized non-Buddhist rites. That group consisted of two sub-groups, the *Iro-shi* (yin) and the *Katana-shi* (yang), who performed the *Matsu-e* and *Onta-sai* ritual festivities, respectively.

The social status of the predominantly Buddhist members was deemed superior to those of the mountain ascetics and of the predominantly Shinto members. That distinction was given legitimacy by a Buddhist doctrine that was actually a framework for the inscription of social power. According to that doctrine, the term "essence" was used to denote Buddhist deities, while the term "manifestation" was used to denote the native deities in whose guise various Buddhist deities were believed to manifest themselves. In other words, Buddhism presented itself not only as an alternative to pre-existing schemata sustaining the interpretation of reality, but as a framework of interpretation including native deities while reducing them to the lower status of local and minor forms of a transcendental Buddha essence. Buddhism thus positioned itself as the dominant—if not domineering—epistemological framework through the use and implementation of such interpretive schemes. Accordingly, but on a social level, the term "essence" was applied to those who associated themselves predominantly with Buddhist temples, while the term "manifestation" was used to refer to those who associated themselves predominantly with Shinto shrines. In other words, the members of the community who specialized in Buddhist doctrine and rites claimed a social status higher than that of those who predominantly worshipped the native deities. Their claim was legitimated by Buddhist doctrine and manifested on yet another social level: Only members of the former group were allowed to marry into the abbot's family.

By the end of the fifteenth century Mount Hiko became embroiled in the civil wars that pitted various warriors' houses, religious institutions, and court-related houses throughout the country against each other; the community of Mount Hiko, therefore, armed itself. Nonetheless, the religious life of Mount Hiko seems to have flourished in that period of unrest. For about one-half of a century starting in 1509, Shugendō doctrine and practice were submitted to thorough systematization by one of its members, Akyū-bō Sokuden (n.d.), who had originally been a member of Mount Futara's Shugendō community at Nikkō. Akyū-bō Sokuden's documents went on to form the bulk of theoretical and practical treatises of Shugendō all over Japan thereafter. These treatises were then circulated among the highest-ranked mountain ascetics and were taught in ascending levels of secrecy to (male) initiates who had undergone grueling tests of endurance in Mount Hiko's temples and in the mountainous ranges of northeastern Kyushu, but they were also circulated among ascetics of other regions in Japan. One of those didactic tracts, the "Secret Directives Concerning the Essentials of Practice in Shugendō," reveals how the body was conceived through the use of spatial metaphors, for a body performing rituals in mountains had to be "oriented."

Body Talk

The body was primarily conceived in terms of its extension in space and needed proper positioning in order to be ritualized and thereby reach the stated goals of its ordered movements through space. Furthermore, the body was encoded so that each of its parts became associated with an element, a shape, a color, a sound, a quality, and the body itself came to be treated as though it were a mandala. These characteristics are clearly stated in Akyū-bō Sokuden's definition of the ritual practice known as *toko-gatame* (solidifying the body position) (see Figure 7.1):

> The following is an instruction regarding *toko-gatame* while coursing through the mountains. The term *toko* [literally, "seat"] refers to the mandalas associated with the diamond and womb courses. It is the *dōjō* of the Land of Cohabitation. The term *katame* [literally, "solidification"] refers to the [diamond-like] solidity of the five elements [forming] the Body of Essence [of the Buddha]. This [terminology implies that] one's body is that of the Buddha. Our Revered Patriarch, the *thatāhgata* Mahāvairocana, is endowed with the inner realization of the realm of essence, is permanent, and pervades the triple world. His essential corporality knows neither beginning nor end, and is perfect and endowed

with a myriad of qualities; it consists of the five elements of earth, water, fire, wind, and ether, each symbolically manifest in the following shapes: square [cube], circle [sphere], triangle [pyramid], crescent [half-moon], and drop [bubble]. These shapes symbolize the following aspects: firmness, humidity, dissipation [like smoke], movement, and absence of obstacle. Furthermore, they are symbolized by five colors: yellow, white, red, black, and blue, and by the five "seed letters" *a-bi-ra-un-ken*. The five elements pervade the ten realms of both sentient and nonsentient beings; they are therefore called "elemental" [literally, "expansive"]. These five elements are the basis on which the bodies of Buddhas and those of common beings are constituted. . . . That is why Shugendo holds the view that one's physical body is the Buddha itself. . . . Recite the following meditation verse:

This very body is *a-bi-ra-un-ken*
Waist and legs, navel, heart, neck, and summit of the cranium.
Below the waist, (𑀅) [a] refers to original nonproduction/
Yellow color, cubic shape, the ground of the Buddha's heart-mind.
In the wheel of the navel, (𑀩) [bi] refers to the sermon beyond language/
White, spherical shape, the water of great compassion.
Set on the heart, (𑀭) [ra] refers to the absence of pollution/
Red, pyramidal shape, the fire of great wisdom.
Below the chin, (𑀳) [un] refers to separation from cause and effect relations/
Black, crescent shape, the power of great wind.
Above the forehead, (𑀔) [ken] refers to absolute spatial emptiness/
Blue, tear-drop shape, the wheel [cylinder] of the great sky [ether].

Thus aiming at visualizing the human body as though it were a *stūpa* conceived not only as the original site of religious practice but as the body of the Buddha, this ritual meditation was usually performed on the first day of coursing through mountains. It was then followed by the performance of a rite called *toko-sadame* (firming the body position), defined in the same text as follows (see Figure 7.2):

—First, form the *toko-gatame* in space (first, diamond; second, womb).
—Next, form the *ōkyōgo* hand configuration; recite the corresponding spell.
—Next, form the *ryūkyōgo* hand configuration; recite the corresponding spell.
—Next, [the practitioner should] lay [on the ground] on the right side,

Figure 7.1 **The body as *stupa***

Figure 7.2 **Position of the body in the horizontal *toko-sadame* ritual**

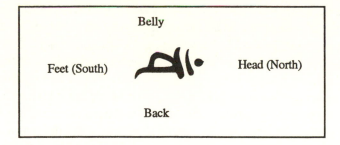

extend the left arm, place it on the hip, and remain firm (*sadame*) in that position (*toko*). This configuration is called horizontal *vam* (𑖪) spell. In the case of the *toko-gatame* ritual, the same configuration is called vertical *vam* spell.[6]

This particular positioning of the body in the form of a *siddhaṃ* graph was related to a symbolic death viewed as liberation from transmigration, for Akyūbō Sokuden goes on to explicitly associate it with the bodily position of the Buddha at the time of his entrance into nirvana.[7] In other words, the body was treated as though it were both iconic (in the semiotic sense) and iconographic, but space and orientation were of the essence.

Late Medieval Shocks

When that text was written in the first half of the sixteenth century, however, Kyushu was divided into three power bases: the Ryūzō-ji, Otomo, and Shimazu warrior houses. One of the ways in which these houses could legitimate their supremacy was to place one of their own members at Mount Hiko by a marriage into the imperial abbacy house. The competition was so fierce that the Ryūzō-ji house burned Mount Hiko's temples in 1568 when it could not succeed in its plans and the Otomo house sent a force of 4,000 soldiers to attack the mountain in 1581, for the same reason. In the course of these disasters that befell Mount Hiko, many valuable documents and records were lost forever, but an important historical record, *Chinzei Hiko-san engi* dated 1572, survived.[8] This document suggests that the community of the mountain was undergoing major religious, social, and political changes at the time. Apparently as a result of the fights for influence and succession that symbolize those changes, a woman was named abbess of the mountain between 1587 and 1601. Shun'yū, the abbot at the time, had no son, but he had a daughter whom he ordered to marry a certain Akizuki Tanenaga. That couple's daughter, Masachiyo-hime, was then chosen as abbess, and she even left Kurokawa to reside on Mount Hiko itself, thus bringing an end to taboos against women and, particularly, against menstruation. A document of the time says that women should feel no shame for their menses and were allowed to go as far as the main Hall of Veneration (at the boundary between the second and third zones). That abbess, however, was dislodged from her position by a warrior named Mori Hisahachirō (in 1587, upon the conquest of Kyushu by Toyotomi Hideyoshi, second of the "three unifiers" of early modern Japan, the entire northeastern part of Kyushu had been given over to Mori Katsunobu). Mount Hiko's community, however, saw the Mori warrior house as an outsider and lodged a complaint against him directly to Fushimi Castle, the seat of the shogunate near Kyoto.

In 1600 the case was brought to trial, and there was a judgment to the effect that Mount Hiko, while retaining its right of no-entry on the part of governmental authority, was to turn its land domains over to shogunate control. As a result, Mount Hiko lost its traditionally land-based economic power and had to turn to its lay followers for economic support, which was the beginning of lay patron sponsorship of Mount Hiko, an important sociopolitical and economic phenomenon during the Edo period. This event was a major turning point in the history of the mountain. Firm in its notion that Mount Hiko was a separate entity out of government control, its members created their own money to be used solely within the confines of the perimeter; visitors had to exchange their cash for that money, which they used to purchase lodging, food, medicine, amulets, and to pay fees to climb the mountain.

Soon thereafter, Hosokawa Tadaoki (a warrior who had become the representative of the central government in Kyushu) granted his support to Mount Hiko: he rebuilt its temples (they stood thus rebuilt throughout the premodern period); his son (adopted, but born from the aristocratic Hino family) was adopted by the abbess and became the next abbot, under the name Chūyū. The Great Lecture Hall of Mount Hiko was dedicated in 1616, and the mountain community was thoroughly reorganized, as is indicated by a legal document signed in 1624 by thirteen administrator monks and consisting of thirty-six regulations. Its salient points are as follows:

- Anybody caught removing wood from the designated sacred perimeter, even in as small an amount as is needed to make a fan, will be condemned to forced labor.
- No dry wood or dead branches for fire use shall be removed from the mountain. People who need firewood will have to go as far as Karagatani to the south and Reisui to the north. It is forbidden to cut wood within the mountain's perimeter, even on one's own residential lot, in order to make furniture.
- It is prohibited to cultivate tea gardens outside of one's residence or to till fields next to the caves where mountain ascetics reside permanently. Those who break this rule will be reported to the monastic authorities.
- Whoever attaches or releases horses on the access roads to the Lecture Hall will be fined 300 copper coins.
- It is prohibited to scatter horse excrement along the village roads or any of the mountain's paths.
- Responsibility for cleaning the access paths will rotate among the town's residents and shall be performed every fourteenth day and every last day of the month.[9]

During the Edo period Mount Hiko was governed by the abbot, two administrative directors, and four directors of ritual affairs. Of these four, one received the special title *nemban* (yearly duty) and specialized in the formulation and control of ritual festivity performances. Below these two yearly appointees were two "controllers of the mountain," one specializing in the protection of the vegetation and the other in its maintenance, two maintenance directors specializing in the maintenance of shrines and temples, and one "town manager" who oversaw both the city of the mountain ascetics and the visitors and inns. Indeed, the Hiko community was not only formed by the year-round residents of the mountain, it also consisted of a huge number of lay patrons (some 350,000 were recorded in 1875) who visited the mountain on a regular basis and who made the donations necessary for the maintenance of the mountain community and proper handling of the visitors; the number of visitors could suddenly jump to 80,000 at the time of the two main ritual festivities. In 1710 the mountain ascetics' village of Mount Hiko had 637 priestly residences and a permanent population of 3,015. Its fame spread beyond Kyushu Island, and emperors sponsored rites and asked for spiritual protection from its deities.

Shugendō thus became a religious, military, economic, and social force that the government could ill afford to ignore, and the shoguns of the Edo period feared its popularity and saw it as a potentially uncontrollable force, should the mountain communities unify across the country. The Edo government therefore decided to undermine its strength by dividing Shugendō into two competitive groups through the promulgation of its *Regulations for Shugendō* in 1613. That policy was intended to "divide and conquer," for it stipulated that all Shugendō temples of Japan must affiliate themselves with either of the two main sects of esoteric Buddhism (Tendai and Shingon) and must immediately place themselves under the direction of head temples located in the Kyoto area: The Shōgo-in Temple would control Tendai-affiliated temples (which would become a Tendai branch called Honzan), while the Daigo-ji Sambō-in Temple would control the Shingon-affiliated temples (which would become a Shingon branch called Tozan). As a consequence, the Shōgo-in renewed its claim dating back to 1181 over Mount Hiko, and treated the religious institution of Mount Hiko as a subtemple. This situation was grudgingly accepted in Kyushu at the time, but in 1651 the Shōgo-in authorities complained to the government that the abbot of Mount Hiko was wearing a purple robe, which it claimed was inappropriate because that color was granted only to Kyoto prelates of imperial birth. Naturally, the abbacy of Mount Hiko objected and requested that Mount Hiko be freed from Kyoto control. After years of arguments, Mount Hiko gained independent status in 1696.

In the seventeenth century the abbots of Mount Hiko wrote that the mountain community "specialized in postulating the fundamental equality of essence and manifestation," by which we must understand that the social rank and community status of the Shinto-oriented members of the mountain was deemed equal to that of the Buddhist prelates, scholarly priests, and their associates. On a translocal level, however, the emerging nativist studies movement resulted in the proliferation of anti-Buddhist representations that had actual material and social consequences, one of which was that by the end of the nineteenth century the Shinto members claimed to have a status superior to that of the Buddhist members, and their rituals came to be performed first (and not last, as had been the case prior to the eighteenth century) and with greater pomp. Throughout the country Buddhist individuals and institutions became the object of derision and criticism, and as the authority of the Edo government waned, there were calls to abolish the shogunate and return the emperor to the head of the state. This was to occur in 1868, the beginning of the so-called Meiji Restoration.

The Meiji Destruction of Mount Hiko

On the eve of the Meiji Restoration, numerous Hiko mountain ascetics sided with the movements to restore imperial authority. This phenomenon was carefully watched over by the pro-shogunate Kokura authorities, north of Mount Hiko. In an attempt to control what it viewed as a dangerous situation, the Kokura authorities encircled Mount Hiko on the eleventh day of the eleventh month of 1863 and arrested the abbot and twenty leading mountain ascetics. Although the abbot and a few mountain ascetics were subsequently released and returned to the mountain, six mountain ascetics remained in jail in Kokura and were executed in 1867.

A few months later the rescript returning the emperor to the throne was promulgated; one of the first directives of the new government ordered that all buddhas and *kami* (the name given to the countless entities that are the object of cult in what are today referred to as Shinto shrines) worshipped in common in sites of cult located all over the country be separated from each other. This order was followed by a movement, more or less popular and attaining various levels of intensity, of rejection of Buddhism. On the sixteenth day of the ninth month, 1868, the abbot Kyōyū went to Kyoto and met with the emperor. He then resigned the abbacy and returned to lay life, but three days later the former Buddhist prelate was installed as the Shinto head priest of Mount Hiko, which immediately set itself under the direct authority of the Jingikan, the supreme office of the government in Tokyo. The Kokura authorities then abandoned the siege of the mountain in reaction to which, on the sixth day of the first month of 1869, a group of radical youths, who called themselves "*Kami* Soldiers" (*shimpei*) and organized themselves on the basis of a code of conduct they swore to uphold, began their destruction of Buddhist emblems and structures on Mount Hiko. The first line of that code reads: "We will cleanse old habits and [ensure that everyone] revere the emperor and the *kami* of Heaven and Earth." In the process of their cleansing actions, they murdered mothers of priests, ordered all temples to slam their gates shut, and destroyed the majority of buildings of Mount Hiko. Some of the remaining structures were subsequently transformed into Shinto shrines. They also removed and destroyed Buddhist statues and ritual implements.

In 1872 the government issued a decree abolishing Shugendō. Soon thereafter on Mount Hiko, the main rites of the mountain ascetics were abandoned and the majority of the mountain ascetics left the mountain, either to become members of the emerging modern Japanese society or to start small-scale religious groups that focused on healing. Some mountain ascetics, however, remained in and around the mountain and continued sustaining their practices in secret, encouraged, apparently, by the fact that the new Shinto head priest (who had taken the truly exceptional name Takachiho) did not favor the absolute destruction of the site of cult.[10] Indeed, his adopted son even acted to quell the activities of the *shimpei* in 1873. Interestingly enough, the lay believers of the area did not reject their beliefs in the same abrupt manner, and they continued to provide economic support for pilgrimages and the main ritual assemblies and festivities at the mountain. We know, for example, that the temple Shōen-bō provided lodging to sixty-nine pilgrims in 1866, to 232 pilgrims in 1870, and to 213 pilgrims in 1871. Furthermore, a number of lay patrons received permission to take care of various Buddhist statues and give them proper worship in their own homes, thus precluding the disappearance of longstanding objects of cult and enhancing the potential for later material presentation of ideological resistance. Finally, we know that some of the new Shinto priests of Mount Hiko placed screens and other devices in front of objects of cult, thus removing them from direct sight and protecting them from what would have been assured destruction.

In 1874, however, the destruction started anew, following the appointment of a Shinto priest who had formerly been an official of the Kokura fief and who declared, "the order to destroy the Buddhas came from the very top and cannot be defied." Whatever bells, statues, paintings, and documents remained on Mount Hiko were gathered and smashed to pieces. An order was subsequently issued to garner all of the objects of cult that had been located in the caves along the various courses around the mountain peaks. All were destroyed. This scenario occurred throughout Japan between 1868 and 1875; it was a major cultural revolution, at the end of which power was radically redistributed and Buddhist authority thoroughly diminished, if not completely wiped out.

In Shōwa 60 (1985), only 109 houses and a population of 328 were recorded in the local census of Mount Hiko; in 1987, 16 priestly residences, 99 lay houses, and a total population of 385 people were recorded in the census.

Altered Landscapes, Practices, and Meanings

We need to make sense of this series of events which befell a great many sites of cult and heralded the appearance of the modern imperial cult and state Shinto as well as the almost complete disappearance of Shugendō. Time and space prevent me from engaging in this question in detail, but I would like to suggest that a fundamental aspect of the new religious imperial system was its view of the division between landscapes and communities, thus instituting a systematic reconstruction of space, the territory, and the social, economic, and political practices that were to "take place" therein. The modern state could not tolerate a discourse on sacralization that did not mesh with its totalitarian notion of territory, with its inscription of new economic and legal codes therein, and with its anti-Buddhist leanings.

On the eve of the Meiji Restoration (which would be better characterized as a cultural revolution),[11] Japan consisted of a large number of fiefs living in relative and uncomfortable peace, and strains were evident in the political, economic, and social domains. When the imperial government was formed, teams of diplomats went to Europe and the United States to study various forms of government constitutions and upon their return to Japan chose those elements they thought might work in the case of their country. France had just gone through its revolution, and one can see some of its effects on Japanese policies: one nation, one language, one territory. Local understandings were to be transformed and put in the background, only to be replaced by a single mode of territorial practice visible to everyone. "Japaneseness" became a dominant obsession of intellectuals who were straining to create a unity out of a variety of modalities of being. All dialects disappeared and were replaced by a single official language. Otherness was reduced to the same. On the level of landscapes, new roads and train lines began tracing different communication lines and practices: The speed of travel was obviously enhanced, but the gaze of the traveler now was a quick glance rather than a long, steady observation of discrete features. Many mountains were either flattened or deforested under the onslaught of the quest for rapid industrialization and its accompanying hunger for natural resources, while masses of people moved from the countryside to the cities. In that context, there were two possible reactions: either the countryside would come to be regarded as distant and backward, or it would become the object of nostalgic representation and adulation. Both reactions can be seen at the time: The new urban population became fascinated with Western technologies and attitudes and began forgetting the past; on the other hand, anthropologists and ethnographers began accumulating immense amounts of data about the past and tried to reconstitute an image of what life in the countryside might have been like. In both cases, however, pre-Meiji Japan became foreign to its own people. Traditional conceptions of nature, of course, became obsolete, exotic, and were romanticized: Japan created its own orientalism. It is becoming clear that an independent social system such as that of the mountain ascetics could not fit the new paradigm, and this is one of the reasons why Shugendō was abolished by the government in 1872. At the end of World War II, some people found in the new constitution, which allowed freedom of religion, an opportunity to restore some sites of cult and form part-time Shugendō groups in various parts of the country; today, one can see where the rediscovery of roots is part of the new call for cultural identity. The landscapes, however, have been radically altered, and there is no sign that Japan will follow France and create a Ministry of the Landscape whose function is to suggest that landscapes are also part of the patrimony.

Future studies of the modern creation of imperial Japan will probably

find it difficult to dispense with local history or with geospecific characteristics; the new nation-state "displaced" or "dislocated" ancient for-
mulations of spatial forms taken by social relations, which is what a
landscape is. In the quest for a unified nation, the lack of tolerance for
local difference was one reason for the destruction of Mount Hiko's
community, the breakdown of its economic base, and the annihilation of
its network of lay patronage. Ascents of Mount Hiko were "programmed"
during the medieval period to lead to intensely mystical experiences
based on fundamental scriptures of Buddhism. Today, Mount Hiko is
little more than a destination for tourists, a mere landscape to be viewed
and photographed, but not lived. Parts of the mountain are now subjected to logging, and a good many slopes are cut through by roads for
tourists in their cars. The rivers' banks are cemented, and one cannot see
what was once an abundant population of trout and other fish, frogs,
crayfish, and rare plants and birds. Parking lots abound. As one descen-
dant of the mountain ascetics remarked wryly during my last visit there
in May 1996, "You see, the mountain has changed very little."

In light of this analysis we can better see, perhaps, how the
government's 1868 claim to return to the pure traditions of the past contained a set of blatant inner contradictions; that claim functioned to hide
the ideological dimensions of the new space and time by which modernity manifested itself, transforming radically different localities into a
single, flat landscape repeating the same message: The state rules, and
mountains and rivers have nothing else to say.

There are encouraging signs, however: People realize how industrialization has fundamentally hurt the environment, and one can see grassroots
political movements of concerned citizens. Nature films abound on televi-
sion. Nature seems to be reclaiming some of the importance it had in everyday consciousness. In the case of Mount Hiko, one can now buy books on
the birds and wildflowers of the once-sacred mountain, and tourists carry
those books, together with cameras and binoculars, during their ascent taking a respite from the frantic lifestyle carried out as a matter of course at the
foot of the mountain. How much of that consciousness and activism are
going to prevail in Japan's quest to remain economically powerful is, however, a wide-open question, and there is no answer in sight.

Notes

1. *Yamabushi* means "those who sleep in the mountains." I will refer to these
practitioners as "mountain ascetics" from here on.

2. This text will appear in translation in my forthcoming book, *The Religion of Space and the Limits of Religion*.

3. A mandala is a graphic diagram used as a support for meditation in esoteric Buddhist schools.

4. See Figure 7.3, which shows Mount Hiko within the limits of its perimeter and the four zones. The map is based on raw material compiled by the Japan National Institute of Geography.

Figure 7.3

5. See Figure 7.4, a simplified drawing of the mandala used in the Lotus Blossom Ritual.

6. "Shugan shūyō hiketsu-shū" in Shugen seiten hensanki, ed. *Shugen seiten* (Kyoto: Sammitsudō shoten, 1968), pp. 239–40 (translations by Allan Grapard).

7. Siddham is the name given to a graphic system now abandoned in India, but transmitted to China, and around the eighth century c.e. to Japan, where it is still used in Esoteric Buddhism to write spells and the esoteric names of divinities.

8. This text will also appear in translation in my forthcoming book, *The Religion of Space and the Limits of Religion*.

9. Nagano Tadashi, "Hiko-san seiiki (shizen) wo hogoshita Shugendō," in *Kyōdo Tagawa* 32 (1989), p. 40 (translation by Allan Grapard).

10. Takachiho is the name of the southern Kyushu mountain onto which the first emperor would have landed after his descent from heaven according to the traditional, but wrong, chronology some 2,600 years ago.

11. See my article, "Japan's Ignored Cultural Revolution: The Separation of Shinto and Buddhist Divinities in Meiji, and a Case Study, Tonomine," *History of Religions* 23, no. 3 (February 1984): 240–265.

Figure 7.4

—— 8 ——

Big Water, Great River: Two Ways of Seeing the Columbia

William L. Lang

"The eyes explore the visual field and
abstract from it certain objects, points
of focus, perspectives."

—Yi-Fu Tuan[1]

East of Portland, Oregon, the Columbia River runs through a 3,000–
foot-deep gorge in the Cascade Mountains on its westward course to
the Pacific Ocean. Nearly at the end of its 1,210–mile run from the
Canadian Rockies, the river cuts the only sea-level passageway through
the chain of volcanic mountains that rise along the western edge of
North America. It is a spectacularly scenic landscape. Rising steeply
on the south bank, volcanic cliffs clothed in hemlock, fir, oak, spruce,
and cedar loom over the river and elevated escarpments on the north
bank. Dozens of glacier-fed streams fringe the precipices, dropping
their waters hundreds of feet in falls and cascades to the Columbia.
Formed by millions of years of catastrophic geological and hydrologi-
cal forces, the "Gorge" has impressed, even stunned, every generation
since it was first described in journal entries written by explorer William Clark in 1805. Immigrants on the Oregon Trail feared its perilous
rapids; nineteenth-century steamboat operators fought its currents; and
twentieth-century tourists regaled it as the greatest "spectacle of nature anywhere in the world," where "the scenery is arranged most effectively" to produce awe.[2]

By the mid-twentieth century, the Columbia River Gorge had become emblematic of the river's scenic character; upriver from the Gorge the Columbia had been transmogrified into a chain of manipulated reservoirs, where one can only see falling water when it is released over the spillways or drops through the turbines. The Gorge seemingly had been spared many of the changes that characterize modern development on the Columbia, and therefore, it begged for official recognition. During the 1980s, a coalition of conservation-minded groups who revered the Gorge for its aesthetic qualities, especially its spectacular waterfalls and dense forests, lobbied Congress for federal protection, arguing that the area needed a tightly drawn management plan to save it as a special place, as a "national scenic treasure." After years of political wrangling and sometimes volatile disagreements between the protection advocates and local residents, Congress passed the Columbia River Gorge National Scenic Area Act in 1986.[3]

In this singular and unprecedented piece of legislation, Congress identified an officially designated cultural landscape, where the future would be controlled and the effects of time would be managed. The statute defined a narrow band of territory along more than 100 miles of the Columbia in the states of Oregon and Washington as a special place. This act was more reification than creation, for Native Americans and generations of non-Indian tourists had long seen the Gorge as an important landscape. From the viewpoint of Yakama, Wasco, and Klickitat Indians, this stretch of the Columbia was homeland, fishing grounds, and a culturally rich place where the community gave deep meaning to the environment. For Euro-Americans, the Gorge had a unique status: it was a place where nature's power could be observed firsthand and appreciated. The scenic area legislation was, as historian Carl Abbott has cogently explained, an effort "to transform a particular aesthetic and moral judgment into public policy . . . establishing that the natural and/or pre-European environment is more attractive and meritorious than the European-American built environment."[4]

Labeling the "Gorge" as a cultural place with specific qualities was a potent identification. It was a self-consciously nostalgic and largely romantic characterization of place, one that blended the scenic qualities of the river landscape with distant historical events and images. The process had been comprehensive and included numerous landscape studies, political discussions, and community forums; it inevitably raised important and vexatious questions about the meaning of place, the con-

nections that landscapes have with human community, and the historical significance of territorial definitions.

Answering these questions about the investment of human meaning
in landscapes thrusts us into a thick conversation between place and
perception, between the observable physical qualities of the environment and the cultural meanings humans attach to the land. People identify places through their own biographies, through shared events, and
through the larger history that groups apply to the landscape. Places, as
geographer John Allen has explained, are "fusions of experience, landscape, and location." They exist in time and space but are always attached to human awareness through an intricate melding of memory, myth,
expectation, and sensation. Below the surface of our observation, Simon
Schama has recently argued, lies the deeper meaning of places, where
"the veins of myth and memory" give profound cultural meaning to our
perceptions. Digging into the human awareness of place, in other words,
means excavating our cultural texts, thus exposing the content of what
we say about the environment around us.[5]

What we mean when we identify or label a place has everything to do
with our orientation. For an inhabitant, the landscape is sustaining home,
but for the explorer, or traveler, it is often unknown, can be exotic, or in
some sense representative of the "other." At any moment in time, however, a cultural landscape is, as geographer John B. Jackson explains, "a
space or collection of spaces made by a group of people who modify the
natural environment to survive, to create order, and to produce a just
and lasting society."[6] There is nothing in a place, nothing that does not
touch and affect all human activity. A place is a complex, multifaceted,
multilayered, and dynamic connection that humans make with the world
they encounter, and as such it is a product of cumulative memory and
multiple views. Perspective is everything, geographer Yi-Fu Tuan reminds us, because nothing appears quite the same from different van-
tage points. Tuan explains:

> [For the visitor] perception is often a matter of using his eyes to compose
> pictures. The native, by contrast, has a complex attitude derived from his
> immersion in the totality of his environment. The visitor's viewpoint,
> being simple, is easily stated. The complex attitude of the native, on the
> other hand, can be expressed by him only with difficulty.[7]

On the Columbia River, during the first half of the nineteenth century, the distinctions between "resident" and "visitor" took on larger

meaning. This is the period when Euro-Americans invaded the Indians' world. People from divergent and distinctive cultures met, interacted, and began a process that changed the physical landscape and layered on it new cultural meanings. That historical change, which has altered and continues to amend lives in the Columbia River Basin (a 259,000–square-mile drainage area), is a dynamic composed of diverse and powerful forces, including the effects of population growth, capitalistic enterprise, and modern engineering. Before those changes dramatically altered the environment—in large measure a twentieth-century story—Native Americans met Euro-Americans and introduced them to their lands. In the journals of mariners and land explorers we read descriptions of those meetings between English seamen and Chinook Indians at the mouth of the Columbia and between Meriwether Lewis and William Clark and Sahaptin-speaking groups far upriver.[8]

What is striking in these descriptions are the cultural differences among the dozens of native groups and the relative similarity of the Euro-American visitors. The indigenous peoples of the Columbia looked at their land from the inside out, from their own beginnings in human communities, and from their lives as shapers of their place. At the time of first contact with Euro-Americans, Chinook Indians living on the lower river resided in densely populated communities, with as many as 300 persons inhabiting residential structures, while on the plateau the groups were usually fewer than twenty; in the entire Columbia River Basin, population density averaged about one person per square mile. Native people spoke an amazing variety of languages, from Chinookan and Athapaskan on the lower river to Sahaptin and Salish on the upper river, with many as singularly different from one another as contemporary French and Chinese.[9] Their clothing, residences, hunting and gathering strategies, and cultural forms were as diverse as their languages. How these people described and understood their places can best be seen as cultural maps that included an incredibly detailed and intimate knowledge of the region and its resources. These cultural maps disclosed much more than an environmental catalog of resources. They also reflected hundreds or thousands of years of knowledge and meaning. Along the middle Columbia, for example, ethnobotanist Eugene Hunn has documented an incredible richness in botanical names known and used by Sahaptin-speaking Indians, who had memorized more than 200 names to identify plants, their locations, the season for harvesting, and other distinctive characteristics. This ecological map focused on everything that related to humans and the natural world.[10]

Fundamental to these maps are words, for it is with names and their associations that Indians in the Columbia River Basin created and described their place. These names, unlike those applied by outsiders on their maps, come from within a lived space, where human events are connected to land forms, sources of food, sacred areas, home. Some names reflect the physical appearance of the landscape; others document the coincidences between human activity and natural resources. Others serve as guides for travel, the location of medicinal plants, and sites of danger. Hunn records names on the Columbia Plateau, for example, that in Sahaptin translate as "many pestles," "Indian hemp place," "large-scale sucker place," and "swallowing monster." They are names with histories and utility. "Many pestles," for example, refers to a rich area for desert parsley on the plateau east of the Cascade Mountains, a place where Yakama Indian women gathered these plants and pounded the parsley roots into a meal, using basalt pestles and oak mortars. The women's activity, the location of the roots, and the richness of the ground inform this name and invest it with meaning. In like ways, prime fishing spots, stream-side locations where specific families settled in their winter lodges, camps where celebrations were held, and hundreds of other places were named according to experience and meaning. The fishing spots at Celilo Falls, for example, are named by Yakama, Klickitat, and Wasco Indians for the gear used in landing salmon, the families who claimed the locations, and the varieties of fish taken there.[11]

Names and words dominate in the Columbia River Indians' place mapping because it was through language, especially stories, that native people knew their world, the realities of the environment, and the meaning humans attach to creation. Through language, generation upon generation learned the revealed secrets of the world and those revelations constituted a literal map of the region. Creation stories were part of the most dynamic oral traditions among Columbia River tribes. These narratives described the beginning of the world, the exploits of animals in the mythic age, the adventures and misadventures of coyote, and how people should live in this world. They were essentially stories of place that mapped out the core truths about existence. Through these stories, as mythologist Mircea Eliade has explained, "the world 'speaks' to man, and . . . reveals itself in language."[12]

The image of the world speaking to humans is unfamiliar to modernists, who have long since objectified the visible world, but for Indian people on the Columbia, and for many indigenous peoples throughout the world, communication with the land is bidirectional. The place had and continues to have voice. Among the Colville Indians on the upper Columbia River, for example, two coyote stories illustrate the inseparableness of landscape and human community. In the stories, names and cultural prescriptions about human beings and their relationship to place make up important components of the tale.

In the first story, coyote longs to give the people some manner of gift that will elevate them and bind them together as part of creation. He travels for miles down many streams until he comes to a large lake. There he pauses to rest, tired as he was from arduous travel, he drifts to sleep. In his dreaming, he hears the "lap, lap, lap" of the water on the shore, and when he wakes he knows what he shall give the people. On his return, coyote brings the drum as his gift and instructs the people to strike it rhythmically: "thum, thum, thum." When they hear that resonant sound, coyote tells the people they should think about themselves as a whole and remember their duties to each other as people. The image of water, the distances between rivers and lakes on the Columbia River Plateau, and the importance of a healthy environment to the prosperity of the people are intermixed in the story with the cautionary image of prosperity as a consequence of responsible behavior toward the land.

In the second story, coyote again wants to give something to the people. He knows how valuable the salmon have been to the people living far down the Columbia River, but salmon could not make their way far enough upstream to give themselves to upstream tribes. Coyote blasts through an obstruction in the river and leads the salmon to his people, but when he offers this priceless gift he warns the people not to transgress the world and its creatures, not to misbehave and neglect their duties to plants, land, and animals. If they forget or ignore the rules of life, coyote admonishes, he would throw up barriers across the rivers and streams and block salmon from their place. In the rock formations along the tributaries of the upper Columbia today, if you look carefully, you can still see images of salmon in the rocks, where coyote made good on his warnings.[13]

In these stories and others that tell of complicated characters such as coyote or ice changing the world for humans, there are powerful didactic messages about what humans should do with each other and how they should relate to the larger environment. There are also distinctive markers and delineations about the landscape that map out place as more than a three-dimensional, sensory reality. Spiritual themes and ideas are pervasive. Stories carry the strong message that everything in the world has spiritual meaning and that humans must acknowledge the spiritual power vested in an unlimited universe. "People, animals, plants, and other forces of nature—sun, earth, wind, and rock—are animated by spirit," Hunn explains, and "as such they share with humankind intelligence and will, and thus have moral rights and obligations of moral PERSONS."[14]

Columbia River Indians mapped out what modern interpreters might call an "enchanted" landscape, where life forces permeated all things and all things were inherently part of the purpose of life. The burden of living in such a landscape could be endured only if people had some assurance that the world would accommodate them and nourish their existence. The native's map of this world identified safe and dangerous spaces, places with power and places for sanctuary, and places of plenty. Such maps also identified "landscapes of fear," as Tuan has called them, and landscapes of joy. The distinction resides in the bargain of responsibility humans struck with the environment, which included sets of relationships with all creation—animate and inanimate. In exploiting natural resources, native peoples connected their wealth directly to the sacrifices made by plants and animals on their behalf and to the gratefulness and spiritual affinity of the nonhuman world. In the worldview of Native Americans, creation could not be divided into living and nonliving, spiritual and nonspiritual. The Columbia River landscape was an environment of mutual obligation and respect between humans, plants, animals, rivers, land, and atmosphere. Maintenance of this complicated ethical bond informed native peoples and in large measure defined their maps of place.[15]

The contrast between the native people's map of their world and the navigational charts and cartographies created by Euro-American visitors to the Columbia River Basin could not be more extreme. Euro-Americans had no similarly enchanted or spiritual view of this landscape. Their perspective had a larger geographical frame and a more selective purpose. They came as commercial adventurers, representing foreign nations and seeking new pathways to wealth and often the treasure itself. They came initially as investigators and catalogers and later as claimants and occupiers. First by sea and then by land, the explorers looked at the land and drew specialized and instrumentalist maps; unlike the ones created by the Indians, these maps related places as linear representations. The first were drawn in the last decade of the eighteenth century by maritime explorers and traders who charted the river's mouth and its first 100 or more miles. On George Vancouver's exploratory mission in 1792, for example, crew members drew nautical charts, noting sandbars, islands, and other riverine features, while scientists described flora and fauna they observed on their trip up the river. A little more than a decade later, Lewis and Clark drew detailed maps of the courses of the lower Snake and Columbia Rivers and included substantial detail about natural resources, plants and animals they saw, and the character and composition of native groups they encountered. During the first decade of the nineteenth century, David Thompson, a fur trader and explorer in the employ of the Northwest Company, described the Columbia in even more cartographic detail, while he scouted prime fur trapping country.[16]

Of the early Euro-American mappers of the Columbia, Lewis and Clark spent the most time on the river and produced the most commentary about what they saw in the Columbia River Basin. Their inventory of the region has astounded scholars for generations because of the intimate detail included in their reports and the impressive range of subjects they addressed. They had begun with a staggering letter of instruction from President Thomas Jefferson, who had bid them to investigate all flora and fauna, topography, minerals and resources, all native groups and their customs, including language, ceremonies, political organization, and so much more. They were to explore all major tributaries of the Missouri and Columbia Rivers and collect as many specimens from the region as possible. But more than anything else, Jefferson instructed them to pursue commercial relationships with Indian tribes and to evaluate their route as a commercial causeway to the Pacific and the market of Asia.[17]

The two men came into the Columbia River Basin in August 1805 with their minds full of the previous months' experience cordelling up the Missouri and its tributary streams to the Continental Divide *as well as* Jefferson's agenda—especially finding an easy passage between the two great river systems. The explorers entered a *terra incognita* after they left the Mandan villages on the Missouri River in April 1805, but they traveled with an articulated purpose, a list of what they should observe, what they should record, and what questions should be answered. This discovery matrix—the kinds of items they should find and how they should see them—came with them on the journey as part of their intellectual equipment. They were men of the Enlightenment, which equipped them with a well-developed method of observation. That method—in effect a way of seeing the material world—rested on two scientific perspectives: Francis Bacon's definition of exploration as the act of "dwelling purely and constantly among the facts of nature" and Carl Linnaeus's prescribed terminology for cataloging the world's flora and fauna. Their Baconian guidelines assured Lewis and Clark that while wonderment was the spur to investigation it was not its end, that truth lay at the conclusion of factual discovery, precise notation, and creation of an understandable order. The more careful the inspection and recording of the new world the explorers saw, Bacon's prescription promised, the better their map, the truer their portrait of place, and the more complete their demystification of nature.[18]

Lewis and Clark's journalizing also owed much of its form and content to Linnaeus's methodological perspective on the botanical and zoological world. The captains looked at the Columbia River Basin landscape as part of a broader, continental natural history, which emphasized the categorization of plants and animals into a known and regularized outline. The system strove to create, as one scholar has called it, a "general table of relations" for what we find in the world.[19] Carrying two illustrated volumes of Linnaeus's works with them on their westward journey, Lewis and Clark applied the taxonomist's system to record an impressive list of newly named flora and fauna species in the Columbia River Basin. Among the dozens of animals the explorers added to the Linnaean matrix were Clark's nutcracker, the mountain goat, Franklin's grouse, Townsend's chipmunk, the candlefish, and the whistling swan. They cataloged a similarly impressive list of flora, including huckleberry, bitterroot, camas, broadleaf arrowhead, and yarrow.[20]

Because of these two methodological perspectives, Lewis and Clark saw the landscape in a much different way than the natives they encountered. They focused on specifics and recorded what they hoped to find—answers for President Jefferson about geography, newly observed flora and fauna, and Indian languages and social relations. More important, at least in applying the Linnaean system, they reported what they discovered on the Columbia as part of a universal catalog that promised to reduce the world to a systematized, measured place. Distinguishing one plant from another, in large part, meant counting its stamens, petals, and leaves, and measuring its height and conformation. The method "enabled discovery through observation," as Pamela Regis has concluded, "but like all methods, [it] defined what would be observed and how."[21]

Lewis and Clark came as visitors and composed pictures of the landscape that portrayed the environment as fundamentally a place of utility, where human action was seen as separate from the landscape rather than part of the landscape. Throughout the journals, the explorers related their observations to a known and utilitarian world, and consistently in their journal and field note entries they ignored activities and evidence that depicted phenomenon beyond their experience and imagination. Jefferson had instructed them to record details on religious beliefs among the Indians, for example, but there is scant information in the explorers' journals on the subject. When it is recorded, it is often tinged with bewilderment or disgust. On October 9, 1805, along the Clearwater River near present-day Spalding, Idaho, for example, Clark wrote: "A woman faind madness etc. etc. Singular acts of this woman in giveing in Small potions all She had & if they were not received She would Scarrify her Self in a horrid manner etc."[22]

What may have been an expression of spiritual belief and the acting out of religiously informed behavior was cast as "faind madness," her belief system ignored in Clark's dismissive "etc. etc." added to the description. Beyond their experience and comprehension, the spiritual world of Indian peoples they encountered escaped notation in their copious detailing of the Columbia River landscape, while they meticulously described the Indians' technologies, commercial relationships, wealth, personal habits, and willingness to trade. The unexpressed meaning is unmistakable. For the explorers, the spiritual lives of native people, especially when it exposed animistic beliefs, existed outside of the anticipated relationships between Indian and non-Indian people. The spirit world of the natives had no functional meaning for the captains.[23]

Part of Lewis and Clark's neglect of Indian spiritual beliefs was due to their preconceived ideas about Indian belief systems, which had permeated Enlightenment culture for more than three generations. Jefferson and other like-minded scientists understood indigenous peoples more as part of the environment and a legitimate subject for natural history than as comparable human communities. Lewis and Clark followed this viewpoint, noting the numerical strength of Indian groups, their relative locations, comparative behaviors, and relationships to each other, much in the way they described and categorized plants and animals they encountered. Native peoples, in short, were listed and described as part of a larger matrix of natural history in the Columbia River Basin. Embedding Indians in the natural world had profound implications, for it iden-

tified them as part of the material environment and thereby more mal-
leable, functional, and utilitarian than Lewis and Clark saw fellow Euro-
Americans. Ironically, listing native peoples as part and parcel with the
environment acceded to the Indians' own worldview, but for the explorers and their Enlightenment cohorts, making humans part of natural history had a much different meaning.[24]

The physical maps drawn by the explorers reveal their commercial
and instrumentalist orientation perhaps better than any other documents
related to the expedition. There were several cartographic missions included in Jefferson's instructions to Lewis and Clark, especially to allay
concerns about territorial claims made by Great Britain's fur trading
activities, cultural to which were the drainages east of the Continental
Divide that might originate in British possessions north of the forty-
ninth parallel. In addition, Lewis and Clark hoped to sort out the pattern
of rivers represented only in an imagined cartography depicted on Nicho-
las King's map of 1803. The maps that Lewis and Clark compiled at
Fort Clatsop during the winter of 1805–1806 focus on the physical relationship between the river courses in the Columbia River Basin, partly
from observation and partly from information they acquired from native peoples.

In the end, they misinterpreted the courses of the present-day Snake,
Willamette, and Clark Fork Rivers, while they documented the mainstream of the Columbia and Clearwater Rivers with exceptional accu-
racy. This was especially true at critical points along the Columbia
River, as at the mouth of the Snake and The Dalles-Celilo area, where
the river compressed into a narrow channel and plunged over sharp
escarpments. The detail provided on the maps, the intimate cartography of specific places, and the misunderstanding of the larger drainage pattern reflect Lewis and Clark's principal orientation toward rivers
and the landscape. The course of the rivers, their pattern of confluence,
and their potential for trade all amounted to a geography of power in
which the cumulative importance of a river system was most palpable at
its estuary, where it joined the waters of the world. For Lewis and Clark,
the power and conformation of the Columbia system became most important and most instrumental at its mouth—where they spent their hor-
rible winter but also where they recommended building a major trade
entrepot.[25]

The differences between the native maps of the rivers and Lewis and
Clark's cartographics are distilled in their respective views of water.

Indian people in the Columbia River Basin honored water as the source of life, as the most important of sacred foods. The rivers brought water to the people and existed as both a physical reality and as part of an enchanted universe, where the material and spiritual worlds commingled and coexisted. The Euro-American viewpoint also assigned importance to water for human sustenance, but it added the power of work and utility to its definition and did not include a sacred role. The difference and the change of perspective is what social geographer E.V. Walter calls a "topomorphic revolution." Revolutionary changes in the structure of spaces, Walter argues, redefine place by radically changing the "system of mutual immanence" that exists between people and their environment. Such changes affect, among other things, how sustenance is related to residential patterns, how wealth is determined in society, and how landscapes are understood. Adopting a Euro-American viewpoint, which sees the Columbia River as a causeway of extractive commerce, for example, reorders nearly all relationships with the river that were understood by native populations. More important, though, this topomorphic revolution vested transportation value in the water itself. Such valuation led directly to the assumption that human engineering could improve upon nature. For native peoples who used the river for transportation, the water itself never became objectified.[26]

The topomorphic revolution on the Columbia, which began during the early nineteenth century, expanded quickly and gained enormous power by mid-century. Lewis and Clark, David Thompson, Hudson's Bay Company traders, and other mappers of the region increasingly defined the place in instrumentalist terms.

The Dalles-Celilo area, for example, ceased being an enchanted and cultural place. No longer a place where fishing merged easily with spiritual life, it became a strategic and commercial place where the flow of goods was the truest measure of the river's power. This instrumentalist viewpoint mapped out a geography of power, as cultural geographer Cole Harris labels it, in which the Euro-American patterns of exchange, political relationships, and evaluations of status were laid over the landscape.[27] The Hudson's Bay Company established central trading forts— which were supplied from distant ports by maritime transport—and connected them to interior outposts for the extraction of furs. The system fed toward a central entrepot, where power concentrated and could be wielded throughout the company's claimed territory.[28]

The Hudson's Bay Company's invasion of the Columbia River Basin was only the beginning of a process of domination by Euro-Americans that has continued to the present day. The fur men and the latter-day settlers would not have accomplished their goals so rapidly, of course, had not the advance agents of this topomorphic revolution—virulent pathogens—swept the region, decimating native populations. In what anthropologists call the Northwest Coast cultural region, the native population declined by more than 80 percent between 1774 and 1870. Although the loss of life east of the Cascade Mountains was relatively less, smallpox, measles, diphtheria, tuberculosis, and other diseases left Indian groups physically, culturally, and spiritually wounded, making them much less resistant to the invading Euro-American forces. Many of the Indians who survived the pestilential onslaught became participants in the establishment of the new institutions of power in the region, first in the fur trade and then as hired laborers for white entrepreneurs.[29]

The rapid overlaying of this geography of power engendered similar additional overlays by Euro-Americans during the first half of the nineteenth century. By the 1850s, the Hudson's Bay Company had begun its retreat to British possessions north of the forty-ninth parallel and American entrepreneurs had put steamboats on the lower Columbia River as adjuncts to an active economic development of the region. The river served the steamboat men as a wondrous source of income and exorbitant profits. The Columbia, as seen from the instrumentalist perspective of entrepreneurial investors such as the incorporators of the Oregon Steam Navigation Company, looked like a way to wealth, not like a homeland. A generation and more later, the descendants of those incorporators and their fellow non-Indian residents of the Columbia River Basin could see the landscape as home and understand it empathetically and to identify themselves with the place. Nonetheless, the viewpoint was distinct from the native perspective, where place was seen as the locale of spirit and not as mostly a means to wealth. The invading population brought with them patterns of land use and viewing the land that had been developed in other places and for other purposes. In the most essential ways, the new residents of the Columbia River Basin translated the newly discovered landscape into a known place by imposing a geographical understanding from another place. The topomorphic revolution on the Columbia came with the outsiders.[30]

The changes that continually remade the Columbia River Basin landscape during the century beginning in 1850 added newer perspectives, newer patterns of use and applications of power. Engineers looked at the river as a place to be controlled, altered, and harnessed. The Columbia's powerful current and volume of water became the focus of investment and a characterization for the river itself. By the time the Columbia River Gorge Scenic Act passed Congress in the mid-1980s, the image of the river had become a collage of competing portraits, ranging from a "working river" of hydroelectric turbines and towboats to a "recreational river" of sports fishing and windsurfing. Behind these newer perspectives on the Columbia, as the justification for the protective legislation made clear, was an older and much more distant image of the river as a unmitigated place, where Indians fished at Celilo Falls and the water ran unimpeded to the sea. The irony is inherent in the Scenic Act's attempt to freeze the Gorge into a romantically understood place, a landscape of nature and history that possesses the intrinsic qualities to evoke the Columbia's earliest history. In the midst of modernity, the Scenic Act suggests that the Columbia is still the river Sahaptin speakers called *Nich'i Wana*, but its rules and regulations remind landowners in the Gorge that the Columbia is every bit the Great River of the West that early entrepreneurs and contemporary engineers have defined.

Embedded in the Columbia River Gorge National Scenic Act is this binocular-like perspective on the river that draws strength from both viewpoints: the native and the visitor. The legislation and the politics that surrounded its enactment remind us that no place has a singular cultural meaning, that there are many ways of looking, many ways of "seeing" a river.

Notes

1. Yi-Fu Tuan, *Topophilia: A Study of Environmental Perception, Attitudes and Values* (Englewood Cliffs, NJ: Prentice-Hall, 1974), p. 11.

2. Edward S. Jordan, *A Tribute to Portland* (Portland: Portland Chamber of Commerce, n.d.); Henry Finck, *The Pacific Coast Tour* (New York: Charles Scribner's Sons, 1890), pp. 183, 189.

3. Carl Abbott, Sy Adler, and Margery Post Abbott, *Planning a New West: The Columbia River Gorge National Scenic Area* (Corvallis: Oregon State University Press, 1997), pp. 18, 218.

4. Ibid., p. 379.

5. John L. Allen, "Lands of Myth, Waters of Wonder: The Place of the Imagination in the History of Geographical Exploration," in *Geographies of the Mind: Essays in Historical Geography*, ed. David Lowenthal and Martyn J. Bowden (New York: Oxford University Press, 1975), p. 39; Donald Meinig, "The Beholding Eye: Ten Versions of the Same Scene," *Landscape Architecture* 66 (Winter 1976): 47–54; Simon Schama, *Landscape and Memory* (New York: Alfred A. Knopf, 1995), pp. 13–15.

6. John B. Jackson, "In Search of the Proto-Landscape," in *Landscape in America*, ed. George F. Thompson (Austin: University of Texas Press, 1995), p. 43. For an extended discussion of place and environment on the Columbia River, see William L. Lang, "From Where We Are Standing: The Sense of Place and Environmental History," in *Northwest Lands, Northwest Peoples: Readings in Environmental History*, ed. Dale D. Goble and Paul W. Hirt (Seattle: University of Washington Press, 1999), pp. 79–94.

7. Tuan, *Topophilia*, p. 63.

8. The most relevant among the many maritime and exploration accounts include Gary Moulton, ed., *The Journals of the Lewis and Clark Expedition*, 8 vols. (Lincoln: University of Nebraska Press, 1983); John Kirk Townsend, *Narrative of a Journey Across the Rocky Mountains to the Columbia River* (rep., Lincoln: University of Nebraska Press, 1978); Alexander Ross, *Adventures of the First Settlers on the Columbia* (1849 rep.; Lincoln: University of Nebraska Press, 1966); Barbara Belyea, ed., *Columbia Journals: David Thompson* (Montreal: McGill-Queens University Press, 1994); David Douglas, *Journal Kept During His Travels in North America*, ed. W. Wilks and H.R. Hutchinson (1914 rep.; New York: Antiquarian Press, 1959); J.B. Tyrell, ed., *David Thompson: Narrative of His Explorations in Western America, 1784–1812* (Toronto: Champlain Society, 1916); F.W. Howay, ed. *Voyages of the "Columbia" to the Northwest Coast, 1787–1790 and 1790–1793* (Boston: Massachusetts Historical Society, 1941); George Vancouver, *Voyage of Discovery to the North Pacific Ocean and Round the World*, 4 vols. (1798 rep.; New York: De Capo Press, 1967).

9. Laurence C. Thompson and M. Dale Kinkade, "Languages," in *Handbook of North American Indians, Northwest Coast*, ed. Wayne Suttles, vol. 7 (Washington, DC: Smithsonian Institution, 1990), pp. 30–51; William Elmendorf, "Linguistic and Geographic Relations in the Northern Plateau Area," *Southwestern Journal of Anthropology* 21 (Winter 1965): pp. 63–77.

10. Eugene S. Hunn, *Nich'i Wana, "The Big River": Mid-Columbia Indians and Their Land* (Seattle: University of Washington Press, 1990), pp. 58–69, 96–99, 333–358.

11. Eugene S. Hunn, "Native Place Names on the Columbia Plateau," in *A Time of Gathering: Native Heritage in Washington State*, ed. Robin K. Wright (Seattle: Burke Museum and University of Washington Press, 1991), pp. 170–177.

12. Mircea Eliade, *Myth and Reality* (New York: Harper, 1963), as quoted in *Coyote Was Going There: Indian Literature of the Oregon Country*, ed. Jarold Ramsay (Seattle: University of Washington Press, 1977), p. xxiii.

13. Stories told by Adeline Fredin, Colville Confederated Tribes, Nespelem, Washington.

14. Ramsay, *Coyote Was Going There*, pp. xxv–xxxiii; Hunn, *Nich'i Wana*, p. 230.

15. Yi-Fu Tuan, *Landscapes of Fear* (New York: Pantheon Books, 1979), pp. 47–50; J. Baird Callicott, "Traditional American Indian and Western European Attitudes Toward Nature: An Overview," *Environmental Ethics* 4 (Winter 1982): pp. 293–318.

16. American trader, Robert Gray, was the first to describe the Columbia and enter it from the Pacific, which he accomplished on May 11, 1792. Gray drew a rough chart of the estuary and passed it on to George Vancouver, who detailed Lieutenant William Broughton to survey the river. Broughton took a dozen men in a cutter and rowed up to near present-day Camas, Washington, in November 1792. Broughton's chart was published in Vancouver's *Voyages* in 1798. For the background of these explorations, see Howay, *Voyages of the "Columbia" to the Northwest Coast*; Belyea, *Columbia Journals*, "Introduction"; Moulton, "Introduction to the Journals," *The Journals of the Lewis and Clark Expedition*, vol. 2 (introduction is in vols. 1 and 2).

17. Thomas Jefferson to Meriwether Lewis, June 20, 1803, in *Letters of the Lewis and Clark Expedition, with Related Documents, 1783–1854*, ed. Donald B. Jackson (Urbana: University of Illinois Press, 1978), pp. 61–66. See also, Michael P. Malone, Richard B. Roeder, and William L. Lang, *Montana: A History of Two Centuries* (Seattle: University of Washington Press, 1991), chap. 2.

18. Francis Bacon, *The New Organon*, as quoted in Wayne Franklin, *Discoverers, Explorers, Settlers: The Diligent Writers of Early America* (Chicago: University of Chicago Press, 1979), p. 9. For the connections between Baconian thought, exploration, and Jefferson's America, see Franklin, chap. 2.

19. Michel Foucault, *The Order of Things* (New York: Vintage, 1973), p. 142, as quoted in Pamela Regis, *Describing Early America: Bartram, Jefferson, Crevecoeur, and the Rhetoric of Natural History* (DeKalb: Northern Illinois University Press, 1992), p. 14.

20. Paul Russell Cutright, *Lewis and Clark: Pioneering Naturalists* (Urbana: University of Illinois Press, 1969), pp. 196, 212, 225–226, 244–245, 307.

21. Regis, *Describing Early America*, p. 21.

22. Moulton, *The Journals of Lewis and Clark Expedition*, vol. 5, p. 253. On Lewis and Clark's reaction to the environment, see William L. Lang, "Lewis and Clark on the Columbia: The Power of Landscape in Exploration," *Pacific Northwest Quarterly* 87 (Summer 1996): 141–148.

23. James P. Ronda, *Lewis and Clark Among the Indians* (Lincoln: University of Nebraska Press, 1985), pp. 162, 252–255.

24. For discussion of Indians as natural history objects, see Regis, Describing Early America, pp. 79–105.

25. Moulton, *The Journals of Lewis and Clark Expedition*, vol. 6, pp. 9–12; Meriwether Lewis to Thomas Jefferson, September 23, 1806, in Jackson, *Letters of the Lewis and Clark Expedition*, vol. 1, pp. 319–322. For discussion of Lewis and Clark's interpretation of the rivers and their comparison with known and imaginary geographies of the area, see John L. Allen, *Passage Through the Garden: Lewis and Clark and the Image of the American Northwest* (Urbana: University of Illinois Press, 1975), especially chaps. 4, 13, 14.

26. Hunn, *Nich'i Wana*, pp. 91, 208; E.V. Walter, *Placeways: A Theory of the Human Environment* (Chapel Hill: University of North Carolina Press, 1988), pp. 23–25.

27. Cole Harris, "Geographies of Power" paper presented at the conference, "Hudson's Bay Company's Northwest," Center for Columbia River History, Vancouver, WA, September 1995.

28. For a recent discussion of the patterns of Hudson's Bay Company control over interior posts, see Theodore Stern, *Chiefs and Chief Traders: Indian Relations at Fort Nez Perces, 1818–1855*, vol. 1 (Corvallis: Oregon State University Press, 1993), especially chaps. 2, 10, 11.

29. Robert T. Boyd, "Demographic History, 1774–1874," in Suttles, *Handbook of North American Indians*, vol. 7, pp. 135–136; Stern, *Chiefs and Chief Traders,* pp. 113–121.

30. Amos Rapoport, *The Meaning of the Built Environment: A Nonverbal Communication Approach* (Beverly Hills: Sage, 1982), p. 62.

9

The Role of Government Intervention in Creating Forest Landscapes and Resource Tenure in Indonesia

Nancy Lee Peluso

Forest resources the world over are subject to multiple claims by government officials, entrepreneurs, and forest-based or forest-dependent people. These intersecting claims take various forms within the same country or state not only because of different policy environments and forest characteristics, but also because local, regional, national, and global processes differentially affect people using particular forests.

This chapter discusses three examples of divergent forms of government intervention in forests also managed in various ways by local people in Indonesia. The cases illustrate three outcomes in the structures of subsequent physical and social landscapes; each of which were unexpected and unintended by government policies. The case involving the least intervention and the most cooperative government attitude toward local people's forest use resulted in what appears to be the most well-managed forest, largely because of the sustained interest and involvement of local people themselves.

The first case involves the teak forests of Java. These plantation forests, occupying a primary production zone in the eastern-central portion of the island of Java, provide nearly the whole of the revenue of the State Forestry Corporation of Java (SFC), a government parastatal agency that manages some 3 million hectares of forest land on the island, less than one-third of which produces teak. Though interplanted with other species in the early stages of plantation establishment, by the time the teak trees are ten years old, planned thinning and natural shading render the plantations monocultures. Under ideal conditions, that is, unless they are destroyed by natural forces or carried away by unauthorized harvesters, these monocultural tracts of teak continue to grow for an additional seventy years before they are girdled and clear-cut. Teak forests in various stages of development, as well as would-be tracts of teak land (which local people consistently use to grow farm crops), dominate the landscape of the teak zone of Java. This dominance has ecological, managerial, and political economic aspects, as discussed below.

Teak forest management is included in this analysis as an example of a major government intervention that involves significant monetary and personnel commitments as well as the use of force to protect the resource. Government foresters in the SFC are directly involved in the creation of management plans for the long-term protection and production of teak, as they were under the Dutch colonial government from the early nineteenth century. The nature of teak management is highly centralized and exclusionary, in that government policy severely curtails local people's access to land in the teak zone and their access to marketing rights to teak. Teak production, because of its long rotation (60 to 100 years) offers limited opportunities for regular local employment in forests, but is located in heavily populated rural Java. Most local people do not derive *legal* economic benefits from the production of teak, although an extensive black market flourishes and does benefit many local people. My theme in this case is the *persistence* of local claims to forests despite centuries of government intervention. The outcome of government intervention here has been a failure to prevent what is defined as forest degradation and deforestation despite intensive and coercive government control.

The second case is the dipterocarps production forests of Kalimantan (Indonesian Borneo). I focus specifically on those parts of these vast forests where "patches" of ironwood (*Eusyderoxylon zwagerii*) grow among the dipterocarps.[1] These primary and secondary forests represent a mix of "natural" processes and clear management by local people.

Since the late 1960s and early 1970s, local forest management systems in Kalimantan and throughout "outer" Indonesia have had government regulation and industrial systems of "scientific" forest management superimposed on them. The main objective of these new systems has been the "efficient" management of forests for commercial timber harvest. As discussed below, although the timber concessions do not generally include rights to harvest ironwood, their presence and the changes they make in the physical environment have had a significant impact on local people's management of ironwood.

The case study of government intervention affecting ironwood production illustrates the unintended consequences of indirect government intervention. Government influence is indirect in the sense that timber concessions for cutting dipterocarps are leased out to large capitalist firms, and these firms neither have rights to ironwood, nor are they formally involved in its production. However, technological innovations and roads have increased market access for ironwood and have had major impacts on local property rights. Timber-extraction policies have therefore contributed to the localized depletion of ironwood stocks. My theme in this case is the *transformation* of local property rights in ironwood, and the role of changing property rights in depleting the forest.

The third case is a forest in coastal West Kalimantan where management is intensive and almost entirely carried out by local people. Similarly managed forests are distributed widely throughout the province (Padoch 1994; Salafsky et al. 1993). The village under discussion is located on a well-paved road running from the coastal city of Singkawang to the interior town of Bengkayang. The village is unable to expand beyond its current land area because it is bounded by the nature reserve to the south (part of which was carved out of the village's traditional lands in the 1930s), a Catholic mission to the west, and to the east and north more recently sited settlements for retired military and police as well as for Javanese transmigrants. These transmigration settlements and many neighboring native villages have markedly different landscapes from the study village because they contain hundreds of hectares of high-yielding rubber, managed within government and private plantations called nucleus estates.

This case illustrates the unintended consequences of direct and indirect government efforts to both sedentarize people (i.e., to tie them to a particular place) and to restrict their access to reserved forest land. Local people have created a new "forest" on the lands to which they were confined, while continuing limited production of agroforestry products inside the reserve border. My theme in this case is the *creation* and *contestation* of property rights because of the power, wealth, and meanings represented by the trees and land of this social forest.

These three cases from three different parts of Indonesia are valuable in a comparative framework of state-local relations and their respective interactions in creating social and physical landscapes. In each case, *access* to the forest or its products is contested by multiple parties; market opportunities have influenced the physical landscapes and social relations among the actors; and the intentions of policy did not materialize. In the remainder of the paper, the three cases will be discussed in greater detail. In each, I outline the environmental and policy settings; the interactions between local people, the state, and the market in relation to local forest resources; and the political-economic forces causing policies to be contested and landscapes transformed. Because of the limits of space, only sketches of the most important aspects of the cases can be provided.[2]

Teak Forest

Foresters working for one kind of ruling body or another—the VOC (United East India Company), the Dutch colonial state, or the Indonesian government—have been around the teak zone of Java for more than 200 years. Today, forest rangers and guards function more as police than as technical planners and implementers of policy.

Villages in the region are nearly all outside the formal borders of the forest; over the past century or so, colonial and contemporary foresters made great efforts to eliminate all enclaves of private land from inside the political territory called "forest." However, a bird's-eye view shows small villages appearing as if they were carved out of the state teak forest. All teak grown on state forest land is the property of the state. Legally, local people's rights to teak are minimal; they even have constrained rights to teak grown on their own land, as the state claims the right to tax teak grown on private land, when it is marketed or transported from the area where it grew. Local people's rights to teakwood and its byproducts (bark, leaves, small branches, deadwood, stumps) have become more and more constrained over the generations.

In a teak forest, the government maintains total control. For example, Cepu is a forest district and is mostly located in the civil administrative district of Blora. Forty-four percent of this district is under forest and therefore is controlled directly by the SFC. Cepu, an interior location that tends to be less densely populated than other parts of the teak forest, and where some of the best teak forest remains, had average population densities of about 800 people per square kilometer in the mid-1980s.

Because so much land is tied up by the SFC, population densities per kilometer of agricultural land were nearly double that.

It might seem that after 130 years of strict legal constraints on access to teak and the teak forest, and several generations of less stringent exclusions by the VOC and the early Dutch state (preceding the development of formal forest laws), most local people would recognize that teakwood and those forests "belong" to the government. That is not the case. Local people still believe they have rights to teak. Most of their claims are for subsistence uses of teak: for firewood, fencing, furniture, and housing. Many of these subsistence uses were recognized as rights under colonial forest law (see Table 9.1). Besides their historical rights of access to the teak, people have very real needs for teak, because other materials for housing and fuel are not available or are much too expensive to be purchased by poor forest villagers. Teak in the teak forest is the dominant species; it is monocultural; and the environment in which teak thrives—thin soils on limestone bedrock with a long, distinct dry season—is not good for many other species.

As a result, people are forced to "steal" teak saplings and to sell or make teak charcoal to cook with; they make fences and agricultural tools from teak; and most important of all, they make their houses. Virtually all houses in the teak forest are make of teak. One legal complication with preventing this is that it is not illegal to *have* a teak house, but it is illegal to build one. The value of teak for house construction—a value placed on the wood by people all over the island—makes the story much more complicated. Today, there is a huge black market in teak; one estimate in the mid-1980s was that 45 percent of the teak made into furniture or sold as boards came from the black market. There are numerous and complicated systems for acquiring, hiding, transporting, and making bribes to get teak. These black market networks require the tacit participation of thousands of people—including all those villagers who are not directly involved in its acquisition but know all about it and do not say anything to the authorities.

What has this lack of perceived government legitimacy done to the physical and social landscapes encompassing the teak forest? First, it has contributed to a strong feeling of distrust and suspicion between foresters and villagers. The insistence of the foresters on the impermeability of borders between forest and village, and the continued emphasis on centralized control of forest lands and on full government control of teak production at any cost, makes any kind of formal negotiation for

Table 9.1

Changes in Local People's Legal Access to Teak in Java

Time period	Ruler	Progression of rules/laws
Seventeenth century	Javanese kings	Allowed collection of teakwood for housing, fencing, fuel—except in forests or sacred sites such as royal cemeteries. Swiddening* by Kalangs.
Seventeenth-eighteenth century	United East India Company (VOC)	Allowed subsistence uses as above and teak used in the construction of boats for personal use; sale of shipbuilding timbers was reserved for VOC.
1808–1811	Dutch colonial Daendels (governor-general of Java)	Allowed collection of deadwood, nontimber forest products, stumps of cut trees up to 1 meter in length; government monopoly on commercial teak production; teak theft formally made a crime against the state; Board of Forests had jurisdiction over villagers and their forest lands.
1811–1815	British colonial Raffles (governor of Java)	Rescinded government monopoly but reserved largest and best forests for state; leased other forests to private contractors; forest land given as gifts to elites.
1816	Dutch colonial state	Resumed government monopoly; tax on teak transport; peasants allowed to cut wood for boats, carts, for own use—restricted to trees 6 "thumbs" wide and 20 feet high; could take waste wood, stumps, roots, underbrush; charcoal manufacture forbidden.
1822		Allowed collection for fuel and timber for house construction and agricultural tools.
1838		No wood for fuel or house timber allowed.
1842		Allowed to construct riverboats and carts for personal use.
1851		Need permit to cut subsistence wood.

*"Swiddening" is a verb form of swidden cultivation. Kulangs are an old extinct group, believed to be either an ethnic group or occupation group, who served as forest workers for the sultan of Solo in the precolonial and United East India Company (VOC) periods of Javanese history.

1865		Peasants allowed branches, fallen wood, from forest thinnings in some government forests, stumps.
1875		All uses except those allowed in 1865 were declared crimes against the state.
Post-1960	Indonesian government	No rights to waste wood from thinning forests; stump size reduced in the new cutting regulations (stumps in the 1980s were about 1 inch above the ground); allowed to collect deadwood, small branches.

Source: Peluso 1992a.

access to part of the revenues from forest products nearly impossible. At the same time, formal negotiations to provide villager access to forest lands and products is taking place on forests not planted with teak, in the form of social forestry programs (Barber 1989; Peluso and Poffenberger 1989; Sunderlin 1992). The strictness of teak management policy, however, does not alleviate conflicts over access within the most productive teak forests.

Moreover, the teak resources themselves are experiencing degradation, despite intensive government patrolling and management. Data collected in the mid-1980s showed that nearly 40 percent of the teak forests were under twenty years of age; in an "ideal" plantation, forests under twenty years old should amount to only 24 percent (Peluso 1992a). Despite heavy and at times coercive government controls on access to teak forests, people cannot be kept out of the forest and away from the species so heavily guarded by the government.

Ironwood Forest

Because ironwood is found within Indonesia's most valuable hardwood-producing forests, some background on the politics of Kalimantan timber production is important to this discussion. Prior to World War II, nontimber forest products in Kalimantan were produced in far greater volume and for greater value than timber (De Beers and McDermott 1989; Peluso 1992c). Laws such as the Basic Agrarian Act of 1960 and the Basic Forestry Act of 1967 facilitated the process by which timber became the primary product extracted from the Kalimantan forest. Building on the declaration by the Dutch colonial state known as *Domeinverklaring* and passed in 1870 and claiming all "unalienated" lands (defined as lands not under cultivation within the past three years), these laws gave the Indonesian state control over the nation's forest land and resources. In practical terms, they gave the state jurisdiction over "the forest lands and all the resources within" (Indonesian Constitution 1945), which in turn gave the state the legal basis for allocating timber rights to foreign and domestic firms.

The timber of Kalimantan is very important to the Indonesian political economy. The island contains 34 percent of Indonesia's forest area and 41 percent of its potential timber (Potter 1996). It is also home to half of Indonesia's 594 timber concessions (*Tempo*, November 1991). More than 50 percent of the nation's plywood factories are located in Kalimantan. Indonesia dominates the world market in plywood.

A key effect of the laws favoring timber production has been the criminalization of many customary uses of the forests. The second effect of such laws and policies is that they do not recognize the nuances of local agroforestry systems, beginning with swidden agriculture and extending to local people's management of multiaged and multicomposition forests. When timber companies build roads or log in a forest village's territory, they are required to pay compensation only for fruit and nut trees (Zerner 1990)—which are generally regarded as agricultural products. They are not required to compensate for so-called forest species such as resin-producing trees (e.g., Agathis spp.) or ironwood trees because local people's roles in their management are not recognized. From the villagers' point of view, of course, their management of these forest species should accord them rights with the government, as it does within their locality. Villagers invest a great deal of labor in protecting or otherwise managing individual forest trees that they have found, claimed, and protected (Padoch 1994; Peluso 1992c; Weinstock 1983). Indeed in some villages, the ancestors of current residents planted the current stocks of ironwood over 100 ago (Padoch and Peters 1993). By focusing on regulating access to the various species of dipterocarps harvested for their timber, the forest laws ignore the more holistic and diverse approaches of local management systems.

The third effect of laws and policies favoring industrial timber extraction relates to the distribution of forest benefits. In just twenty-odd years since the earliest timber concessions were issued, the flow of economic benefits from forest land in Kalimantan, as in all of Indonesia, has become extremely concentrated.

Timber concessions in Indonesia are not automatically given rights to cut or sell ironwood unless they account for such activities in a management plan. Some resist the option to include ironwood in their plans because the wood is difficult and expensive to transport (it does not float like the other tropical hardwoods being exploited) and because local people's claims to ironwood have been so strong historically.

However, the logging of other tropical hard woods has had a major impact on ironwood-rich forests, primarily because concessionaires have built roads through or near these areas and have made chainsaws widely available throughout the provinces of Kalimantan. As logging roads have come through, networks of ironwood collectors, traders, and truckers have evolved. Collectors, traders, and truckers come from both nearby localities and distant towns.

In the early 1990s, the government decided it wanted to tax the lucrative trade in ironwood. To this end, they made it mandatory for villages to be organized into cooperatives in order to obtain newly created "legal" rights to cut. The fees paid for the right to harvest constituted a kind of tax. The government also made it mandatory for traders to have government-issued permits to buy wood from specific village organizations. The fees paid by the traders also constituted a tax. As a conservative measure, limits were put on the size of ironwood allowed to be cut. Standing trees with less than sixty centimeters (cm) diameter at breast height (DBH) were off limits. In addition, regional district governments put restrictions on the transport of ironwood logs out of their district territories to prevent losses of the valuable construction wood.

These laws could not be implemented. Logistically, they were difficult to enforce—there simply were not enough government foresters to supervise their proper implementation. Moreover, villagers also had difficulty—and no formal government support—preventing locally unauthorized ironwood cutters from outside their villages either from cutting in their forests or from making individual deals with their fellow villagers. The difficulties with implementation led to a retraction of the law and a vacuum in the allocation or recognition of legal rights to ironwood. As one official commented, the government was simply not able to derive any portion of the flow of benefits from the harvest and trade in ironwood (Peluso 1992b).

From the villagers' point of view, the changes taking place in their access to ironwood and their ability to protect it for future use had to do as much with incongruities in their local systems of exerting property rights to ironwood as with changes in the legal system and in the means of gaining physical access to the wood and transporting it. In the days

preceding the logging roads, people had claimed ironwood trees by building swidden fields around them. This entailed slashing the other timber
and brush, allowing it to dry, and burning it during a relatively prolonged dry spell (in this part of West Kalimantan such dry spells often
lasted from one to three weeks). Ironwood is resistant to fire, so burning
the forest around ironwood trees did not mean destroying the standing
timber. Forest clearance imparts perpetual land rights to the clearers and
their descendants, and ironwood trees standing within a swidden field
were inherited as well. Moreover, within the forested territories claimed
by whole villages, trees standing unclaimed (i.e., in forests that were
not yet cleared for cultivation) were considered the "common property"
of the village. In some places, if outsiders wanted to cut down the trees,
they would have to pay the village or village head a "tax" of 20 percent
of the ironwood cut in the village or longhouse's territory. Thus, the
management and allocation of these trees were governed by both private and common property principles. Because most forest territories
were claimed by surrounding villages, there was little, if any, ironwood
that could be considered a completely unclaimed resource.

In one village where I have been working, private or individual
claims to ironwood have become much more widespread than group
claims and have changed in form. In the past, an individual claim
required the investment of labor either by immediately cutting down
a claimed ironwood tree or by building a swidden around it; by the
1990s, all it required was to go out and paint your name on the tree.
After a road was built, providing easier extraction, it was not long
before all the trees in the village territory were claimed by people
who had painted their names on them; thus, virtually all of the
community's commonly owned reserve trees became privatized.
Roads and this new way of privatizing the village's common property (in reserved ironwood trees) thus led to the loss of the village's
revenue from the 20 percent tax on the harvest when outsiders came
in to cut village trees. Outsiders—ranging from individual woodcutters to shopkeepers and other wood buyers—could now strike
deals with the individuals whose names were on the trees, rather
than negotiating access through a representative of the village as a
whole. And, whereas in the past individuals kept some of their ironwood trees standing for future use in their swiddens and swidden
fallows, now the opportunity to readily sell their claimed trees for
cash caused many people to sell access rights to the trees.

All sorts of local marketing arrangements arose to take advantage of the changing structure of property rights—arrangements such as chainsaw "rentals" and the purchase of gas to run the chainsaws (paid for with cut wood) and "loans" of food to support the woodcutters during their stay in the forest (to be repaid with cut wood). These arrangements in effect, gave outsiders access to locally owned trees. Traders made arrangements to buy the rights to uncut trees that had a villager's name painted on them. Villagers made cooperative arrangements to rent trucks for wood transport. All transport vehicles paid "access fees" to security guards for the timber company that had constructed the road. As a result of these and other new arrangements giving outsiders access to some of the benefits flowing from the control, production, and trade in ironwood, the balance of rights was shifted from common to private property arrangements, and the flow of benefits, which had previously been directed toward both the village and individuals, was now directed toward individuals exclusively.

The use of chainsaws also meant that many villagers no longer had access to the increasingly valuable resource of ironwood. Whereas the previous manner of claim (by building swiddens) and the technology of exploitation (the ax) had been basically family or household oriented, claims were more easily realized by those who had access to chainsaws and by those who could physically handle them. This meant that older people and virtually all women lost access to the flow of benefits from ironwood, particularly that portion of the monetary benefits spent by male laborers on their subsistence while in the forests and on all the "extras" bought by the woodcutters from the shopkeepers with whom they associated (leather jackets, blue jeans, and expensive ready-made cigarettes).

In this case, the government failed to get involved to the benefit of the villagers, even though their regulations for village access to ironwood may have required it. But foresters alone, either officially or unofficially, cannot work against the interests and actions of officials involved in the exploitation of ironwood—even the police and the army garrison in the district capital were said to be receiving "users fees" for the logging roads from the entrepreneurs bringing their nocturnal trucks into the forest. The outcome of all this has been the depletion of local stocks of ironwood and the losses of much of the villagers' future supplies of ironwood. It has also emphasized the individual aspects of a multiple-rights resource allocation system.

Locally Managed Forest

The heavily managed forests of West Kalimantan, dominated by trees that produce fruit, rubber, and resin, are highly diverse. They differ from other kinds of standing forests and from each other in the ways they were created, how they are managed, and what they produce (Padoch and Peluso 1995). At present, the most important tree crops in the managed forests of Bagak Sahwa, a small village not far from the coast of West Kalimantan are durian, langsat, and other fruits, mixed with rubber. Because the village is located along a main road, residents have several options for selling their fruits and rubber: Traders come into the village to buy during fruit season; villagers take their fruit to market in Singkawang, about a half-hour's ride by minivan; and local and urban traders buy rubber.

The people who own and manage the forests have long been essentially sedentary, even when shifting cultivation was their primary land and forest use. Access to the resources of various types of managed forest is typically controlled by complex and changing property relations enforced at the local level. The reserved part of the forest is under the formal jurisdiction of the Department of Forest Conservation and Nature Preservation (PHPA). The reserved forest is very loosely managed, lacking even annual visits by foresters from the Singkawang office. Bagak had a resident forest guard whose guiding management policy was to prevent fires and radical transformations of reserve lands (such as clearing for agriculture), mostly along borders. He turns a blind eye on low-impact uses such as the collection of bamboo shoots, fruit, and rubber from within the reserve.

The ancestors of the ethnic group Salako Dayaks of this village lived for several hundred years in longhouses near the upper slopes of Setipa Mountain just outside what is today the Gunung Raya Pasi nature reserve. Living in the mountains allowed them to diversify their production while defending themselves from their enemies. Unlike their more well-known Iban neighbors, these Salako did not make war and hunt heads in order to expand their resource territories, although they responded to war parties' depredations with counterattacks of their own. Every twenty to fifty years, the villagers moved their longhouse sites short distances or split off into separate longhouses (e.g., when population expanded, when the trees near the longhouse had grown too large, or when illness struck the occupants and the site was considered inauspicious). When they left a site, additional durian and other fruit trees were planted in the space left by the house structures. These were the bases of highly "social" forests. Dominated by fruit trees, they were also populated by useful species allowed to live when people cleared the area around trees to prepare for the harvest. The Dayak's landscape until 1930, then, was one in which large patches of ancestral fruit forests, marking former longhouse locations, dotted the surrounding land in various stages of swidden fields and fallows.

While the Dayaks practiced swidden agroforestry on the dry slopes of Setipa Mountain, the swampy lowlands to the north of the mountain were farmed by Hakka-speaking Chinese agriculturalists. Their village, Sahwa, may have been established as early as the late eighteenth century, soon after the Chinese began mining gold for the sultan of Sambas at nearby Montrado (see Chew 1990). The Chinese cut the lowland forest and dug canals to drain the swamps and plant rice. The Dutch colonial policy passed in 1870, mentioned above, prohibited Chinese and other "nonnative" peoples from owning land. It ignored the Chinese role in converting this forest to productive irrigated agriculture and thus ignored their own criteria for recognizing land rights: continuous cultivation and the conversion of "unproductive" forest to "useful" crops. The Chinese could, however, acquire usufruct rights to the land, through agreements that were effectively long-term leases. Although they did not formally own the land, the Chinese continued to alter it, improve it, and make it productive. Chinese planters also leased rights from the Dutch colonial government to the drylands between the wet-rice fields and the mountaintops called Patengahan. There they built houses and eventually planted fruit and rubber. They were the first non-Europeans in the area to grow rubber, a crop with solely commercial value. The Salako generally maintained control of their forest and land resources, except for occasional tribute payments to the Malay sultan of Sambas. The community sold or bartered agroforestry products with Malay and Chinese traders.

In 1920, the Dutch initiated plans to turn the upper slopes of the Gunung Raya Pasi complex, including Setipa Mountain, into a nature reserve—a watershed protection and water supply area for the growing urban area of nearby Singkawang. The initial line for the reserve border was drawn where a water catchment device was to be constructed, encompassing all of the village's current and former living sites—in other words, the sites of their ancestral forests and lands. The longhouse occupants had to move off the mountain and forfeit their ancestral rights. Not surprisingly, the villagers were not happy with the colonial government's new plans. Dutch officials worked with local leaders to convince the Salako that they had no choice but to move from the upper slopes of Setipa to the lower slopes near the areas where the Chinese had planted rubber and fruit. Eventually, people moved out of the longhouses into single-family dwellings lower on the mountain, which they built for themselves. The housing units were generally large enough to accommodate extended families.

The villagers' unhappiness with the new spatial arrangements caused some families to remain on the mountain (inside the reserve) until approximately 1940, eight years after the nature reserve was officially established and mapped. These families moved only because a subdistrict government official threatened to jail them if they refused to leave or continued to make swiddens above the reserve boundaries. The head of the new village continued to negotiate with the Dutch to change the reserve boundaries to recognize the rights of local people who had planted trees or converted land there. According to local accounts, the Dutch eventually moved the reserve boundary above the old longhouse sites, restoring a good deal of the people's territory and constituting a victory for the local people. Nevertheless, the reserve still took up several hundred hectares of local people's land.

The intervention of the colonial state in the arrangement of the village's social and productive space did more than superimpose a new set of rules about land and forest use. Real and imaginary boundaries were imposed for the first time on the villagers' access to the lands and land uses they had always preferred. However, the villagers have continued to "push back" this border in less organized, informal ways. Villagers harvest rubber, durian, langsat, rambutan, angkaham, cempedak, and other fruits planted by their ancestors within the border. During periods when the intensity of government forest surveillance has waned due to other more pressing political issues (e.g., the Japanese occupation from 1941–1945, the Indonesian revolution, and the early years of Indonesian independence), villagers have cleared forest and made swiddens within the reserve boundaries, planting rubber and fruit in the fallows. By planting productive tree crops, people were also staking their claims in the future control of the hillside's upper slopes. Villagers continue to blur this border by planting fruit and rubber trees within the reserve, creating an informal buffer zone between the reserve forest and their 'village forest. They also hunt the occasional deer and collect the products of various self-sown species such as bamboo shoots, candlenut, and rattan, from within the borders of the reserve.

Government interventions such as evicting people from the reserve land, consolidating village borders through legislation, and siting alternative land uses around the village, sparked Salako interest in planting rubber. After people were denied legal access to the extensive tracts within the reserve and on the mountain and alternative locations for a new village were becoming more densely populated, it became difficult for everyone to find enough swidden land to produce their families' food. Before World War II, a few Dayaks had experimented with planting irrigated rice near the Chinese paddies but gave up—the time and labor demands of wet-rice production interfered too much with their other productive activities. Rubber was much less labor intensive and thus was allegedly stolen, bought, or otherwise acquired from the Chinese planters already producing it. Rubber's other biological characteristics made it an attractive crop: Latex could be collected and marketed in virtually all seasons except the rainiest weeks. Uncollected latex did no harm to the tree's productivity. Until the Confrontation with Malaysia (1963–1966), it could be carried without spoilage to Sarawak (Malaysian Borneo) and sold or exchanged for goods there, or it could be sold along the road to Singkawang, widened by the Dutch in the 1930s.[3] Rubber trees increased the value of their land and widened a household's diversity of economic options. When the first Dayaks moved down from Setipa, none planted rubber. Gradually, more acquired it; today, 85 percent of the villagers own productive rubber trees.[4]

As the village's resource territory was shrunken by direct and indirect government intervention, the relative intensity of land use became increasingly important. Because of the combined impacts of the loss of land for expansion and the response to market opportunities for rubber, by the mid-1960s many people were no longer able to produce their year's supply of rice on their hill land; they had to buy rice. To feed their families, the marketing of forest and agroforestry products assumed a more important role in people's subsistence strategies.

These stresses on land and changes in production perhaps contributed to local people's willingness to participate in the forced eviction of the Chinese from the lands they and their ancestors had transformed and managed—despite the strongly held local belief that labor invested in land management and forest conversion imparted inheritable rights. In

1968, the Indonesian army, assisted by local Dayaks, violently forced the movement of the Chinese from the agricultural areas to urban centers such as Sambas, Singkawang, and Pontianak.[5] In the village under discussion alone, approximately 150 hectares of paddy lands, plus productive rubber and fruit gardens were left behind by the evicted Chinese.

Important changes in the landscape of resource control began to emerge at this time—once again, largely because of the ways the state had intervened in the allocation, formalization, and enforcement of property rights in land. First, when it became clear that the Chinese would not be allowed to reclaim their land, a council divided the irrigated fields and fruit and rubber gardens they had cultivated among local Dayaks. The council was organized by civil and military officials from the subdistrict and included the village head of Bagak, the head of customary law, and some informal village leaders. Claims were made official at the agrarian office, where people paid nominal registration fees for their land certificates. Not long afterward, the village's physical borders were sealed much tighter than they had been. Transmigration areas for retired police and retired air force personnel were established on the eastern border of the village. Around 1980, some 4,000 Javanese were settled just to the north of the village, and a rubber plantation was established.

The early 1980s saw a second surge in rubber planting in the village, when a government project to fund small production of high-yielding rubber was introduced. The state's role in this project is changing its relationship to the nature of land rights. Land converted to high-yielding rubber production changed its status from village land to state land, while people maintained rights to the high-yielding rubber trees. Thus, while landed property was increasingly important to ownership of trees in village forests, individually owned trees were gaining in importance on lands converted to state property.[6] Once the loans extended by the government for the rubber production inputs were paid off, the owner received a land title. Rubber was now both a means by which people put relatively long-term claims on a piece of land and a way for the state to temporarily reclaim land from the villagers, while permanently retaining some rights over it as the authorizer of title.

In addition to these changes, the land use revolution has also entailed an expansion of land use categories and a change in the locations where fruit trees are planted. Easy access to the urban markets of Singkawang and Pontianak, facilitated by the paving of the road in the 1960s and the entry of Japanese vehicles (motorcycles and vans) in the 1970s, added additional incentives for tree planting. Durian, the most expensive and locally valued fruit, is no longer found only in the "social forests" of former living sites or in current houseyards; durian trees are encroaching on swidden fallows and rubber gardens (which were themselves planted in swidden fallows). Some 97 percent of sample households have planted durian trees in swidden fallows; at least 41 percent have planted durian in or adjacent to their rubber gardens.

At the same time that the ecological and economic importance of trees has been increasing within the landscape, forest-garden land has risen in value both because of the trees planted there and because of the increasing degree to which individuals plant clusters of trees, tying up land for much longer periods than they had in the past.

In sum, the relationships between land, trees, and the systems of tenure around them have been revolutionized by major changes in the political ecology of the region, particularly market opportunities, changing population structures, and changes in the nature of access to the forest —changes in which the state has been directly and indirectly involved. In this village, these have included the sedentarization of borders, the fluctuating enforcement of the nature reserve's borders, the introduction of two forms of rubber at two different times, the eviction of the Chinese and appropriation of some 150 hectares of irrigated rice paddy land, and the booming market for fruit brought on by political economic change and the improvement and expansion of transport facilities. Each of these changes either constrained villagers' access to resources or expanded the markets for local products. The outcome of change was reflected in the landscape at different historical moments in two ways: shifting spatial relations between forests and fields and the mechanisms of access to trees and fields particularly new property rights in these. The changes also altered the ways some people valued the mix of resources and led to new types of property relations for many people.

In response both to their eviction from their lands and in response to increasing access to markets (via the road) and sedentarization, Bagak villagers have "filled in" their hillsides with economic and other useful trees. In effect, they transformed what was a swidden agriculture landscape, consisting of swidden fields and fallows, to a fruit- and rubber-dominated forest. People began to plant and protect more trees in places where trees were not previously planted. They planted mostly rubber and fruit—but in the same tracts protected self-sown timber, wood for fuel, and medicinal species for their use. Very little of the hillside area is planted today with rice. Rubber, collected year round, has become the main crop; fruit in good production years has become a source of wind-fall profits.

By planting productive tree crops, people inside and outside the re-serve boundaries are also staking their claims in the control of the hillside's upper slopes, negotiating new forms of old territorial and re-source claims. Whereas in the past, they had claimed the lands in the reserve by clearing forest for swiddens, now they are currently trying to reclaim them by planting long-living trees.

Conclusion

These three cases have shown that government intervention in forest management through policy—particularly policies that directly or indi-rectly serve to alter the means of physical and legal access to the forest —does not operate within a vacuum. Local claims on and objectives of forest use, as well as local interactions with local, regional, and global markets, will always influence the ways government policy plays out.

In the first case of direct and intensive government forest manage-ment, neither the physical landscape nor the cognitive landscape of lo-cal people who are dependent on forest resources have adapted to the policy appropriations intended by total government control of the for-est. In this case, both the ecology of the teak forest and the value of the wood—which underlies the development of the thriving black market in teak—have facilitated the persistence of people's claims to teak for their subsistence needs.

In the second case, the policies and physical infrastructures put into place by both the government and the timber industry have facilitated the extraction and marketing of a formerly difficult-to-access timber. Market opportunities, technology, and a failed government protection policy led, in the case of ironwood, to the transformation of local prop-erty rights. Rights to the wood have suddenly and radically shifted from a mix of community, family, and individual rights to individualized pri-vate property.

Similarly in the third case, the village's proximity to roads and urban markets softened the blow of the government's appropriation of ances-tral lands by providing incentives for people to commercialize their pro-duction of diverse tree crops and sacrifice their food production. Other seemingly unrelated government policies spurred by the social and political upheavals of the late 1960s freed up valuable rice-producing land, although today this land is not cultivated by all who have rights to it (some choose not to do so, as their other productions are lucrative enough). Nevertheless, the case illustrated the variety of ways these local people contested government claims on their lands and created new forests or new claims within new government forests for themselves.

In sum, three lessons of value to people thinking about forest management anywhere in the world can be learned from these cases of forest management in Indonesia. First, government intervention through policy instruments rarely has the totalizing effects expected. Second, sometimes those people who are denied access to resources are in a position to create new resources despite external controls. And finally, in these and any other cases, you never really "see" a forest by only looking at the trees.

Notes

1. Patches are not dominated by a single species (ironwood in this case); rather, as in other parts of the tropical everwet forest, a very diverse mixture of species exists in each hectare.

2. For more background and detail on the teak forests of Java, see Peluso 1992a, 1993a, and 1993b. On the ironwood situation, see Peluso 1992b, 1993c, and Colfer 1983. On indigenous social forests see Padoch 1994; Peluso 1993c; Peluso and Padoch 1995; Peluso n.d.; Salafsky, Dugelby, and Terborgh 1993; and Sather 1990.

3. The "Confrontation" (*konfrontasi*) was a conflict between Malaysia and Indonesia that took place between 1963 and 1966, and that stemmed from Sukarno's opposition to the formation of the Federation of Malaysia.

4. This contradicts the findings of Dove (1993), who maintains that swidden production was preferred over rubber production as a means of resisting external control.

5. The complexities surrounding the social and political relations of this violent period and the circumstances surrounding the exile of the Chinese have been difficult to research from fieldwork and oral histories alone. Moreover, research on ethnic conflict of any sort is strongly discouraged, even forbidden, by the Indonesian government. Without having access to archives from this period, it is impossible to tell the nuanced story this tumultuous period deserves.

6. Although in reality, the People's Bank of Indonesia owned the trees until the loans were paid off.

Bibliography

Barber, Charles V. 1989. "The State, the Environment, and Development: The Genesis and Transformation of Social Forest Policy in New Order Indonesia." Ph.D. diss., University of California, Berkeley.

Chew, Daniel. 1990. *Chinese Pioneers on the Saswak Frontier, 1841–1941*. Singapore: Oxford University Press.

Colfer, Carol. 1983. "Change and Indigenous Agroforestry in East Kalimantan." *Borneo Research Bulletin* 15 (1): 3–20, (2): 70–86.

De Beers, Jenna, and Melanie McDermott. 1989. *The Economic Role of Non-Timber Forest Products in Southeast Asia*. Amsterdam: IUCN.

Dove, Michael R. 1993. "Rubber Resisting Rice, Rice Resisting Rubber." Paper presented at Agarian Studies Program, Yale University.

Padoch, Christine. 1994. "The Woodlands of Tae: Traditional Forest Management in Kalimantan." In *Forest Resources and Wood-Based Biomass Energy as Rural Development Assets*, ed. William Bentley. Lebanon, NH: Science Publishers.

Padoch, Christine, and Charles Peters. 1993. "Managed Forests of West Kalimantan, Indonesia." In *Proceedings of the American Association for the Advancement of Science*. Washington, DC: American Association of the Advancement of Science.

Padoch, Christine, and Nancy Lee Peluso, eds. 1995. *Borneo in Transition: People, Forests, Conservation, and Development*. Kuala Lumpur: Oxford University Press.

Peluso, Nancy Lee. 1992a. *Rich Forests, Poor People: Resource Control and Resistance in Java*. Berkeley: University of California Press.

———. 1992b. "The Ironwood Problem: (Mis)-management and Development of an Extractive Rainforest Product." *Conservation Biology* 6, no.1 (June): 210–219.

———. 1992c. "The Political Ecology of Extraction and Extractive Reserves in East Kalimantan, Indonesia." *Development and Change* 23, no. 4 (October): 49–74.

———. 1993a. "Traditions of Forest Control in Java: Implications for Social Forestry and Sustainability. *Natural Resources Journal* 32, no. 4 (October): 884–918.

———. 1993b. "Coercing Conservation?: The Politics of State Resource Control." *Global Environmental Change* 3, no. 2 (June): 199–218.

———. 1993c.*The Impacts of Social and Environmental Change on Indigenous People's Forest Management in West Kalimantan, Indonesia.* Forest, Trees, and People Monograph Series. Rome: Food and Agriculture Organization of the United Nations.

———. 1996. "Fruit Trees and Family Trees in an Indonesian Rainforest: Property Rights, Ethics of Access, and Environmental Change." *Comparative Studies in Society and History* 38 (3): 510–548.

Peluso, Nancy Lee, and Mark Poffenberger. 1989. "Social Forestry on Java: Reorienting Management Systems." *Human Organization* 48, no. 4 (Winter): 333–344.

Salafsky, N., O.L. Dugelby, and J.W. Terborgh. 1993. "Can Extractive Reserves Save the Rainforest? An Ecological and Socio-economic Comparison of Non-timber Forest Product Extraction Systems in Peten, Guatamala, and West Kalimantan, Indonesia." *Conservation Biology* 7(1): 39–52.

Sather, Clifford. 1990. "Trees and Tree Tenure in Paku Iban Society: The Management of Secondary Forest Resources in a Long-Established Iban Community." *Borneo Review* 1, no. 1: 16–40.

Sunderlin, William. 1992. "The Equity Mandate in the Java Social Forestry Program." Ph.D. Diss., Cornell University, Ithaca, NY.

Weinstock, Joseph. 1983. "Rattan: Ecological Balance in a Borneo Rainforest Swidden." *Economic Botany* 37 (1): 58–68.

Zerner, Charles. 1990. *Legal Options for the Indonesian Forestry Sector*. Jakarta: United Nations Food and Agriculture Organization.

—— 10 ——

China's Environment: Resilient Myths and Contradictory Realities

Vaclav Smil

An understanding of China's environment poses a challenge of doubly difficult interpretation. To the general problem of disentangling complex environmental realities—a task done poorly by many Western experts even in their own countries—one must add the challenge of understanding the intricacies of a civilization whose inner workings are far from the Western experience and whose history mingles reverence and abuse of nature.[1] Not surprisingly, this combination has resulted in memorable misinterpretations, ranging from pardonable, indeed unavoidable, mistakes to inexcusable apologies of a dictatorial regime as well as frightening visions of impending doom.

My personal experience has made me immune to any infatuation with ideologies proffering incomparable worldly salvation through "great thoughts," no matter what "-ism" they embody. And my scientific preferences—unprejudiced studies of complex systems proceeding from first principles—has made me suspicious of any simplistic solutions, all-encompassing claims, and biased interpretations of reality. Consequently, my understanding and my interpretation of Chinese realities affecting the state of the country's environment ran against the prevailing Western infatuation with the Chinese model of development during the 1970s.

As the aim of this chapter is to illustrate the contradictory trends in the Western understanding of China, rather than to document the relevant developments, I have not burdened it with scores of references. An interested reader will find all detail and all appropriate citations and notes in the sources listed at the end of the chapter.

They do so again now, in the late 1990s, when the newest, and totally opposite, vogue is to see China as the planet's greatest environmental threat, irreparably damaging the global commons and poised to drain the world of its food surpluses.[2]

I will illustrate these misinterpretations with a detailed example for each of the two periods. The first case will expose the Western adulatory naiveté of the Maoist period by looking at China's afforestation programs. The second one will focus on recent catastrophic appraisals of China's future food production.

Misunderstanding China: The Era of the Maoist Spell

The mixture of the long-lasting Western fascination with the affairs of the Middle Kingdom and of the more recent awe at the great social experiment produced some astonishingly naive paeans to Maoism, widespread suspension of critical reason, and embarrassing adulation of vastly exaggerated (and unsustainable) achievements. Yet another powerful factor enhanced these uncritical appraisals. Reopening China after a long spell of self-imposed Maoist isolation did not result in an immediate open access to its realities. During the 1970s access was highly controlled, and the best guarantee that Western emissaries would be chaperoned on their travels by "responsible comrades" was to write glowingly (and if criticizing, then apologetically) about China. These privileged travelers were only too eager to believe every fabulous claim made by Beijing bureaucrats, or to describe atypical experiences of a few show places as the national norm.

Then the first "Communist emperor"—and if there was any doubt about that designation, Li Zhishui's memoirs, *The Private Life of Chairman Mao*, make (too graphically) clear that it is a most fitting one—died in September 1976. Mao Zedong's death was almost immediately followed by the arrest of the scheming empress and her accomplices (again, a replay of deadly dynastic foibles), but then nothing dramatic happened for the next year or so. However, 1978 was a different year, as Chinese newspapers and broadcasts began to include news items implicitly criticizing many past policies of the Chinese Communist Party. The tide turned formally just before the end of the year, when the unsinkable Deng Xiaoping regained power for the third time and turned the country toward radical and rapid economic reforms.

Realities that critical Chinese scholars always knew about but could not document in extensive detail and could not quantify in nationwide terms had finally begun to surface. Some surprisingly bold early exposés in China's newspapers and weeklies were followed by official admissions of past fake claims and figures, and by publication of more realistic statistical reports. Contrasting this new critical information with the flood of Maoist propaganda, and with its often too eager Western embrace, is a fascinating, but ultimately a saddening, exercise.

Chinese Afforestation

Chinese afforestation has never been just about planting trees. In Maoist China, where, as in all communist countries, every activity was subject to politicization, annual mass tree-planting campaigns were a natural domain of the overblown official propaganda and a perfect tool for the regime's effort to "mobilize masses" in order to "change nature." The Communist propaganda machine delighted in stressing the scales of this enterprise: In the course of every year more than 100 million schoolchildren, peasants, and factory and office workers fanned out on designated days to transform old, deforested China into a green paradise. The reports of overfulfilled planting targets added up to hundreds of thousands, even millions, of hectares planted every year.

Singling out some choice quotes from writings of Western students of China seems almost unfair: Who was not deceived and who was not astonished by this gargantuan transformation? But two quotes are truly irresistible as they come from men who should have known better than wide-eyed reporters "opening up" the country to the West after years of Maoist isolation. The first comes from one of America's best-known liberal economists, John K. Galbraith, the other from a forester, Jack Westoby, who was at that time a senior official in the Food and Agriculture Organization of the United Nations. Observing from the windows of Beijing-Guangdong train, Galbraith concluded in 1973 that "the hills of China, which I had always heard of as being bare, are no longer so."[3] And in 1979, Westoby claimed that "the mightiest afforestation effort the world has ever seen" means "that the balance between man and nature, lost through centuries of reckless forest destruction, is being steadily restored."[4]

Post-1979 reporting has given us a very different appraisal of the country's much-extolled afforestation program. While the central bureaucracy has not stopped issuing bloated annual totals and revealing plans whose enormity guarantees their failure, critical analyses by foresters and more accurate field surveys have provided a more realistic picture of the great transformation.

Official Chinese afforestation claims, if true, would add up to the biggest revegetation effort in human history. Between 1950 and 1957 (the period of postwar economic reconstruction and the first Five-Year Plan) claims of newly afforested areas totaled 15.7 million hectares (Mha). An identical total was claimed for 1958–1960, the years of the Great Leap Forward (Mao's irrational attempt to accelerate the course of China's economic advancement). The total for the first half of the 1960s came to 10.5 Mha, followed by 48.3 Mha between 1966 and 1976 (the decade of the Cultural Revolution—a misnomer for a period of intensified Maoist persecution and mismanagement).

Before the end of the 1970s official afforestation claims added another 13.8 Mha, making up the grand total of 104 Mha of new plantings during the three decades between 1949 and 1979. If true, these official afforestation claims meant that the country's forest cover more than doubled in thirty years. Compared with forest coverage in other countries this claim is truly stunning: 104 Mha of new plantings is an area about 20 percent larger than all existing forests in Western Europe!

Realities concerning China's forestry that have been gradually disclosed since the late 1970s have been quite different from the Maoist propaganda, and the afforestation accomplishments have been the subject of one of the greatest revisionist rectifications of the post-Mao era. By far the most outrageous was the claim of 15.7 Mha of new plantings (an equivalent of all forests in France) during the three Great Leap years (1958–1960). As we know now, during the three years between 1959 and 1961 China had suffered the greatest famine in human history. This largely man-induced catastrophe resulted in about 30 million deaths. The first two years of the Leap were actually a period of massive deforestation driven by Mao's delusionary goal of boosting China's iron output through a mass charcoal-fueled smelting of locally mined iron ores in primitive "backyard" furnaces.

When it resumed its publication in 1980 (after more than two decades of inactivity), China's *Statistical Yearbook* carried a comprehensive series of post-1949 afforestation claims that were clearly incompatible with other official statistics and with new admissions by the Ministry of Forestry. The first set of new official statistics put China's fully stocked forested area (the canopies of which cover at least 30 percent of the ground) at 122 Mha. Clearly, this inventory would have had very different totals if the official afforestation claims were even half true.

Official statistics put China's 1949–1979 timber harvests at 1.01 billion cubic meters (Gm^3), but the actual removal was about five times larger. This large disparity is due to the fact that the official statistics do not include either felled wood that was not removed from forests or wood used for fuel, whose harvests actually amounted to more than half of all wood. An average annual increment of at least 150 million cubic meters (Mm^3) would have produced about 4.5 Gm^3, which means that, without any afforestation, China's forested area should have remained roughly stable. The increase to 122 Mha implies afforestation of 27–39 Mha since 1949, rather than the officially claimed 104 Mha.

An apparent afforestation success rate of less than one-third is not at all surprising when one appreciates common shortcomings of Chinese statistical reporting in general and some bizarre "afforestation" practices in particular. Fudging the numbers in order to meet the centrally allocated targets has been very common. Many bureaucrats reported afforested areas by simply estimating based on the numbers of available seedlings or saplings, no matter if the young trees were actually discarded, buried in trenches, planted upside down, or even uprooted and replanted in order to boost the total claim. Huge numbers of trees were actually planted—but, as later admissions revealed, their survival rates were extremely low for a number of reasons: careless planting (such as bare-root saplings put into dry rocky or sandy soils); no or highly inadequate watering during China's frequently prolonged dry spells; no weeding; no protection against grazing animals; and planting of species unsuitable for the climate or for local soils.

This shoddy, careless work was quite satisfactory in a system whose standard criterion for afforestation success until the late 1970s was merely survival on the day a tree was planted. With such a criterion it was easy to create the world's most successful afforestation campaign. There is little doubt that since the early 1980s the quality of many new plantings and their subsequent care have been incomparably better than during the decades of Maoist mass campaigns. New private contract plantings in southern provinces have been relatively more successful. And by far the most ambitious project has been the state-directed planting of a massive shelter belt (called the Great Green Wall) designed to check the advancing desertification across China's northern provinces.

But average afforestation success rates, especially in state-sponsored plantings, remain relatively low, and even false afforestation claims did not disappear during the 1980s—but now we do not have to wait two decades to learn the extent of these gross exaggerations. A survey by the Northwest Institute of Forestry in Xian indicated that half of the reported national afforestation claims during the mid-1980s were false and that the survival rate of planted trees was no higher than 40 percent.

And even the properly planted trees have had great difficulty surviving the combined impacts of prolonged droughts (both their duration and frequency have increased in most of northern China during the 1980s), pest infestation, and fires. During the 1980s the annual economic loss caused by insects was said to equal the state's total investment in forestry. Poor fire-fighting capabilities were most dramatically demonstrated by the huge Da Hinggan Mountains fire in Heilongjiang. In total, between 1949 and 1989 the northeastern forest fires burned or damaged an area roughly eight times the size of the region's newly afforested area. The best nationwide estimate is that about one-third of successfully established new plantings was eventually damaged by fires. A combination of false reporting, early sapling mortality caused by poor planting and inadequate care, and pest and fire damages means that the real annual net afforestation gain during the late 1980s was no higher than about two-fifths of the officially claimed totals.[5]

Nobody familiar with the existence of these trends was surprised when the results of a survey conducted by the Ministry of Forestry, released in 1989, found a combination of declining forested area, diminishing growing stocks, and poorer quality timber. Areas of state-owned forests shrank by almost 25 percent during the 1980s, with mature growth accounting for 60 percent of this large decline. In December 1990 the Ministry of Forestry decided that although the total forested area had increased rather substantially, wood consumption continued to surpass the growth rate and in order to remedy this imbalance timber harvests should be limited during the next five years. Wood shortages already forced China to prohibit many uses of wood (including for floors, stairs, and windowsills) and to become a major timber importer spending the equivalent of more than US$1 billion a year since 1985. Yet by 1992 the Chinese media was claiming that afforestation had achieved a surplus of timber. And in December 1993 the numbers presented, if true, would mean a fundamental reversal in a single decade, with the 1989–1993 annual surplus being equal to exactly one-quarter of all tree felling.

If we are to believe the results of Chinese surveys, the total 1981–

1991 rise in annual growth would be approaching 50 percent and China's 1993 wood harvest-to-growth ratio would have stood at 80 percent of total growth in 1993, just marginally worse than the percentages of such prodigious, and heavily forested, producers of wood as the United States or Finland (respectively, 75 percent and 73 percent in 1990). This comparison alone should alert us to the fact that the Chinese figures are not really what they seem to be. But even if we were to assume that most, or even all of the gain was real, its practical import appears in a different light once one realizes the changing composition of China's forest biomass and the spatial distribution of its harvests.

Because of the rising share of new plantings in the total coverage, 82 percent of China's timberland in 1990 were young or middle-aged stands. The growing stock ready for harvesting in mature forests amounted to less than 1.5 billion cubic meters, which could be completely harvested in just seven to eight years. In the last decade or so of this century, reserves approaching maturity will decline by more than 50 percent.

Many new plantings may be doing well, and their growth will be reflected by the rising volume of the standing stock, but the state record in replanting principal commercial logging areas has been poor. This neglect is creating a major resource crisis: Of the 131 state forestry bureaus in the most important timber production zones, twenty-five had exhausted their reserves by 1990 and forty can harvest until the year 2000. By the year 2000 almost 70 percent of China's state forestry bureaus will have few trees to fell. Among the collectively run forest districts, 250 counties were suppliers of commercial timber in the 1950s, but only about 100 were delivering by 1990.

Prospects are made even more worrisome by a low productivity of new plantings. The official figure for the average growing stock in forest plantings—28.27 cubic meter per hectare (m^3/ha)—makes it quite clear that the new plantings, whose trees may be now yielding a statistical wood surplus, offer little hope of replacing the felled mature forests (generally more than fifty years old), whose growing stock would be at least 70–80 m^3/ha, for many decades. The inevitable conclusion is that even if real, the recent quantitative growth of Chinese forests hides a major qualitative decline.

In sum, China's pre-1980 afforestation achieved a limited amount of success while wasting an enormous amount of resources. Improvements during the past fifteen years have brought some encouraging advances, but more has to be done to assure sustainable productivity of forests.

Further improvements in the quality of afforestation, better fire preven-
tion, and more complete utilization of felled timber should be the key
measures.

Misunderstanding China: The Era of Second Thoughts

The afforestation story seen through Western eyes is an ideal illustration of
wishful thinking, of uncritical elevation of flimsy evidence to sweeping
judgments. Considerable complexity of the story—requiring, in this case,
sound understanding of China's realities ranging from environmental limits to bureaucratic habits—is a common attribute of all of China's history.
Neglecting these complex realities can lead not only to overly optimistic
conclusions but also to exceedingly pessimistic interpretations.

This negativist, or even catastrophist, slant has become much more
prominent after 1989. First, the brutal suppression of student demon-
strations in June 1989 was interpreted by many foreigners as a major
change of China's modernization course. Fortunately for the Chinese
people, the Western seers proved to be wrong: Economic modernization
actually accelerated after a brief pause, and political repression never reached
the extent and intensity widely anticipated in the late spring of 1989.

Then, as China's economy began posting double-digit gross domestic product growth rates, worries about precipitous degradation of the
country's environment came to the fore. These concerns became conflated
with the fashionable scare of a rapid global warming: China, already the
world's second-largest emitter of greenhouse gases, will almost certainly
become the world's largest producer of CO_2 , CH_4, and N_2O within the
next thirty years. These increased emissions will more than offset even
the largest predicted reductions attainable by the industrialized countries of Europe and North America. I will take a closer look at the latest
scare, at what many people now believe to be an unavoidable emergence of China as the ultimate destabilizing factor in the global food
market.

China's Food Production

The first wave of American visitors rediscovering China in the early
1970s brought back encouraging reports of remarkable food self-sufficiency buttressed by photographs of well-nourished children gathered
in communal kindergartens. The naiveté of those reports and the falsity

of countless official statements about an ever-better state of China's farming was exposed by Deng Xiaoping's radical rural reforms after 1979.

In just five years after the beginning of privatization China's average per capita food supply vaulted to within less than 10 percent of the Japanese mean. Moreover, this quantitative rise was accompanied by impressive qualitative gains. Rice became whiter, and traditional nonstaple food favorites became, once again, commonplace. Pork consumption ceased to be a rarity reserved for a few festive days, and fish sales rose sharply.

All food rationing was eventually abolished as the Chinese media continued to highlight the boast that China feeds one-fifth of the global population from just one-fifteenth of the world's arable land. The largest grain harvest in China's history was recorded in 1984, and the next year the country actually became a net exporter of grain. Grain harvests, always the greatest preoccupation of the Chinese rulers, stagnated after the 1984 record crop. A new record harvest in 1990, however, surpassed the 1984 yield by almost 10 percent, and yet another record was set in 1993.

But in the spring of 1994, Lester Brown, president of the Worldwatch Institute, wrote an article arguing that China is rapidly losing the capacity to feed itself, and in 1995 he expanded this warning into a book, *Who Will Feed China? Wake-up Call for a Small Planet.* Other publications released a flood of gloomy to outright panicky papers and newscasts about China's food future. Brown believes China's grain output will drop by at least 20 percent by the year 2030. China's increasing prosperity will move the country up the food ladder as consumers will demand more meat, plant oils, and sugar. As China's population, currently just above 1.2 billion, will almost certainly surpass 1.5 billion by the year 2025, it will be impossible to satisfy its huge food demand by domestic production, and the country's rising imports, potentially much larger than today's global grain exports, will inflate worldwide prices of grains, oils, and meat.

Moving up the food chain—that is, eating less staple grain, but more meat, fish, eggs, and dairy products—has been a universal trend clearly discernible in all modernizing countries with rising personal incomes. China has been no exception. Since 1980, major per capita consumption increases in all of these categories have brought its dietary pattern closer to East Asia's three richest economies, Japan, South Korea, and Taiwan.

Because China has only a limited area of good-quality grasslands, it does not have the North American option of producing large amounts of range-fed beef. Because most of the world's major fishing grounds are already heavily overexploited, China cannot follow the Japanese path of securing a large share of high-quality animal protein from the ocean. Consequently, China's meat, whether from farm animals or from aquatic species, will have to come overwhelmingly from grain-fed sources.

Losses of farmland are a global phenomenon and a longstanding Chinese problem, but the rapid post-1980 modernization greatly increased the annual rate of loss through a combination of new rural and urban housing construction, the unprecedented expansion of export-oriented manufactures, and the expansion of highways. Because Brown believes that China's farmland losses will follow the previous East Asian rates of decline, which have averaged 1.2 percent a year, his conclusions are extremely bleak. Should China follow the pattern, its farmland would be reduced by half by 2025. Even if the Chinese could somehow slow down the rate of farmland losses, their future harvests would be limited by shortages of water and by difficulties in raising average crop yields.

Brown foresees only further aggravation of water scarcities already so obvious throughout north China as growing cities and industries compete with agriculture for limited supplies. And while he allows that future yields may rise, he believes that they will do so slowly that year-to-year changes will be hardly perceptible. Because Brown considers all of these trends to be virtually unstoppable and irreversible, his conclusions add to a sequence of correspondingly catastrophic prospects.

As incomes rise, China's demand for feed grain will continue growing from less than one-quarter of the country's grain output in 1994 toward one-half, or even more, of the shares typical for industrialized countries. The only way to satisfy the soaring demand will be through massive and increasing imports of grain, and China will, at best, make food dear for all nations and, at worst, will be the cause of global food shortages.

Although Lester Brown has a longstanding reputation as an unreconstructed catastrophist, it would be a mistake to dismiss his concerns about China. One needs to consider the issues without ignoring realities and possibilities that add up to a very different kind of conclusion. Most importantly, there are no fundamental biophysical reasons why China's crop yields should not be increasing much faster than at Brown's barely perceptible rate.

To begin with, virtually all of China's official yield statistics are wrong because of substantial underestimates of the total cultivated area. This underreporting occurred during the times of communal farming in order to meet and to surpass the state-prescribed yields and quotas, and it is continued by private farmers eager to avoid taxation and to minimize compulsory deliveries to state. This figure stands now at about 95 Mha, or a mere 0.08 hectares per capita. Among poor and populous (more than 100 million people) countries, only the Bangladeshi mean is as low. But in reality (revealed by satellite monitoring and, more accurately, by detailed country-wide sample surveys) China's cropland amounts to about 140 Mha, almost 50 percent more than the official total.

This does not mean that all officially reported crop yields are inaccurate by about one-third. Reported figures are fairly reliable for rice from central and eastern provinces, but they may be up to 50 percent too high for crops in hilly interior regions where the underreporting of farmland has been particularly extensive. The bottom line is that China's current average staple grain yields are still below the Korean or Japanese means, and hence the country's potential to improve crop productivity is higher than the official figures would lead one to believe.

Validity of this conclusion is only strengthened by considering an array of inefficient agricultural practices that can be improved by a combination of more realistic pricing, better management, and technical fixes. Just as the capacity of fossil fuel resources to provide useful energy can be greatly expanded by more efficient uses, the environment's capacity to support higher crop harvests can be increased by rational farming. I have likened the current situation in agricultural efficiency, and not only in China, to the situation in the world's energy consumption in the early 1970s when low prices militated against any major efficiency gains.

There are enormous opportunities in increasing efficiency of irrigation and fertilizer use. About two-thirds of China's irrigation water is wasted, mostly because it is not priced right: Peasants obtain it at unrealistically low prices (often less than one-tenth of the real cost)—prices equivalent to those paid by heavily subsidized California farmers. Many price-induced water savings do not need high capital investment. More appropriate matching of crops with available moisture, irrigation scheduling optimized with the use of inexpensive sensors and microcomputers (which do not have to be individually owned—a single laptop belonging to an advisor can serve hundreds of farmers), and better-lined canals to prevent seepage are among the readily applicable remedies. Raising the mean irrigation efficiency from 30 to about 50 percent (a level still far below the rates achievable with investment in today's best irrigation techniques) would expand China's agricultural water supply by 40 percent without tapping any new sources.

Gains in fertilizer efficiency should come first of all from gradual shutdowns of small fertilizer factories making ammonium bicarbonate. This compound—still about one-third of China's total output of synthetic nitrogenous fertilizers—is highly volatile, and a large share of it is lost because of its shoddy packaging and careless distribution and storage even before it is applied to fields. This, and the underestimated farmland, means that actual applications of nitrogen are substantially lower than implied by official statistics—and hence the potential to raise yields by increased fertilization is commensurably higher.

Further opportunities lie beyond the fields. Considerations of food prospects are almost exclusively about increased supply, with too little said about great opportunities for reducing waste along the whole food chain: Environmental management in agriculture should not end with crop harvests. China's performance has been particularly poor in this respect. A recent five-year survey of grain losses in leading cereal-producing provinces found that about 15 percent of the crop is lost annually during harvesting, threshing, drying, storage, transport, and processing. Table waste in hundreds of thousands of labor-unit mess halls and losses during inefficient animal feeding and fermenting to alcohol almost doubles that total to more than 50 million tons (Mt) of staple grain equivalent a year. Reducing this waste by just one-third would boost annual grain availability by almost 20 Mt, more than the annual total of recent grain imports.

Raising the efficiency of pork production has to be a key ingredient in this effort. Most of China's pigs are still not fed well-balanced mixtures but all kinds of locally available plant matter deficient in protein. Not surprisingly, they take at least twice as long to reach slaughter weight as American pigs (twelve versus six months), and even then their carcasses are, on the average, 40 percent lighter. And hundreds of millions of chickens roaming the country's farmyards take three times as long to reach, again lower, slaughter weight than American broilers. Availability of mixed feeds and better breeds can lower today's feed-to-meat ratios from well over 4:1 to just over 3:1 for pigs and from much above 3:1 to just over 2:1 for chickens.

Finally, there is the possibility of smart nutritional choices. As we have finally learned with energy consumption, demand management should be at least as important a concern as the growth of supplies. In nutritional terms it means not only steering the consumption toward more efficient and well-established foods but also promoting nontraditional foodstuffs. By far the best opportunity for the first option in China is to produce more high-quality animal protein from both freshwater and marine aquaculture. Intensive fish production will also require good mixed feeds, but carp are much better converters of feed than warm-blooded animals.

In the second category nothing would make more difference than substantial per capita intakes of dairy products. In terms of feed conversion efficiency, milk is, of course, the best animal product supplying high-quality protein. Every kilogram of concentrated feed can produce one kilogram of milk, or twice as much food energy as feeding it to the most efficient broilers. The fact that the Chinese, like all East Asians, have a very high incidence of lactose intolerance, which makes it difficult to digest large quantities of fresh milk, is no barrier to such a dietary shift. This biochemical peculiarity does not prevent most people from drinking smaller, but nutritionally significant, volumes of whole milk, and it is largely irrelevant for eating fermented dairy products: Yogurt has less lactose than raw milk, and ripe, hard cheeses contain mere traces of the milk sugar. The Japanese experience is excellent proof that neither the widespread lactose intolerance nor the traditional absence of milk in a nation's food culture are obstacles to healthy dairy intakes: Japan's per capita mean consumption of dairy foods is now well over 50 kilograms per year. Chinese milk consumption is still very low in the countryside, but it is already rising sharply in cities.

No single measure will do, but a combination of gradual improvements harbors a potential for impressive gains. Its key ingredients are more efficient use of water and fertilizers, reduction of stunning postharvest waste, improved production of pork, reliance on broilers to supply most of the additional demand for meat, and expanded output of freshwater fish and dairy products. This combination can bring annual food gains not only surpassing China's population growth but also going far to meet the anticipated improvements in the country's nutrition without necessitating enormous imports of foreign grain.

Many Chinese top-level agricultural experts are well aware of these potentially large gains, and their greatest ally in impressing the ruling party with the need for adequate financing of agricultural research and farming development will be the often-repeated preference of the Chinese government to avoid any excessive dependence on food imports.

Never a Normal Country?

China's history and size (now not only of its population but also of its economy) inevitably put the country into a class of its own. But that indisputable uniqueness should not provide any excuse for failing to recognize universal limits and opportunities. Consequently, assessments of China's claimed achievements should be always carried out with a searching criticism so routinely applied to other nations, while appraisals of the country's aspirations should recognize many realistic opportunities available to meet tomorrow's needs.

Such an approach will repeatedly show that China is not so unique after all and that what has so often passed for an expert analysis of its achievements and prospects has been more a reflection of Western biases, misinformation, and wishful thinking rather than the reflection of complex—often exasperating but certainly not hopeless—Chinese realities.

Notes

1. For more on these contradictions, see the chapter by Xiaoshan Yang in this volume.
2. For an example of such a pessimistic outlook, see Rhoads Murphey's contribution in this volume.
3. Galbraith, John K., *China Passage*. (Boston: Houghton Mifflin, 1973), p. 27.
4. Westoby, Jack, " 'Making Green the Motherland': Forestry in China," in *China's Road to Development*, ed., N. Maxwell (Oxford: Pergamon Press, 1979), p. 231.
5. This estimate seems to be confirmed by contrasting two sets of recent Chinese afforestation figures. Totals provided by the Ministry of Forestry in 1990 showed China's forest cover declining from 121.86 Mha in the mid-1970s to 115.28 Mha during the years 1977–1981, and then increasing to 124.65 Mha by 1988. Plantations accounted for 19.4 percent of the total in the first period, 24.2 percent in the second, and 30.7 percent in the third. These shares mark a steady decline of China's mature forests, and they present afforestation gains averaging about 1.2 Mha a year.

Bibliography

For afforestation:

Richardson, S.D. *Forests and Forestry in China*. Washington, DC: Island Press, 1990.
Ross, L. *Environmental Policy in China*. Bloomington: Indiana University Press, 1988.
Smil, Vaclav. "Afforestation in China." In *Afforestation Policies, Planning and Progress*, ed. A. Mather. London: Belhaven Press, 1993, pp. 105–117.

————. *The Bad Earth*. Armonk, NY: M.E. Sharpe, 1984.

————. *China's Environmental Crisis: An Inquiry into the Limits of National Development*. Armonk, NY: M.E. Sharpe, 1993.

Westoby, J.C. " 'Making Green the Motherland': Forestry in China." In *China's Road to Development*, ed. N. Maxwell. Oxford: Pergamon Press, 1979, pp. 231–145.

For food production capacity:

Brown, Lester. *Who Will Feed China? Wake Up Call for a Small Planet*. New York: W.W. Norton, 1995.

Smil, Vaclav. "Feeding China." *Current History* 94, no. 593 (1995): 280–284.

————. "Who Will Feed China?" *China Quarterly*, no. 143 (1995): 801–813.

————. "China's Agricultural Land." *China Quarterly* 158 (1999): 414–429.

Part IV

Moving Beyond Boundaries

As we struggle to make sense of current environmental "crises" and the conditions in which they are produced, we must simultaneously refine and re-examine the very terms by which we define these conditions. Historically more dominant "Western" views of environment, landscape, and aesthetics, or even science and technology, may gain a great deal by considering "Asian" perceptions and practices, while Western ideas of conservation and "ways of seeing" nature may resonate in Asia. The final essays move beyond traditional disciplinary and cultural boundaries. In unique ways, each applies experimental and theoretical approaches in their exploration of the relationship between landscapes and communities

Alan McQuillan pushes beyond the traditional bounds of science with a consideration of theories of chaos and their potential resonance with the Taoist concepts of *te* and *wu-wei*. In a different, but similarly integrative approach, Scott Slovic explores the potential for nature writing in Japan, as inspired by the popularity and power of nature writing in the United States.

———— 11 ————

Dancing with Devils: Finding a Convergence of Science and Aesthetics in Eastern and Western Approaches to Nature

Alan Graham McQuillan

The problem raised by seeking sustainable landscapes and communities is the matter of being able to predict the outcome of our decisions and the actions that follow from those decisions—large or small scale, spatially broad or narrow, short or long term—in general, the problem of "planning." Whether planning for an economic and ecological relationship between people and the land; planning for relationships between communities, regions, nations, and continents; planning for growth; planning to avoid natural disasters; or planning the management of forests and wildlands, the modernist approach to planning attempted over the past century or so has largely been a failure. The grand schemes of planning of the Progressive Era, which engulfed both Europe and North America (and in the United States are associated with individuals such as Teddy Roosevelt, Franklin D. Roosevelt, and Lyndon B. Johnson), were based on the assumption that, because science was successful at explaining how observed effects resulted from discernible causes, science could be equally successful at predicting the outcomes of actions under consideration. On this basis planning could proceed and succeed.[1]

As things turned out, unforeseen events almost invariably rendered plans (land-use plans, community or economic plans, and so on) obsolete long before they had reached their anticipated ends. These devastating and "chaotic" events could be natural (hurricanes, volcanoes, floods, landslides, forest fires, or insect and disease attacks), but they were just as likely to occur within the human sphere (warfare, economic boom or bust, unexpected technological discoveries ranging from the internal combustion engine to radioactive fallout and from the computer chip to genetic engineering, or even changing moral and aesthetic values).

Today there are many who, lamenting this failure of modernism, seek to blame science and technology and pine nostalgically for some earlier time when life was thought to be simpler, more sustainable, more localized, and more "in touch with nature."[2] Some see tribal life as the epitome of a sustainable relationship between community and landscape. The mere fact that tribal life has largely succumbed to the spread of global capitalism and the world marketplace, however, is testament to the unsustainability of that system in the face of external perturbations. In the same vein, the demise of feudalism and mercantilism in the Western world is testimony to the premodern world's lack of resilience as a system for mediating relationships between people and nature. Today, it appears inevitable that any system that purports to engender a sustainable relationship between community and landscape (a term that implicitly emphasizes *locality*) must do so within the larger global context, which is one of technological as well as cultural change, one of increasingly free trade and movement of peoples, one of "extranational" capitalism. This is a challenge that faces Asia just as surely as it faces the Western world.

One who has both criticized Western dependence on science and made useful comparisons with Chinese approaches to nature is Roger Ames, a professor of philosophy at the University of Hawaii.[3] Ames begins by criticizing the Western world's emphasis on what he calls "logical construction," which stresses abstraction and reduction. In this view, things are recognized atomisticly as separate individuals, but only insofar as they exhibit generalized characteristics that "conform" to preconceived "blueprints" (the scientific method). Ames has been joined by many others who have criticized Western science for its reductionism and "atomism," which ignores the interdependence of all things that share the planet—an omission that has led to poor decision making and unsustainability of human ventures.[4] He compares the Western method with the Chinese system, which emphasizes *polarity*; it is a system that recognizes that nothing exists in isolation, that everything exists only in relation with other things.[5]

· In contradistinction to the failure of "logical construction," Ames finds hope in a Chinese approach to nature that he calls "aesthetic composition." This stresses the primacy of relationships, a view that he believes is conducive to fostering desirable human-nature relationships. According to Ames the six features of aesthetic composition are:

1. It begins with the uniqueness of the one particular as it collaborates with other particulars in an emergent complex pattern of relatedness, and as such, will permit of no substitutions: Plurality is prior to unity and disjunction to conjunction.
2. It takes as its focus the unique perspective of a concrete, specific detail revealing itself as productive of a harmony or an order that is expressed by a complex of such details in their relationship to one another.
3. Given that it is concerned with the fullest disclosure of particularity for the emergent harmony, it necessarily entails movement away from any universal characteristic to the concrete detail.
4. It is an act of "disclosure"—the achieved coordination of concrete details in novel patterns that reflect their uniqueness—and hence is describable in the qualitative language of richness, intensity, etc.
5. In that it is not determined by preassigned principles, it is fundamentally anarchic and contingent, and as such, is the ground for optimum creativity, where creativity, is to be understood in contradistinction to determination.
6. "Rightness" in this context refers to the degree to which the insistent particularity of the detail in tension with the consequent unity of the specific details is self-evidently expressive of an aesthetically pleasing order.[6]

As we shall see, he goes on to explain these features in terms of his understanding of certain Chinese concepts, principally *te* (potency) and *wu-wei* (a complex term having to do with non-action, defined below).[7] First, however, I would point out that the "logical construction," for which he criticizes Western civilization in general is more properly a criticism of what I would call modernism, the predilection for atomistic reductionism and simplified abstraction that characterized Western science and Western civilization's approach to nature from around the time of Isaac Newton until late into the twentieth century. The slow decline of "atomism" in the West is seen, for example, in the development of "ecology," which stresses the importance of relationships and interdependencies. It is also seen in a so-called poststructuralist epistemology, which views symbolic relationships (instances of "writing" and "reading") as the only empirical evidence we have of the regular world, since all communicable, empirical knowledge, and experience are necessarily filtered through symbolic concepts (whether in ordinary language, "body language," or some other system of signs).[8] And this is seen, I hope to illustrate, in emerging Western science itself, in the work of research scientists such as Ilya Prigogine and Stuart Kauffman who see all physical exchange relationships (which necessarily occur in accordance with the second law of thermodynamics) as being the very source from which ordered life springs forth, out of primeval chaos.[9] What is more, this postmodern science of "complexity theory" actually allows us to understand (explain) the failure of modernist approaches to planning and is generally suggestive of an aesthetic approach along the lines advocated by Ames.[10]

Thus, what I hope to persuade the reader is that, while Ames is correct in bringing to our attention the Chinese (or more precisely Taoist) emphasis on aesthetic construction, one can actually find evidence of a sympathetic move already under way in the Western mainstream. One can go so far as to suggest that we are witnessing a convergence—in fact a double convergence: not only of Eastern and Western thought, but also of Western arts and science. This, I believe, allows for a certain measure of optimism for achieving some form of sustainable relationship between community and landscape within the context of a still-globalizing capitalist economy.

And, as Ames perhaps melodramatically expresses in his fifth principle, this process of aesthetic construction is a "fundamentally anarchic and contingent . . . ground for optimum creativity." That is, far from any positivist pursuit of the "good life" that proceeds linearly and logically from starting conditions toward some utopian goal (the modernist project), we are suggesting that pursuing community and landscape in a complex, chaotic world is more on the order of a "dance with devils," an active, by no means assured, and possibly dangerous irreversible engagement with a "wicked," "wretched," and ultimately unknowable otherness that we call nature.[11] There is, so far as we know, no other way it can be. Before we approach Ames's work more directly, it is necessary to establish a context for this inquiry.

Knowledge of Nature

What Westerners mean by "nature" has been defined and redefined. Some of this history has been interpreted by Michel Foucault.[12] Only since around the Enlightenment of the eighteenth century has Western civilization held a view of wild nature as the cradle of civilization, an "awesomely wonderful" and intricately ordered system of "ecological" relations, and only since Darwin, a century later, have people come to view themselves as a naturally evolved product of that system (which can presumably exist without people, but without which people cannot exist).

In recent years, it has become more difficult to come to terms with the idea of nature. We used to ignore the "problem" of language and did not consider that how we went about gaining knowledge of things could actually affect the knowledge that was gained. We had the idea that nature existed independently "out there" and knowledge could be discovered "like rocks." It did not matter from what direction we stumbled into those rocks; the same rock would reveal itself in the same way, whether approached from above or below, from north or from south. It was transcendentally "real." This idea that knowledge was of objects, was "objective," because objects existed independently of the people who came to do the knowing, is an example of the atomism and logical construction that Ames criticizes. Since Sigmund Freud, Werner Heisenberg, Jacques Derrida, and Ilya Prigogine, we have come to realize that knowledge is the result of a relationship between the knower and that which is known, between the subject and the object. Ontology has given way to epistemology. How we go about looking (scientific method), how we go about expressing what we see (language), and, even more fundamentally, how we are constructed as lookers (psychologically and culturally) affects what we find nature to be, at least as much as (if not more than) whatever nature actually "is." In fact, because it is impossible for any of us to go "out of our minds" and "see" (at least while maintaining any claim to "sanity"), we can never know what nature "really is." Thus, all we really have is the relationship, the report, the reflection.

This epistemology (which can be described as poststructuralist), comports with Ames's notion of the primacy of relationships, of things in relations, rather than of things independently. Curiously enough, this postmodern epistemology (which can be most clearly associated with Derrida and his followers) has often come under attack from those same people who castigate modernist science and technology. Those same people who commonly agree with the idea that humans have presumed to know too much, that Western civilization has arrogantly assumed certainty of scientific knowledge and consequent predictability of planning (when no such confidence was warranted), are often found attacking postmodernism for its admission that we cannot ever presume to "know" nature, that all we really have is discursive (relational) knowledge.[13] There is considerable irony in these criticisms, for these individuals attack postmodernism from a position that presumes to know what "real nature" is all about.

There is not space, however, to dwell on the debate between poststructuralists and Western nature lovers. It is sufficient for present purposes to point out that there is considerable agreement between poststructuralism's acceptance of the slipperiness of language (what postmodern philosopher Jean-François Lyotard calls "glissement") and the unpredictability of complex systems (what Lyotard calls "indetermination") outlined by the likes of Prigogine. This is what causes Prigogine and Lyotard to focus on the importance of particularities or singularities, something that is also in keeping with Ames's principles of aesthetic construction, as we shall see.

Prigogine believes that the West is heading toward "a new synthesis, a new naturalism" that will merge Western emphases on experimentation and quantitative formulation with an originally Taoist view of the cosmos as spontaneously self-organized.[14] Citing Joseph Needham, Prigogine considers the regularity of phenomena experienced in nature to be, not due to the design of any external authority, but rather an expression of a nonconcerted harmony of process.[15] He sees this as a profound change that "leads to a new view of matter in which matter is no longer the passive substance described in the mechanistic worldview but is associated with spontaneous activity."[16] Where the classical model of science was a mechanistic one, he sees the emerging model as more like a dance: a "search for a junction between stillness and motion, time arrested and time passing."[17] His criticism of earlier Western science, which resulted in nature being "treated as an independent being," would comport with that of Ames, I believe.[18]

Order: Complexity and Regimentation

Let us take up with the concept of order. It is quite clear that human beings are order-generating agents. We know of no human beings, tribal or "civilized," that live without culture—a set of norms for mediating relations, a form of social ordering. A shared characteristic of the human species is its predisposition to natural language (of one form or another)—language being a highly complex amalgam of surface and deep structures that permits humans to be creative (that is, to use order to generate new forms of order, which they imbue with *meaning*).[19] Art is itself a creative act, and art criticism (which includes discourse of aesthetics) is perhaps a more complex order of ordering, wherein one symbolic structure is brought to bear upon another to elicit yet more meaning.[20]

It is apparent that order generated by language is entirely of human making, once we accept the existence of language itself. Yet, we also see all other creatures as generative of order, everything from ant colonies and bird nests to spider webs and coral reefs. Indeed every form of life is an order-generating mechanism, which is why it is tautological to point out that life itself flies in the face of the second law of thermodynamics (and why economist John Maynard Keynes was correct to point out that "in the long run we are all dead").[21] Furthermore, there is no reason to suppose that order-generating behavior is an attribute only of living things.

A current theme in both physical and biological science is the discovery that, not only can order arise spontaneously from chaotic natural systems, but that order can be expected to arise in such systems. These are systems that are at far-from-equilibrium thermodynamic conditions ("dissipative structures," as Prigogine called them), such as systems like the Earth that receive radiation from external sources, in our case the sun. On this basis, the entire evolution of the universe since the "big bang"—which produced any number of far-from-equilibrium thermodynamic subsystems—can be thought of as a tension between entropy-producing and energy-hoarding, self-ordering processes.[22] While in closed thermodynamic systems (the universe in general, the solar system approximately) all exchanges of energy are accompanied by an unrecoverable loss (in the form of heat) and all exchanges of information are accompanied by an unrecoverable loss (in the form of "noise"), in open, far-from-equilibrium systems (for example, on earth) the external source of energy (the sun) is seen to result in "negentropic" effects (whereby useful energy and information become stored in "dissipative structures" that dissipate energy at the slowest rate compatible with their external conditions).[23] Despite loss of energy or production of noise at each instance of exchange (because no physical process can be 100 percent efficient) order arises nonetheless, seemingly spontaneously out of disorder or chaos.[24] This is one of the most important aspects of complexity theory.

There are of course other explanations for the origins of order, the most frequent and perhaps the oldest being the postulation of a super-natural creator of order, often known as "God." To the Enlightenment thinkers of the eighteenth century, the existence of God could be "proven" because no reasonable person at that time supposed that order might be expected to arise spontaneously. For example, the philosopher Francis Hutcheson frequently used the term "author of nature" for "God" and wrote, "We see this confirm'd by constant Experience, that Regularity never arises from any undesign'd Force of ours; and from this we conclude, that where-ever there is any Regularity in the Dispositions, there must have been Design in the Cause."[25] A counter voice in the nineteenth century was Marx who held that *geogeny* or *generatio aequivoca* "is the only practical refutation of the theory of creation."[26] While nothing in contemporary science prohibits belief in a God (who can still be postulated as the grand author of the entire universal scheme), the necessity of an "author" of the natural order no longer appears logically compelling in the light of complexity theory.

All species create order, and in order to do so, they frequently destroy orderings made by other species. Humans are no exception, and if the order is not even perceived, then there can be no possibility that it will be consciously protected by the likes of humans.

There are, of course, many orders of order. Simple regimentation—the seemingly endless repetition of sameness as, for example, in a column of soldiers—is one order. Euclidean geometric form (squares, circles, and triangles) is of a similar simplistic nature. Modernist aesthetics, epitomized by the Bauhaus school of design (which produced among other things office cubicles and the apartment projects of Mies van der Rohe[27]), eulogized simplified Euclidean form. Postmodernist critic Jean Baudrillard has vilified this as a "cold order" of aesthetics, an annihilation.[28] While such regimentation might be impressive, it contains less information (it is more "boring" and therefore has a higher associated entropy level) than more complex and "interesting" forms of ordering. The geometric forms found most often in nature (as Benoit Mandelbrot has shown) are more likely to be "fractal" than Euclidean.[29] While Euclidean dimensionality is restricted to integer values (between zero and three), fractal dimensions in nature can be any "real number" (with endless decimal places) between zero and three. Thus, living structures in nature are typically more complex (carrying more information and correspondingly lower levels of entropy), than structures of similar mass constructed by people.[30] There is a direct link between fractal geometry and complexity theory in the sense that fractal patterns are frequently the result of dissipative behavior, the residue or "trace" of self-organization in complex systems. This turns out to be instructive to an understanding of Ames's principles of aesthetic construction.

Pattern, Interest, and Aesthetics

There can be little doubt that we find patterns interesting; this appears almost tautological.[31] If we find something interesting and we cannot say or point to what it is, then we are unable to communicate our interest to others. If we can communicate to others what it is we find interesting, then we must be pointing to an ordering, a pattern of some sort. This is the very nature of words in language (identity and difference); they identify some things as being like others and those things as being in some way different from everything else. It is a process of discrimination.

Now, works of art are by definition perceived as orderings or discriminations. That is what qualifies some human creations to be called works of art rather than just a mess of material, something to be cleaned up. And this is as true of abstract expressionism as of representative or any other form of art.[32] It is consistent therefore with the notion that humans are negentropic agents, preferring order to chaos and the persistence of order to ephemerality, to conclude that humans feel an urge to prevent the destruction of order where it is perceived—at least unless such destruction is deemed necessary to create some new or higher form of order.[33] To the extent that we perceive order that is not of our making (order in nature), to the extent that we are able to make such discriminations, then we might presumably feel a similar urge to prevent the destruction of the rich source of our discriminations, the source that we take to be nature itself.

If we allow that order, information and pattern are intimately connected, and if we acknowledge that these are the stuff that human beings find *interesting*, then the question remains: What is the relationship between aesthetics and beauty? Francis Hutcheson in 1725, at the dawning of the Enlightenment, before he embarked on a career in ethics and before aesthetics entered the English language, wrote:

> The figures which excite in us the Ideas of Beauty, seem to be those in which there is Uniformity amidst Variety. There are many Conceptions

of Objects which are agreeable upon other accounts, such as Grandeur, Novelty, Sanctity, and some others, which shall be mentioned hereafter. But what we call Beautiful in Objects, to speak in the Mathematical Style, seems to be in a compound Ratio of Uniformity and Variety: so that where the Uniformity of Bodys is equal, the Beauty is as the Variety; and where the Variety is equal, the Beauty is as the Uniformity. This may seem probable, and hold pretty generally.[34]

Notwithstanding what was said above about Hutcheson's remark on God being the author of nature (understanding of self-organizing systems was still far in the future), this observation, on the sense of beauty as the perception of uniformity amid variety, is remarkable. If we postpone the question of beauty for a moment, and concentrate only on the question of what things "excite in us ideas"—which can only mean "what things interest us"—we see that Hutcheson considered that what interests people is (among other things) the perception of "uniformity amidst variety." And interest level increases as variety increases, so long as we are still able to perceive some degree of uniformity. That is, we find complexity (variety) more interesting than regimentation (simplicity), but only insofar as we are able to make "sense" of the complexity (find uniformity or some unifying theme within it). If something is so complex as to cause nothing but confusion, we would prefer simplicity. The ecologist who makes sense of (interprets) the complexity of nature for us enables us to "see" nature in a way that enhances our interest. This is likely to cause us to prefer (appreciate) the complex whole to some simplified reduction. The same can be said of the art critic. These acts of interpretation (criticism) which lead to appreciation can be seen as fostering a "sense of aesthetics." Aesthetics here is broadly construed to pertain to all qualitative, sense-based discriminations that do not rely on reasoning, not just those that deal with beauty.[35] Nonetheless, as inferred by Hutcheson, beauty is one important type of discrimination.[36]

The connection between interest level and beauty is not so easily drawn, and space will not permit a full explication. Beauty is an affective response to sensory stimuli (as Hutcheson's cohort and acquaintance, the philosopher of science and empiricism, David Hume would have pointed out). As an affective response, today's understanding of post-Freudian psychology would require that we draw the link to *desire* —a link that is drawn by Derrida and Lyotard among others.[37] As human creatures born into language, and separated by the "disjunctive bar" (along with separation from the mother and human society's incest taboo), we live out our lives in experience of "the lack." This lack, which can be thought of as that which separates each of us as individuals, we seek to fill with "little objects" that give us pleasure.[38] Our desire for pleasure, to put it all too bluntly, is what causes us to find beauty in things that interest us. These things do not have to be physical, they can be ideas, concepts, or instances of language.[39] Hutcheson recognized the beauty of mathematical and other theorems,[40] and he was also consistent with poststructuralist epistemology to the extent that he avoided "essentialism" or reification of nature. That is, he did not suppose that beauty existed "in" things themselves, but held that the perception of beauty arose as a result of the relationship between the perceiver and the perceived. Unequivocally he stated, "All beauty is relative to the sense of some mind perceiving it."[41]

Another who has written of the propensity of people for finding beauty in nature—that is for experiencing aesthetic pleasure in relationships with nature—is the ecologist and sociobiologist Edward O. Wilson. Wilson, like his predecessor ecologist Aldo Leopold, has linked aesthetics to ethics in constructing what they see as a prudential approach to dealing with human-nature relationships.[42] Wilson recognized the prudential value of aesthetics when he wrote, "Mathematics and beauty are devices by which human beings get through life with the limited intellectual capacity inherited by the species." He, too, avoided an essentialist interpretation by adding, "Elegance is more a product of the human mind than of external reality."[43] According to Wilson, aesthetic awareness and ethical behavior are characteristics that have been selected in human evolution just as high speed and sharp claws were selected in the evolution of tigers. The prudential affinity of people for nature is what Wilson has dubbed "biophilia."

The relationship between human survival, Prigogine's dissipative structures, complexity theory, and aesthetics has also been noted by the cultural critic, Frederick Turner, who concluded, "What capacity could be better adapted than our aesthetic sense to the complex, context-rich work of ecological invention, which must harmonize into a higher unity large masses of mutually dependent information?"[44]

Sensitive Dependence

To complete the groundwork necessary for an examination of Ames's idea of aesthetic construction from a perspective of emerging Western science and poststructuralism, it is necessary to review what has been called the "butterfly effect." Originally credited to the meteorologist Edward Lorenz, this effect (more accurately described as "sensitive dependence on initial conditions") is now broadly accepted as a common phenomenon of complex, nonlinear systems (which include systems known as dissipative structures).[45] Earlier, scientists thought that small errors were inconsequential in practice. Natural systems (which include "economic systems" and so on, as explained at the outset) were thought to be generally stable or "in equilibrium." If displaced by small amounts, they would either return to their starting position or would move to some new equilibrium in an orderly manner. This was known as "negative feedback." It is the desirable condition when designing control systems (for example, thermostats, whether of the domestic heating or the human bodily-function variety). By contrast, positive feedback is the term used to describe a system where small displacements "feed on themselves" to produce progressively larger displacements, culminating rather rapidly in total instability. An easily understood analogy is a tall beer bottle: standing upright, it will return to that position if pushed slightly out of vertical; balanced on its top, a small displacement will cause it to topple.

What Lorenz and his successors have found is that in nonlinear systems there are a huge variety of possible system states that affect whether small displacements will produce negative or positive feedback. Some states are locally stable, others locally unstable, and still others wildly chaotic. Think of a mountain river: out in the main current, the direction of movement is strong and unidirectional; a stick dropped into the water at this point will be washed downstream without doubt. At a bend or by the shore there may be eddy currents. Close to the shore the water may be moving consistently upstream; a stick dropped in here will float slowly upstream.[46] However, this current may be unstable at a slightly different temporal scale, in the sense that a small raising or lowering of the water level (after a heavy rainstorm, say) may radically change the eddy current (while the main current will continue to flow downstream). Between the eddy current and the main current there is likely to be a chaotic zone where, if a stick were dropped, it would be virtually impossible to predict its immediate direction of travel. This last state is referred to as close to boundary conditions. The boundary demarcates the onset of chaotic ("wild") behavior.

These zones of behavior are both spatially and temporally scale dependent. Cream stirred into a cup of coffee might yield unstable patterns of behavior over the course of a few seconds, yet be perfectly predictable over the course of a few minutes (the patterns merging into uniformity). Similarly, the behavior of the solar system might be perfectly stable over the course of a few millennia (allowing us to send rockets to planets with remarkable success), yet be unstable over the course of a few billennia.

An important corollary of sensitive dependence is that science can no longer link the ideas of determinism and predictability as it did in the past. We were brought up to think that if a system was deterministic (cause and effect) then it was (in principle) predictable, while only systems incorporating random behavior were unpredictable. We know that the behavior of cream being stirred into coffee is entirely deterministic (the movement of each molecule is determined by the forces acting on it), but during the period of its instability the movement of each molecule is likely to be perfectly unpredictable for the simple reason that it is much too complex.[47] The upshot for ecologists, and others interested in the future of landscapes, is important: Over the time scales that are of interest to human beings (years, decades, and centuries) and over the spatial scales that are of interest (acres to square miles and more), most complex systems that we call "ecosystems" are likely to be chaotic. Much the same is true for the behavior of economies at the community and national scales over the course of years and decades. This is why modernist planning failed and why a little "tweaking" (of predictive models) is not likely to produce much improvement in methodology.

If all of this seems rather dismal, there is another aspect that is anything but dismal. Although this branch of complexity theory has been dubbed chaos theory, this is something of a misnomer, since, as Mandelbrot, Prigogine, and so many others have shown, chaotic states of behavior in complex (or nonlinear) systems frequently produce traces that are very highly ordered—that is, they produce what we recognize as patterns, sometimes very intricate and interesting, and often perceived as beautiful. Things that we recognize as trees, animals, river systems, human faces, poetry, sea shells, galaxies, intestines, ripple marks on the beach, insects, soil structure, graphs of stock market movements, plants, fishes, prose, bark structure, lung surface, neural networks, blood capillaries, and art are all examples of the patterns thus generated. These discriminations or differentiations, these deviations from neutrality or "gray mush," these storage sites of potential energy represent relatively low states of entropy. The more the information (per unit of mass) the lower the entropy.

It is unsurprising then, that from Hutcheson to Wilson, certain human beings have commented upon the apparent propensity of human beings in general for perceiving "uniformity amidst variety." And although it is unproved, Wilson's suggestion that this stirring of human (admittedly culture-bound) aesthetic sensibility has, in fact, been an attribute "selected" in the natural evolution of human society appears entirely plausible. When Wilson goes on to suggest that this aesthetic sensibility has prudential value for amicably mediating human relationships with nature (an extension of seeing the trait as being a result of Darwinian natural selection), he approaches the position of Ames, as we shall see.

There is one important caveat, however: While it is plausible to link the desire for perceiving "uniformity amidst variety" to what the Western world has considered (for about 200 years) to be aesthetic sensibility, we must not assume that that which is accorded aesthetic approbation necessarily relates to complexity, naturalism, or any other particular "set" of patterns. Aesthetic "values" are undoubtedly culturally determined and liable to change over time; if one wishes to disparage them, one has only to allude to their ephemerality by calling them tastes or fashions. The modernist aesthetic of minimalism, epitomized by the Bauhaus School, and criticized by Baudrillard (as cited above), is a clear example of an aesthetic order that could be referred to as "antinaturalistic." And just what constitutes "naturalism" in aesthetics has periodically changed in the Western world—as evidenced, for example, in the movement from the "serpentine" or curvilinear ideas of naturalism popularized in eighteenth-century England by the landscape gardener Capability Brown to the "rustic" interpretation of Humphry Repton, which became a romantic ideal of naturalism that held for most of the nineteenth century.[48] Between romanticism and twentieth-century modernism came a brief period of "organic" naturalism, variously called the "arts and crafts" movement or art nouveau. There is no reason to suppose that our current conceptualization of nature in the West will now be our last.

Thus, while the arguments of sociobiologists such as Wilson are appealing (and perhaps not without merit), we must recognize the shifting nature of "nature," as interpreted by human culture (and who among us exists outside of culture?). While birds, for example, very seldom change the design of their nests, humans frequently do. Bauhaus-style minimalism can be viewed either as a vain attempt to free ourselves from nature or as an attempt to conform to an idea of nature that we no longer accept.[49] In language-bound (human) culture there can be no aesthetics without criticism. The role of the critic is to attempt to influence society's tastes and preferences. It is in this vein then (as critics), that we must view Wilson, Ames, and any others when they would have us adopt complexity-based naturalistic aesthetics on the grounds that it will enhance our ability to maintain sustainable relationships with the natural world upon which we depend. As human beings, we cannot escape the indeterminacy of culture.

How does this last statement comport with a view that any and all "real" biophysical systems (natural and human) might be, at bottom, entirely deterministic?[50] The "indetermination" that is central to the ideas of Lyotard and other poststructuralists in no way conflicts with this notion. Precisely because complexity theory separates determinism from predictability, the ground is opened up to what we might choose to call creative endeavor. Because nonlinear systems are so sensitively dependent (not least the operation of the human brain), actions that appear to be entirely novel and unexpected are entirely possible (even if at some neurological or particulate level cause and effect were still at work). The development of an idea (almost "out of nowhere") is an example of positive feedback at work.

What is more, the indetermination (or ambiguity) of language (Lyotard's glissement) is what opens up an otherwise closed tautological system of language to *meaning*. Meaning slips in as a result of our *desire* (for meaning). As every reader undoubtedly has realized, if one looks up any word in a dictionary one is going to find its "meaning" defined in terms of other words. Looking up these words leads to still more words to be looked up, and so on, seemingly without end. The search for meaning only stops when one says, "Ah! I know what that means. I understand." The meaning is not contained in any word, but is mapped onto language from somewhere deep down in our past, probably when each of us individually first developed self-consciousness and "understanding."[51] Thus, indetermination opens up what I would call the "glade" in which we dance with "devils." This is the site of meaning, where we engage with the ultimately unknowable otherness that we call "nature," the terrifying and the serene, the sublime and the beautiful. As an individual divorced from contact with anything else, each of our lives could have no meaning; meaning depends on the dance, the relationship, the polarity, the I with the other.

Ames's "Aesthetic Construction"

At last, the groundwork is laid for an examination of Ames's aesthetic construction. His first principle, cited above, emphasizes the uniqueness of any "one particular as it collaborates with other particulars in an emergent complex pattern of relatedness." This emphasis on particularity is entirely consistent with complexity theory. Because of sensitive dependence, each and every particular (or singularity) constitutes a "starting condition" that can have profound effect on the development of the whole. Particulars can be indeterminably small (in accordance with Ames's principle of individuation); like Benjamin Franklin's "want of a nail," the outcome of something as large as a war or the birth of a nation can hinge on a particular as small as the proverbial grain of sand. This is the connotation of the name "butterfly effect"—the idea that the fluttering of a butterfly's wings can lead to a hurricane hundreds of miles away. It is out of these particularities that complex patterns or traces can emerge, the fractal patterns so prevalent in natural as well as human systems. Each and every particular in a chain of· events constitutes a new starting condition and as such comports with Ames's principle of integration; the integrated whole is a multidimensional "daisy chain" of particulars.

Ames's second principle speaks of the production "of a harmony or an order that is expressed by a complex of such details in their relationship to one another." The idea of harmony might connote balance, but this must not be taken to imply the now-disparaged idea of a "balance of nature," meaning either stasis, equilibrium, or stability.[52] While local (spatial or temporal) stability is entirely possible, the boundaries of such "islands of stability" are usually shifting and ultimately unknowable. As Lyotard puts it, "A field of perception has limits, but these limits are always beyond reach."[53] The patterns traced by complex systems (emergent behavior) often appear harmonious and reveal "strange attractors"—loci about which system states appear to revolve without ever exactly repeating a previous path, like dancers circling the floor. But one never knows when the dance might end. The devilish dancing partner is chaos, turbulence, the wildness, madness even, of far-from-equilibrium, open thermodynamic systems. At best, stability implies the absence of both stasis and stumbling; it is the dynamic, uncertain equilibrium of the dance. It implies not falling down or, most fundamentally, survival itself.

But survival of what? Ames's third principle refers to "movement away from any universal characteristic." This is certainly consistent with the postmodern idea that we have abandoned the "grand narratives" or utopian ideas of modernism. But Ames, like Wilson, adopts an environmentalist position that seeks survival of both nature and the human species, while Lyotard also, for all his postmodernism, desires the survival of (inhuman) intelligence beyond even the inevitable burning out of the sun. Lyotard asks, "What else is left to resist with, but the debt which each soul has contracted with the miserable and admirable indetermination from which it was born and does not cease to be born?"[54] For Lyotard, the task is to bear witness by "writing, thinking, literature, art," which is perhaps what the poet Dylan Thomas was doing when he wrote: "Rage, rage against the dying of the light." For Ames, this raging should take the form of an aesthetic composition.

The apparent inescapability of grand narratives, in one form or another, despite all attempts at resistance, is an irony that we must accept. Just as we would hardly be "sane" to say that because language is slippery, because the "real" is ultimately unknowable, the sun does not exist. Maybe it *ex*-ists only when we recognize it as existing, but that has to be a sufficient cause for action, for living. Maybe I eat only because my brain conjures up the symbolic notion of hunger (based perhaps on electrical signals transmitted by the stomach), but that has to be a sufficient reason to eat.

By simple extension, we may suppose that the rotation of the Earth on its axis once a "day," and the Earth's rotation about the sun once a "year," has generated rhythms that have become a part of human metabolism. Having thus evolved with such rhythmic structures, it could well be that the human perception of beauty evolved naturally (a "direct sense" as Hutcheson called it), just as language evolved naturally, despite our inability to separate this from the aesthetic discourse that, as we have seen, can only be considered a cultural construction.

Ames's fourth principle of aesthetic construction, that " 'disclosure' . . . in novel patterns . . . is describable in the qualitative language of richness, intensity, etc.," might at first appear to be problematic. "Disclosure" implies an active subjectivity on the part of nonhuman (and inanimate) things, willfully disclosing themselves to others. But he encloses this word in quotation marks, and he does not say that "richness, intensity, etc." *ex*-ist; rather, he says they are describable in language. That is, they are attributes, qualities that subjective humans attribute to that which they see.

Ames's fifth principle describes aesthetic composition as "not determined by preassigned principles," as "fundamentally anarchic and contingent, and as . . . the ground for optimum creativity, where creativity, is to be understood in contradistinction to determination." Certainly, the dependency of creativity on indetermination is consistent with Lyotard, but how can a principle establish something as anarchic, as not being dependent on principles? It is true that I have been using the word "principle" where Ames used the word "feature" as descriptive of his six "criteria." But they are principles nonetheless. The problem is similar to the criticism leveled against the architecture critic, Charles Jencks, who was chided for having the audacity to promulgate "principles of postmodernism," when the postmodern was supposed to be devoid of principles. To this I would respond, "But is a requirement of being devoid not itself a principle?" How can Ames suppose that an aesthetic composition is both "productive of a harmony or an order" (number two) and "fundamentally anarchic" (number five)? The answer can only lie in indetermination itself, in fact, in the very essence of complexity theory's contention that order can and does arise spontaneously out of chaos.[55]

In his sixth and last principle, Ames holds that " 'rightness' . . . refers to the degree to which the insistent particularity of the detail in tension with the consequent unity of the specific details is self-evidently expressive of an aesthetically pleasing order." Once again the words "insistent" and "self-evidently expressive" appear to connote subjectivity on the part of nonhumans. An appropriate response would be that, once we suppose that all we "really have to go on" is the relationship, then the subject-object dichotomy breaks down. In this sense I would suggest that a Taoist approach is actually an improvement on much of the poststructuralist discourse on subjectivity. If we accept that (as Charles Peirce laid out in his semiotic construction of the subject) the subject, the I, is actually constructed by each of us in relation to the other, then the subject-object relationship is seen as being primary to even the subject itself.[56] This notion of "self-evidencing"—as an interdependency rather than the expression of a subject (speaking in a vacuum as it were)— is crucial: The Chinese equivalent, *tzu-jan* (self-evidencing) is frequently translated as "nature." This relational interpretation of nature is what Ames refers to as "polarity," in distinction to Western "dualism." I might suggest that we maneuver around the dualistic concepts of existence and insistence by speaking simply of "sistence."[57] That would be consistent with Ames's translation of *tzu-jan* as "spontaneous" and consistent with complexity theory's spontaneous creation of order from disorder and yet would avoid the problematic subjectivity of nature implicit in "self-evidencing" and in Ames's word "insistent."[58]

By "rightness" (which Ames puts in quotation marks) and "an aesthetically pleasing order," I take him to mean something akin to the later Ludwig Wittgenstein's notion of fitness or correctness, something the individual accepts because it appears to work, "comfort" perhaps over "beauty" *per se.*[59] This concept of fitness or fittingness is consistent with the ecologists' notion of *niche*, where the environment and the organism are in a workable, sustainable, pragmatic, symbiotic, and "comfortable" relationship with one another. It is unsurprising that ecologists (and others) see these particular "dances" as beautiful.

Polarity

The Chinese principle of polarity, which, as stated above, Ames distinguishes from Western dualism ("a world of 'things' characterized by discreteness"[60]), is, in fact, not so different from a poststructuralist position. According to Ames, polarity is the concept "that each 'pole' can be explained [only] by reference to the other. *Left* requires *right, up* requires *down, yin* requires *yang*, and *self* requires *other.*"[61] Such "an explanation of relationships," he says, is characterized by "interdependence, openness, mutuality, indeterminateness, complementarity, correlativity, [and] coextensiveness." Similarly, for us, each word is capable of conjuring meaning only to the extent that it is able to establish identity and difference. Yet, words remain ambiguous; the length of the pole remains slippery; "light" becomes "dark" at a point that is fundamentally indeterminate, thus requiring an act of interpretation on the part of the "reader."[62] And, rather than things *ex*-isting (in a vacuum as it were), they are intuited only by our relationship with them.

In *Forests: The Shadow of Civilization*, Robert Harrison provides an example of such interpretation when he shows how, in Western history, the word "civilization" is inseparable from the word "forest"—the latter being that which has delimited the former—the interface being the edge where wild nature takes over and man's influence leaves off.[63] The forest is "not civilization," and civilization is "not forest"—just as black is not white and white is not black. Yet the edge is always blurred.

To assert the larger unity of a system of polar opposites (such as yin and yang) is not to assert that the distinction between the poles should be eliminated. The dance requires the dancers. Ames's point lies deeper, however. If we follow Taoist scholar Angus Graham's method of denoting one set of poles as "A" (yang, male, hard, light, active, strong, etc.) and the other as "B" (yin, female, soft, dark, inactive, weak, etc.), then, Graham says: "as has long been recognized, China tends to treat opposites as complementary, the West as conflicting. . . . The West strives to abolish B and preserve only A."[64] Graham points out that Ames and coauthor David Hall "suggest that the whole reductionist enterprise in Western philosophy may be seen as the conquest of B by a transcendent A."[65] One could certainly find many instances in Western history of attempts to deny one pole while championing the other: Christianity has associated God and love with everything that is to be retained and devils (in the personification of Satan) as an evil to be driven out. In our modern world, people came to view human death as something to be avoided at all costs (even to the debasement of life); disagreements or strife were to be papered over with polite cordialities (even to the debasement of communication); and in nature certain creatures (wolves, for example) were labeled "bad" and marked for eradication while others (like elk in Yellowstone) were labeled "good" and worthy of protection (even to the point of starvation induced by overpopulation).

Graham points out "the Chinese tendency to divide down from a wider whole" and "our own tendency to start from the thing itself."[66] This Western tendency is the dualism that Ames criticizes in favor of polarity. However, as stated at the outset, recent Western trends toward "holism" and ecological thinking now run counter to this history of atomism, and Ames's own work is a case in point.

The necessity of maintaining both ends of each pole in order to maintain polarity (accepting that life needs death, light needs dark, up needs down, etc.) was asserted by Lao-tzu using a process of reversal. Graham compares this with Derrida's deconstruction, stating:

> The reversals in *Lao-tzu* have a [post]modern parallel in Jacques Derrida's project of deconstructing the chains of oppositions underlying the logocentric tradition of the West. The parallel is indeed so striking that there is danger of missing the differences. . . . Starting from the abolition of the signifier from thought [Descartes' unself-conscious use of language] . . . the West has aspired . . . to dissolve B in the pure being, the full presence of A. . . . The affinity of *Lao-tzu* and Derrida is that both use reversal to deconstruct chains in which A is traditionally preferred to B, and in breaking down the

dichotomy offer us a glimpse of another line which runs athwart it—for *Lao-tzu* the Way, for Derrida the Trace.[67]

According to Graham, the difference between the two lies in differences in the structure of Chinese and Western language, so that, unlike Derrida, the Chinese would never say: "There is nothing outside of the text." However, Graham foresees resolution of this difference if and when the West overcomes its attachment to the idea of transcendent reality: "Perhaps *Lao-tzu's* Way is how the Trace will look to us when we are no longer haunted by the ghost of that transcendent Reality the death of which Derrida proclaims."[68]

Potency

The concept of the Taoist *te* is a central focus of Ames's discussion because of *te*'s relationship to particularity. Ames states that *te* has been translated as "virtue" or "power," and Graham translates it as "potency."[69] Ames suggests that *te* "denotes the arising of the particular" and is "characterized by an inherent dynamism."[70] He states:

> For the Chinese classical philosopher, the world of particulars is alive in the sense that they are aware of and hence "feel" or prehend other particulars in their environment. The expression "self-evidencing (*tzu-jan*)" is a physical and a psychical characterization which means that reality is self-causing and self-aware. And to be aware is to invest interest and thus value other things. The range of its particularity is variable, and is contingent upon the way in which it interprets itself and is interpreted.[71]

While the self-causing nature of nature is now acceptable in Western science, the contention that nature and things in nature (both animate and inanimate) are also self-aware, that they "feel," and psychically "value other things," is another matter entirely. This is to assert a world of animism that would not be embraced by (post)modern science and epistemology. What are we to make of this statement by Ames? Graham discusses the great difficulty of translating between Chinese and Western ontologies and states: "The ancient Chinese think of the cosmos as like an organism, but this is consequence not cause of thinking correlatively."[72] He appears to be suggesting that (by being a consequence of thinking correlatively) Chinese "organicism" is metaphorical.

Te is the potency that sets things moving; " 'life' is Potency's lighting

up," says Graham.[73] Ancient Chinese cosmology identified several po-
tencies: wood's potency for catching fire, fire's potency for reducing to
ashes, water's potency for nourishing wood, and so on.[74] Potency can be
thought of as the "working out" of potential energy, of evolution (of the
big bang perhaps); it neither implies self-consciousness nor intentionality in nature. Ames's choice of words appears unfortunate in this instance.[75] The *te*, in self-conscious human beings, might be interpretable
in English as the Freudian "drives" or in French as the Lacanean
"pulsions"; the drive or pulsion comes before intention (being from the
subconscious rather than the conscious) in this understanding. Just what
is the equivalent of this notion of the *te* for the rest of nature is a question that the West is still not in a strong position to answer.[76]

Ames's statement about the holographics of *te* is more in keeping
contemporary Western understanding:

> When *te* is cultivated and accumulated such that the particular is fully ex-
> pressive of the whole, the distinction between *tao* and *te* collapses and *te*
> becomes both an individuating concept and an integrating concept. . . . *Te*,
> when seen as a particular focus or event in the *tao*, is a principle of indi-
> viduation; when seen as a holograph of this underlying harmony, diffusing
> in all directions in coloration of the whole, it is a principle of integration.[77]

Te energizes each and every particular, and the flowing of energy
integrates the whole. The traces of this activity constitute *li*, which is
"pattern." Besides pattern, *li* is also translated as "texture" (wood grain,
etc.), "reason," "logic," "natural science and physics," "rightness," and
"the fitness of things."[78] It would seem that there is a similarity between
li and Wittgenstein's aesthetic of correctness mentioned above.

Wu-Wei, an Aesthetic Criterion

One of the most important upshots of Ames's work is his argument that
human activities in relationship with nature should be approved according to an aesthetic criterion: the degree to which they are *wu-wei*. Ames
tells us that the two Chinese characters that compose the term *wu-wei*
are "formularistically rendered as 'nonaction.' "[79] In what seems at first
to be an oxymoron, *wu-wei* means nonaction but refers to action (*wei*)
nonetheless. *Wu-wei* and *yu-wei* represent two poles (polar opposites)
along an axis of action. Neither is less active than the other; the difference has more to do with the attendant relation between the actor and

the acted upon. Where *yu-wei* activity is more along the lines of labor and dominance, *wu-wei* activity is "a negation of one particular serving as a 'means' for something else's 'end.' "[80] Ames writes, "*Wu-wei* as 'making' is irrepressibly participatory and creative." Given the polar nature of the relation between the actor and the acted upon, each "makes" the other. If the *te* of each is to achieve its nature (*tzu-jan*, self-evidencing), then the actor must remain open to the *te* (potency) of the material. Ames continues: "In human terms, the integrity that must be sustained in the project of self-disclosure requires an awareness that uncoordinated action between oneself and one's environment not only deprives environing particulars of the possibilities of 'self-evidencing,' but further, impoverishes one's own possibilities."[81] Hence, in a move reminiscent of both Wilson and Leopold, Ames finds an ethical imperative in an aesthetic criterion.

For Graham, man is spontaneous when his action is *wu-wei*, which means that his action springs not so much from his "distinguishing and classifying" (which I take to be Lacan's symbolic) as from somewhere deeper within, what the Taoist master Chuang-tzu called "'impulse' or 'impulse from heaven.'"[82] Graham continues: "Taoism does not however, as Buddhism was later to do, wholly refrain from calling [the source of *wu-wei* action] 'desire.' All names being inadequate, this name too may be used and undermined by paradox, as in the first stanza of *Lao-tzu*, which requires us to be 'constantly without desire' yet 'constantly have desire.'"[83] The project of being *wu-wei*, of being spontaneous or impulsive (Graham) while also being "aware that uncoordinated action . . . deprives" (Ames) suggests that the conscious and the subconscious have to be "in tune" with one another, perhaps as the musician's fingers have to be in coordination with his emotions.

The call to act *wu-wei* is certainly not a call to refrain from acting. Rather, to act *wu-wei* is to act in consort with the acted upon (which includes materials, the environment—living and nonliving—and other human beings). This is the dance; it encompasses all. As Ames states, "Just as there is no *wu*—no 'pure creativity'—without a specific context, so there is nothing that is not subject to creative transformation."[84] It is all a matter of the quality of the transformation, its fittingness. Fitting transformation works *with* the *li*, the natural pattern or the grain, and avoids destructive meddling: "The essential thing is not to interfere when things are already running well by themselves."[85] Regarding politics, Graham quotes the ancient Chinese legalist, Han Fei:

> Therefore observing it in terms of pattern, if employing a great multitude you keep changing things around you achieve few results, if storing a great vessel you keep shifting it somewhere else it will be badly damaged, if in boiling a small fish you keep on meddling with it you rob it of freshness, if in ordering a great state you keep altering the laws the people will suffer from it. This is why a ruler who has the Way values stillness and does not keep on altering laws.[86]

There is no conflict between the notion of *wu-wei* action and *wu-wei* stillness; in Taoism, remaining still or inactive at the appropriate time is just as much an active response (to a situation) as what we often call proactive behavior. This is one important difference with the West that is not addressed by either complexity theory or poststructuralism.

As Ames tells us, *wu-wei* is an aesthetic criterion: "We distinguish *wu-wei* from *yu-wei* by the quality of the creative event—the same way that we distinguish a good piece of music from a bad one, or good painting from one that is not good."[87] I would add that we do not always have to like something to say that it is aesthetically good. I can, for example, say, "I do not care for sweet white wine, but this is a particularly fine example of a Sauternes" (if I am sufficiently educated and experienced regarding wine).

Frequently, *wu-wei* might mean "seemingly without effort" or "without appearing belabored." This would accord with Wittgenstein's aesthetic of correctness or fittingness (what I believe Ames means by "rightness" in his sixth principle), or Chuang-tzu's linking of spontaneity to inevitability; an obvious example is the work of a good cartoonist who captures a wealth of expression and emotion with a "casually drawn line"—an action both spontaneous and of which one could say "there was no other way it could be."[88]

By contrast to the ways of the West, Graham says, "The Chinese choice is of an integrated solution of the problems both of placing oneself in the world and of manipulating it for one's purposes."[89] An obvious example is the sailor who works with the immutable tides and winds to get him to where he wants to go. One cannot sail straight upwind any more than Canute could turn back the tide, but that does not mean giving up in despair. Neither does it mean attacking the elements as if we might subdue them. It is all a matter of working with the *li* of the elements, not against them. This type of working—which is seemingly without effort, which "makes it all look so easy"—is also *efficient.* The efficiency arises in the minimization of "laboring" against the elements;

as such, it results in minimal production of entropy.[90] This type of efficiency might be thought of as a lightness, an easiness, as in a dance. In working out a *wu-wei* relationship with the indetermination of "nature," we can only dance our way into the unknowable future one step at a time.

Ames, I believe, has good advice when he tells us that an appropriate criterion for choosing our actions, with regard to nature, is the aesthetic criterion of *wu-wei*. In a similar vein, Graham cites *Lao-tzu* describing *wu-wei* in these lines:

> To generate but without taking possession,
> To do but without presuming on it,
> To lead but without managing,
> This call the Dark Potency.[91]

Optimistically, I see Western science and epistemology as already converging on the right path, toward the middle way perhaps. In seeking sustainable landscapes and communities, adoption of aesthetic criteria in general, and of *wu-wei* in particular, would be one more step in a fitting direction.

We began with a concern for sustainability, in ecosystems and human communities, and wondered how we might pursue such a concern in light of the failure of modern planning, the failure of predictive modeling. What I believe we have learned is that we cannot expect the problems of predictive modeling to be solved, precisely because of the indetermination of nonlinear natural systems or dissipative structures. So does this mean that all planning is worthless? Not so. If we interpret "planning" to mean design, and particularly the design of our relationships with nature (including the design of landscapes), then we can postulate that Ames's Taoist aesthetic criterion, *wu-wei* is appropriate for evaluating our proposed actions. Actions that are *wu-wei* (which appear effortless) are humble in that they seek to have minimal impact on those forces that are extant in nature; in the metaphor of sailing, the sailor does not seek to stop, subvert, or reverse the wind, only to work *with* it to get him where he wants to go. While we can have no assurance that *wu-wei* activities will not produce unexpected results, we can take comfort at last in the idea that the action that has the least impact on natural forces is also the least likely to disrupt nature in some surprising or undesirable way. This is the most that we can expect to achieve in the field of planning.

Activities that are *wu-wei* are also the most likely to promote sustainability. This is because *wu-wei* action is efficient, when measured in terms of entropy production. That is, those actions that are minimal with regard on their impact on natural forces will also be those that produce the least heat (from friction) and those that produce the least noise (meaningless or unwanted signal). Again using our marine metaphor, these actions will move us through the water with the smallest wake. Since they are the least productive of entropy (which leads inevitably to "heat death") *wu-wei* activities, therefore, will be as sustainable as any we could wish for.[92]

Notes

1. See John Friedman, *Planning in the Public Domain: From Knowledge to Action* (Princeton, NJ: Princeton University Press, 1987), for a thorough account of the history of modernist planning. For one example of its failure in the arena of public forestry, see Paul Hirt, *A Conspiracy of Optimism: Intensive Management of the National Forests, 1945–1992* (Lincoln: University of Kansas Press, 1993). For another, see Gerald M. Allen and Ernest M. Gould, Jr., "Complexity, Wickedness, and Public Forests," *Journal of Forestry* 84, no. 4 (1986): 20–23.

2. See David W. Orr, "Virtual Nature," *Conservation Biology* 10, no. 1 (1996): 8–9. See also Paul Shepard, "Virtually Hunting Reality in the Forests of Simulacra," in *Reinventing Nature? Responses to Postmodern Deconstruction*, ed. Michael E. Soulé and Gary Lease (Washington, DC: Island Press, 1994), pp. 17–30. Shepard says that "Derrida, Lyotard, and other deconstructionists have about them the smell of the coffeehouse." Apparently, similar derisory remarks were made about people who consumed warm drinks and read novels rather than breaking their backs at the plough in the late seventeenth century (Michel Foucault, *Madness and Civilization* [New York: Pantheon Books, 1965], pp. 170, 219).

3. Roger Ames, "Putting the *Te* Back into Taoism," in *Nature in Asian Traditions of Thought: Essays in Environmental Philosophy*, ed. J. Baird Callicott and Roger T. Ames (Albany: State University of New York Press, 1989), pp. 113–144. See also Roger Ames, "Taoism and the Nature of Nature," *Environmental Ethics* 8 (Winter 1986): 317–350.

4. The critics have come from many perspectives, including deep ecology and ecofeminism. For examples, see Carolyn Merchant, *Radical Ecology: The Search for a Livable World* (New York: Routledge, 1992).

5. In this system, the whole is composed of interdependent parts, and each part depends for its existence on the existence (or perhaps insistence) of the other. Neither part is superior, is held to be "self-evident."

6. Ames, "Putting the *Te* Back into Taoism," p. 117.

7. Romanization throughout this chapter follows the Wade-Giles system.

8. "Writing" refers to the bringing-to-mind that is a necessary condition of all self-conscious human behavior. As Jean-François Lyotard puts it, "What so-called 'French thought' has been calling writing for a long time [is] what psychoanalysis

calls anamnesis [*sic*]." (Jean-François Lyotard, *The Inhuman: Reflections on Time* [Stanford: Stanford University Press, 1991], p. 55.) Thus, all conscious human activity involves an "inscribing" in the mind which is relational. This is further developed below. It should be noted that language is not restricted to written or spoken words but refers to all communications in some symbolic system (which includes plastic art, dance, mathematics, and so on). And it should be apparent that not all cultures develop "natural language" (such as English, Urdu, and so on) in the same way. The poststructuralists see language and thinking as inseparable—a radical departure from the position of René Descartes, for whom language was "invisible." In Western discourse, language was just coming into (self-conscious) visibility by the time of Karl Marx and became more visible with the development of semiotics by American philosopher Charles Sanders Peirce. Peirce's work was further developed by the structuralists (principally the work of Ferdinand de Saussure in France), which was followed (but not entirely superseded) by the poststructuralists (principally Jacques Derrida, also in France). For this reason, and despite multinational origins, the field has come to be known (and often ethnocentrically disparaged) as "French thought." The term "postmodern" aligns roughly with poststructuralism, although, being broader in scope, it is frequently fought over. (See Jean-Francois Lyotard, *The Postmodern Explained* [Minneapolis: University of Minnesota Press, 1992]).

9. Ilya Prigogine and Isabelle Stengers, *Order Out of Chaos: Man's New Dialogue with Nature* (New York: Bantam Books, 1984); Stuart A. Kauffman, *The Origins of Order* (New York: Oxford University Press, 1993).

10. Although they do not yet embrace aesthetics to any considerable extent (a failing that I would like to see corrected), emerging approaches to planning that incorporate some of the ideas of complexity theory have been coming to the fore. One such approach is called "adaptive management"; (see Kai N. Lee, *Compass and Gyroscope: Integrating Science and Politics for the Environment* [Washington, DC: Island Press, 1993]). Another is called "holistic resource management." An example of ecologists embracing the ideas of complexity theory is found in Robert Costanza, Bryan Norton, and Benjamin Haskell, eds., *Ecosystem Health: New Goals for Environmental Management* (Washington, DC: Island Press, 1992), pp. 28–29. Introductions to complexity theory can be found in Roger Lewin, *Complexity: Life at the Edge of Chaos* (New York: Macmillan, 1992), and M. Mitchell Waldrop, *Complexity: The Emerging Science at the Edge of Order and Chaos* (New York: Simon and Schuster, 1992).

11. Allen and Gould ("Complexity, Wickedness, and Public Forests") quote H.W.J. Rittel and M.M. Webber ("Dilemmas in a General Theory of Planning," *Policy Science* 4 [1973]: 155–169) as follows: "We use the term 'wicked' in a meaning akin to that of 'malignant' (in contrast to 'benign') or 'vicious' (like a circle) or 'tricky' (like a leprechaun)." It is in this pantheistic (rather than Christian) vein, that I am using the word devils.

12. For example, Foucault's *Madness and Civilization* relates how medieval man saw nature, not as the place of "animality," but as the place to be created by man in bringing God's reason and orderliness to the chaotic wilderness. Only later, after the sixteenth century, when Western man began to become disenchanted with civilization, did he start to see nature as the benign source of everything that was good (pp. 77, 157). This coincided with the ideas of John Locke and Jean-Jacques Rousseau who saw the natural state as the original "home" of man and with scientists

(such as Galileo Galilei and Isaac Newton) who saw nature as the source of scientific knowledge. Eventually, in the seventeenth century, philosophers like David Hume established the primacy of empirical (scientific) knowledge (drawn from nature) over that of rationalist or *a priori* knowledge (drawn from within the mind).

13. For an example, see George Sessions, "Reinventing Nature: The End of Wilderness?" *Wild Duck Review* 2, no. 1 (1995): 13–15. Frequently, if we say we cannot know reality we are then accused of assuming that reality can be anything we want it to be, that we presume ourselves to be free of worldly constraints. Such a reading of poststructuralist epistemology is sadly naive. For example, when the poststructuralist Slavoj Zizek says "Nature does not exist," he is making the valid point that nature is a mental and linguistic model of some ultimately unknowable outer reality—that is, that nature does not *ex*-ist (as in outside of ourselves), that knowledge of nature can only be in *relation* to ourselves as knowers, that "our" nature is a construction that we hope adequately mimics (simulates) the way the world works. It would be hopelessly naive to think that Zizek does not believe in "reality." He knows full well that he must eat and sleep and will eventually die; in fact, he discusses at length "the intrusion of the real." (See Chapter 2 in Slavoj Zizek, *Looking Awry: An Introduction to Jacques Lacan Through Popular Culture* [Cambridge, MA: MIT Press, 1991].) Jacques Lacan divided human existence into three provinces—the real, the imaginary, and the symbolic—so, obviously, Lacan cannot be said to have denied the existence of the real. For more on discursive knowledge, see Will Wright, *Wild Knowledge* (Minneapolis: University of Minnesota Press, 1992).

14. Prigogine and Stengers, *Order out of Chaos*, p. 22, quoting the Taoist Chuangtzu (c. 320 B.C.).

15. Ibid., p. 48.

16. Ibid., p. 9.

17. Ibid., p. 22.

18. Ibid., p. 44.

19. Noam Chomsky, *Language and Mind* (New York: Harcourt Brace Jovanovich, 1972). That language depends on structure (is a structure) is not at odds with poststructuralism. Derrida states unequivocally: "Language is a structure—a system of oppositions of places and values—and an oriented structure" (Derrida, *Of Grammatology*, trans. Gayatri C. Spivak [Baltimore: Johns Hopkins University Press, 1976], p. 216).

20. In this manner information can be doubled and redoubled virtually without constraint of resources other than time itself.

21. The second law of thermodynamics posits (and no one refutes) that in closed systems of energy eventually all goes to exhaustion. Temperature equilibrates, and no life is possible. Lyotard recognizes (like John Maynard Keynes) that the sun will eventually burn out, and his passion is that intelligence (an evolved characteristic of life on earth) should evolve further so as to outlive the sun itself (*The Inhuman*, p. 7). In this work, Lyotard was inspired by Prigogine (personal communication, Missoula, MT, November 1994).

22. The chemist Prigogine, an expatriot Russian who works at and founded the "Brussels School" in Belgium, received a Nobel Prize for his work on dissipative structures in 1977, the essence of which was the spontaneous origins of order out of

chaos. In the same year, the German chemist Hermann Haken published on similar phenomena in *Synergetics: An Introduction; On Equilibrium Phase Transitions and Self-organization in Physics, Chemistry and Biology* (New York: Springer-Verlag, 1977). Since then the American embryologist and theoretical biologist Stuart Kauffman (*The Origins of Order*) has gone one step further to suggest that not only do complex systems develop order spontaneously but that they tend toward "boundary conditions" thereby increasing the likelihood of novelty (which in the case of genetics increases the amount of variety available for natural selection processes) and so increasing the rate at which organisms (and other nonlinear systems) are able to "adapt" (through Darwinian processes of natural selection) to changing environments. Kauffman's work has not yet gained the level of acceptance of Prigogine's, but neither has it been discredited. A corollary is that complex systems are not stable *per se*. Only those that endure the trials and tribulations of evolution have the attribute that we would call stability. (And stability is an illusion except in the sense that it appears to us, in terms of our temporal and spatial scale.) See also Bruno Burlando, "The Fractal Geometry of Evolution," *Journal of Theoretical Biology* 163 (1993): 161–172. An obvious example of spontaneous ordering in a nonliving system is the crystalline structure of certain minerals cooled slowly.

23. Ilya Prigogine, *Introduction to Thermal Dynamics of Irreversible Processes*, 2d rev. ed. (New York: Interscience, 1961), p. 85.

24. In terms of botany, an example is photosynthesis—whenever gross primary productivity exceeds respiration losses, resulting in growth.

25. Francis Hutcheson. *An Inquiry into the Origin of Our Ideas of Beauty and Virtue, in Two Treatises* (London: John Darby Printers [W. & J. Innys Booksellers], 1725) Treatise 1, Section 2.

26. Karl Marx. "1884 Economic and Philosophical Manuscripts," in *Karl Marx: Selected Writings*. (Oxford: Oxford Press, 1977), p. 77. Of course, in far-from-equilibrium systems, order arises not so much *ex nihilo* (as Marx held) as from the effects of the external source of energy. A system that was truly composed of nothing could generate no order. Marx apparently believed that life on earth was created by the earth itself, without divine intervention. Today (while belief in divine intervention is not logically barred as an ultimate explanation of the universe), complexity theory holds that the origin of complex structures on earth are a result of the far-from-equilibrium conditions created by the sun. Belief that order springs spontaneously from chaos goes as far back as the ancient Roman philosopher Titus Lucretins.

27. Hans Wingler, *Bauhaus: Weimar, Dessau, Berlin, Chicago* (Cambridge: MIT Press, 1978).

28. Jean Baudrillard, *For a Critique of the Political Economy of the Sign*, Trans. Charles Levin (St. Louis: Telos Press, 1981).

29. Mandelbrot, a French mathematician employed by IBM, is frequently cited for his work, *The Fractal Geometry of Nature* (New York: W.H. Freeman, 1983). In this seminal work, he shows how many of his ideas were anticipated by mathematicians of the nineteenth century—ideas that did not become acceptable until recently.

30. This is a simplification that should not be pushed to extremes or taken out of context: The complexity of deserts and oceans (per unit of mass), for example, might be relatively low, while the complexity of artwork or of information stored in computer chips (per unit of mass) might be relatively high.

31. For example, most books on chaos theory include pages of color inserts dis-

playing fractal patterns that readers are clearly expected to find interesting and even beautiful.

32. Foucault (*Madness and Civilization*) posits the role of art as rebellion (the voice of unreason) against the established political order of reason. However, he does this from a position *of* (or within) reason—that is, he speaks in language and does not babble. Thus, it is implicit in Foucault that his intention is not the destruction of reason (of order) so much as a constructive criticism of the same. That criticism he champions as the constructive role of art.

33. Certainly humans do feel a duty to preserve works of art. For example, there is the famous case of the Nazi general in command of Paris during World War II. Reluctantly accepting the decision to evacuate Paris in advance of Allied forces in 1944, Hitler wanted the city razed. He asked his general, Dietrich von Choltitz, over the telephone, "Is Paris burning?" Choltitz lied to his Führer that it was—being unable to bring himself to destroy such a monumental work of art. (Max Hastings and George Stevens, *Victory in Europe* [Boston: Little, Brown & Co., 1985], p. 72.) The ethics of aesthetics and nature has been explored by Janna Thompson in "Aesthetics and the Value of Nature," *Environmental Ethics* 17, no. 3 (1995): 291–305.

34. Hutcheson, *An Inquiry into the Origin of Our Ideas of Beauty and Virtue*, Treatise 1, Section 2, pp. 15–16. The word "aesthetic" did not enter modern language until after 1750 and did not enter the English language until around 1800.

35. Taoist scholar Angus Graham states, "The oneness of Taoist vision seems to be of a kind with the 'Unity within Variety' of Western aesthetics" (*Disputers of the Tao: Philosophical Argument in Ancient China* [La Salle, IL: Open Court, 1989], p. 198).

36. From the perspective of ecology, it is notable that Aldo Leopold's (an early leader in American wildlife conservation) "land ethic" was built upon a three-legged stool of "integrity," "stability," and "beauty." (Aldo Leopold, *A Sand County Almanac* [New York: Ballantine Books, 1966].)

37. This link is primarily the work of Lacan and is well explained in Jonathan S. Lee, *Jacques Lacan* (Amherst: University of Massachusetts Press, 1990).

38. For Lyotard, the disjunctive bar is closely associated with the Freudian process of primal repression, the incest taboo, and what Lacan calls "the name of the father" (this is the repression out of which language is born) (ibid., pp. 47–67; Sigmund Freud, *Three Essays on the Theory of Sexuality* [New York: Basic Books, 1962], pp. 41–44). The separation is not just from each other, but from the otherness of nature also. Separation, of course, is necessary for there to be a relation; intercourse requires polarity of some form. In a poststructuralist view, people (who live in the symbolic) cannot be thought of as *in* nature in the same way as we think of other creatures as being *in* nature (despite acceptance of Darwinian evolution of humans from natural origins). Furthermore, if we were to take the word "nature" as indicating "everything, including ourselves," then it would be no different from the word "universe" and would lose considerable sign value. The "little objects" (Lacan's "object-a") are not little things *per se*; they are everything that is the stuff of our individual lives—objects big and small; ideas, schemes, and other symbolic constructions; our loved ones; and our enemies.

39. An excellent reference is Roland Barthes, *Pleasure of the Text*. Trans. Richard Miller (New York: Hill and Wang, 1973). Interestingly it was Hutcheson who, among the philosophers of the Enlightenment, first formulated the pleasure prin-

ciple that became the basis of Jeremy Bentham's utilitarianism: the idea of seeking the "greatest happiness of the greatest number."

40. Hutcheson, *An Inquiry into the Origin of Our Ideas of Beauty and Virtue*, Treatise 1, Section 3.

41. Ibid., Treatise 1, Section 4.

42. The ethics and aesthetics of Leopold has been explored extensively in many publications by J. Baird Callicott.

43. Edward O. Wilson, *Biophilia* (Cambridge: Harvard University Press, 1984, p. 60). See also Edward O. Wilson, *On Human Nature* (Cambridge: Harvard University Press, 1978), and Stephen R. Kellert and Edward O. Wilson, *The Biophilia Hypothesis* (Washington, DC: Island Press, 1993).

44. Frederick Turner, "The Invented Landscape," in *Beyond Preservation: Restoring and Inventing Landscapes*, ed. A.D. Baldwin, J. DeLuce, and C. Pletsch (Minneapolis: University of Minnesota Press, 1994), p. 53.

45. James Gleick's popular book *Chaos: Making a New Science* (New York: Penguin Books, 1987), describes the butterfly effect and explains how Lorenz discovered that a seemingly insignificant change in the starting values of a seemingly simple deterministic system (model) composed of just a few equations produced rapid divergences as the model was run iteratively to produce predictions of system behavior over time.

46. Toward the end of the stick's passage upstream it is quite likely to pass into the boundary zone where it will either be washed out into the main current or (depending on its precise movement) be washed once again into the circling eddy current. Such seeming indetermination can amuse small children (and adults) for hours.

47. In principle, chaotic deterministic systems remain predictable. However, they are unpredictable in practice because there is neither enough time nor enough computing power to make a timely prediction of future behavior. The fractal nature of chaos (that chaotic states often persist across scale) is such that faster computers or better research cannot eliminate the problem. While chess is a discrete game (in the sense that both chess pieces and squares are indivisible) so that faster computers can consider more possible moves by the opponent, truly complex systems are fractal so that if we "zoom in" on an island of apparent stability, we are likely to find still smaller islands of imbedded instability, within which there are still smaller islands of stability, and so on ad infinitum.

48. This move is well portrayed by John Stoppard in his play *Arcadia* (London: Faber & Faber, 1993).

49. For support of the latter interpretation, see remarks concerning the Bauhaus architect Ludwig Hilberseimer in Wingler, *Bauhaus*, pp. 496–497.

50. Complexity theory does not depend on the notion that everything is, at bottom, deterministic. Prigogine and Stengers themselves state, "The natural contains essential elements of randomness and irreversibility." And Heisenberg's quantum theory depends on randomness so fundamentally that Albert Einstein objected strongly (in his famous statement, "God does not play dice with the universe"). Further pursuit of this topic, however, lies beyond the scope of this paper. Suffice it so say that, if randomness is indeed intrinsic to natural systems, then Lyotard's indetermination is even less subject to doubt.

51. Any apparent stability of meaning is illusory, slippery, in that it is not based

on any "bedrock," but rather on a plethora of repressed experiences that occurred in early childhood, in advance of anything that we could describe as "understanding." An analogy is the process of constructing buildings of rock in Venice, London, or Chicago, where there is no bedrock; instead wood or other pilings are driven into the mud or clay until they "stick" sufficiently to provide the illusion of stability. In this view, the ultimate source of meaning, the reason why we emerged from early childhood with understanding, is not passive but is the result of activity that is initiated by our desire. As already alluded to, for Lacan, desire is for the absent (m)other, the separation of the subject from "the real" by the "disjunctive bar," which is the "law" that is language (the symbolic); this separation is what constitutes the lack. (The notation "(m)other" is from Ellie Ragland-Sullivan, *Jacques Lacan and the Philosophy of Psychoanalysis* [Urbana: University of Illinois Press, 1986].) As Derrida's translator, Spivak, states, "Derrida's trace (under erasure) is the mark of the absence of a presence, an already absent present, of the lack at the origin that is the condition of thought and experience" (Derrida, *Of Grammatology*, p. xvii).

52. Hamish Kimmins, *Balancing Act: Environmental Issues in Forestry* (Vancouver: UBC Press, 1992).

53. Lyotard, *The Inhuman*, p. 16.

54. Ibid., p. 7. According to Alastair Moles, Nietzsche's will to power transcends humans and even life itself to what I would characterize as the entire big bang process (*Nietzsche's Philosophy of Nature and Cosmology* [New York: Peter Lang, 1990], chap. 5). This is similar to Lyotard's project, it would seem.

55. Taoist scholar Angus Graham notes two stages in the thought of Chuang-tzu (a Taoist philosopher of the third or fourth century B.C.): "(1) All principles for grounding rules of conduct are themselves groundless. (2) At the rock bottom of skepticism there remain spontaneity and a single imperative to guide it" (*Disputers of the Tao*, p. 193). The first of these is reminiscent of what in the West is called Gödel's theorem.

56. Poststructuralism is generally accepting of this construction of the subject (which occurs during the "mirror stage"). For more on this important innovation of Peirce's, see Walter Benn Michaels, "The Interpreter's Self: Peirce on the Cartesian 'Subject,' " in *Reader-Response Criticism: From Formalism to Post-Structuralism*, ed. Jane P. Tompkins (Baltimore: Johns Hopkins Univversity Press, 1980), pp. 185–200.

57. From the Latin word, *sistere* ("to stand; cause to stand").

58. Ames, "Putting the *Te* Back into Taoism," p. 135.

59. G.E.M. Anscombe and G.H. von Wright, ed., *On Certainty*, trans., Denis Paul, G.E.M. Anscombe, and Ludwig Wittgenstein (Oxford: Basil Blackwell, 1969).

60. Ames, "Putting the *Te* Back into Taoism," p. 120.

61. Ibid.

62. Using an analogy from information theory, identifying whether a particular "bit" in a string of digitized information is turned "on" or "off" requires establishing a threshold level that is an (unsure) act of interpretation. Similarly, filtering "noise" from "signal" requires algorithms that constitute (unsure) interpretation. One can choose to minimize either errors of commission or errors of omission but can never eliminate either.

63. Robert Pogue Harrison, *Forests: The Shadow of Civilization* (Chicago: University of Chicago Press, 1992). The word "forest" did not come to specifically refer

to a stand of trees until the modern era, in Diderot's encyclopedia.

64. Graham, *Disputers of the Tao*, pp. 331–332.

65. Ibid. Graham reveals that the situation in China was not quite this simple. Lao-tzu (according to Graham) thought: "[H]uman codes of conduct prefer A, Heaven's Way is to equalize A and B. . . . At first sight one might take Lao-tzu to say that man is unjust but Heaven just. But the point is rather that man always strives to enlarge A at the expense of B, fighting the natural course of things which reverts to B and so balances A and B." (*Disputers of the Tao*, pp. 230–231.) One could say that Lao-tzu was taking note of the second law of thermodynamics and of man's tendency for negentropic activity in the face thereof.

66. Graham, *Disputers of the Tao*, p. 411.

67. Ibid., p. 227.

68. Ibid., p. 228. In a footnote (on p. 181) regarding a story by Chuang-tzu, Graham notes "the Yellow Emperor is himself aware of being remote from the Way because he puts it into words." The disjunctive bar of language (for Lyotard and other followers of Lacan) removes us from the real.

69. Ames, "Putting the *Te* Back into Taosim," p. 121; Graham, *Disputers of the Tao*, p. 13.

70. Ames, "Putting the *Te* Back into Taoism, p. 125.

71. Ibid.

72. Graham, *Disputers of the Tao*, pp. 335, 408–414.

73. Ibid., p. 191.

74. Ibid., p. 341.

75. Another example occurs later in Ames discussion of *wu-wei*. Having told us that *wu-wei* activity is a negation of "teleological purpose" (p. 137), he tells us that, in *wu-wei* activity: "there is an intendedness or insistence of the particular that makes it particular" (p. 139). Surely intendedness is teleological, and the working out of energy, of potency, of *te*—what Ames calls insistence, which I would prefer to shorten to sistence (see above)—cannot be equated with intentionality.

76. Perhaps this potency is Lyotard's "inhuman" indetermination, from which life (development, evolution, negentropic resistance against death, against the second law of thermodynamics) is born "and does not cease to be born." (Lyotard makes passing reference to Chinese thought, Dōgen, founder of the Sōtō Zen school in Japan, and Taoism in several of his works.) See also note 54 above regarding Nietzsche's will to power in nature.

77. Ames, "Putting the *Te*, Back into Taoism," pp. 128–129.

78. Mathews, *Chinese-English Dictionary* (Cambridge: Harvard University Press, 1966), and A.P. Cowie and A. Evison, *Concise English-Chinese Chinese-English Dictionary* (New York: Oxford, 1986). By taking *li* to be both pattern and physics, the word (exemplified by "texture") connotes both the way things appear to be and the way things are. This demonstrates, perhaps, that the epistemological divide in the West (between a subjectivist and a transcendental notion of reality) simply does not (perhaps cannot) occur in Chinese. See text above, in association with note 68.

79. Ames, "Putting the *Te* Back into Taoism," p. 136.

80. Ibid., p. 137.

81. Ibid., p. 138. In a Marxian (or perhaps merchant-style ecofeminist) vein, one might add that *wu-wei* can apply not just between a human and his environment, but

equally well between two human beings, in terms of labor and the relationships of production.

82. Graham, *Disputers of the Tao*, p. 385. One must not confuse heaven in Taoism with the Christian Heaven.

83. Ibid., p. 385. Based on Graham's reference to "habitual desires" on the same page, I take this passage from Lao-tzu to be consistent with Derrida's "desedimentation," which is perhaps a "bucketing out" of "little objects" to open up to the terror or sublimity of the void, the lack. Referring to Chuang-tzu, Graham states, "The Taoist however wants to show that the Way is not that which the sage desires, but the course on which he inevitably finds himself in his illuminated state" (pp. 190–191).

84. Ames, "Putting the *Te* Back into Taoism," p. 139.

85. Graham, *Disputers of the Tao*, p. 232. This is identical to Peter S. Wenz's "principle of Process-Harm" (Peter S. Wenz, *Environmental Justice* [Albany: State University of New York Press, 1988], pp. 300–310).

86. Graham, *Disputers of the Tao*, p. 287.

87. Ames, "Putting the *Te* Back into Taoism, p. 139.

88. Graham, *Disputers of the Tao*, p. 190.

89. Ibid., p. 315.

90. An example is the principle employed in Asian martial arts. In the West, this form of efficiency has perhaps not been applauded because of a Christian tradition that has viewed labor as, first and foremost, a penance for original sin. (See Foucault, *Madness and Civilization*, pp. 55–56, and also John Dunn, *The Political Thought of John Locke* [Cambridge, UK: Cambridge University Press, 1969].)

91. Graham, *Disputers of the Tao*, p. 232.

92. The possible exception is that non–*wu-wei* activities might produce an actual reduction of entropy in any open thermodynamic system. This would be the logical rejoinder of promoters of "development." Such promotion, however, requires that human action be highly predictable in outcome. Such predictability is foreclosed in our notion of chaotic systems, and the development movement thereby falls prey to those who have accused it of a lack of humility and an "arrogance of humanism."

— 12 —

Of Frogs, Old Ponds, and the Sound of Water: Building a Constituency for Environmental Literature in the United States and Japan

Scott Slovic

The Social and Political Implications of Environmental Literature

Henry David Thoreau, in some ways the most direct ancestor of contemporary American environmental writers, died in May 1862. A month later, *The Atlantic Monthly* published Thoreau's essay, "Walking," which begins with the following lines:

> I wish to speak a word for Nature, for absolute freedom and wildness, as contrasted with a freedom and culture merely civil, to regard man as an inhabitant, or a part and parcel of Nature, rather than a member of society. I wish to make an extreme statement, if so I may make an emphatic one, for there are enough champions of civilization: the minister, the school-committee, and every one of you will take care of that. (p. 93)

We surely have enough advocates for nature represented in the pages of this book concerning landscapes and communities in Asia and the Pacific Northwest. What we may need, however, is someone to "speak a word" for literature—that is, for the crucial role of literary artists in helping us to explore the relationship between human culture and the natural world, in helping us to articulate the principles of scientific ecology and the personal experience of contact with nonhuman nature, and indeed, in giving words to the almost indefinable process by which our systems of values are formulated and undergo constant adjustments and reality checks. There are plenty of people who can speak for nature, so I'll speak a word for words, for stories and images, for the literary genre of "nature writing," defined broadly to include not only the usual non-fiction essays, but also poetry, fiction, and drama that scrutinizes the relationship between humans and the natural environment.

Literature and the other arts are the proper media for exploring and communicating systems of values within specific communities and between one culture and another. This is not a particularly novel idea, but it flies in the face of postmodern critical theory, which is frequently criticized for its indeterminacy, its obsession with textual (and metatextual) problematics, and its indifference to real social problems. Many literary scholars in recent years have forgotten the traditional social function of the arts. Some critics, however, are now coming to question this asocial, valueless perspective. For instance, James S. Hans, in his 1990 book, *The Value(s) of Literature*, writes:

> A good number of our current novelists and poets . . . have quite clear commitments to the concerns that developed out of the environmental movement, and yet it is hard to find serious discussions of these concerns in academic journals. We confine ourselves to their words, not to the implications of them, and we have come to think that there is no place in "serious scholarship" to evaluate these "outside" concerns. Our business is with words, nothing more, nothing less, or so it all too often seems. (p. 2)

On the other hand, Hans continues, "If we assume that literature does have an ethical component to it, we must then broaden the ways in which criticism deals with particular texts and with the tradition as a whole. . . . Literature does not exist in its own discrete space, so to limit our discussion of it to its 'literariness' is to denude it of its crucial links to the other systems that combine to articulate our sense of values" (p. 15). This consciousness of the "ethical component" of literature is one of the important tenets of the new ecological literary criticism, or "ecocriticism," which Cheryll Glotfelty has broadly defined in *The Ecocriticism Reader: Landmarks in Literary Ecology* as "the study of the relationship between literature and the physical environment" (Glotfelty and Fromm 1996, p. xviii).

One of the most succinct statements about the role of literature in formulating environmental values in the particular context of the American West is William Kittredge's essay "Owning It All" (in his 1987 book by the same title). "A mythology can be understood," he writes, "as a story that contains a set of implicit instructions from a society to its members, telling them what is valuable and how to conduct themselves if they are to preserve the things they value" (p. 62). He continues this line of thought a few pages later:

> In the American West we are struggling to revise our dominant mythology, and to find a new story to inhabit. Laws control our lives, and they are designed to preserve a model of society based on values learned from mythology. Only after reimagining our myths can we coherently remodel our laws, and hope to keep our society in a realistic relationship to what is actual. (p. 64)

Writers, and artists in general, are trying to craft and communicate such a new story, or multiple new stories, at this moment. In many cases, the "new story" requires the recycling of old, sometimes very old, stories. Back in the mid-1980s, Barry Lopez, one of the most important contemporary American nature writers, said, "I suppose this is a conceit, but I believe this area of writing [nature writing] will not only one day produce a major and lasting body of American literature, but that it might also provide the foundation for a reorganization of American political thought" (Lopez 1987, p. 297). In fact, one of the reasons nature writing has become and continues to emerge as such a powerful force in contemporary literature is that writers such as Lopez and Kittredge—as well as Terry Tempest Williams, Rick Bass, Robert Michael Pyle, Scott Russell Sanders, Wendell Berry, Gary Snyder, and dozens of other environmental writers—understand their work as the effort to achieve not only aesthetic brilliance, but an understanding of human society's "realistic relationship" to the actualities of the planet.

Barry Lopez, who received the American Book Award in 1986 for *Arctic Dreams*, commented explicitly about the social dimension of the arts in a 1990 catalog essay that he wrote for an exhibit of collages by the Maine artist Alan Magee. Confessing that his own expertise is in the literary arts rather than the visual, Lopez nonetheless raises a series of issues that are fundamental to the link between art and environmental awareness:

> What is the meaning of this work . . . to a *community* of people? Is it rich in allusion and metaphorically striking, more in other words than just an

announcement of the artist's presence in the world? Does it disturb complacency or stimulate wonder? Does it awaken anger or compassion?

> These questions, I think, are more social than aesthetic. They proceed . . . from a feeling that if art is merely decorative or entertaining, or even just aesthetically brilliant, if it does not elicit hope or a sense of the sacred, if it does not speak to our fear and confusion, or to the capacities for memory and passion that imbue us with our humanity, then the artist has only sent us a letter that requires no answer. (Lopez 1990, p. 1)

This concept of the social responsibilities of art will require a basic paradigm shift for most viewers, listeners, and readers, a shift that broadens the attention from mere "aesthetic brillian[ce]" to the moral dimension of the work or works in question. Such a perspective is not unique to Lopez or to environmental writers. In fact, there is considerable activity today in environmental film, music, theater, and the visual arts. For instance, the Spring–Summer 1994 issue of the journal *Theater* is devoted specifically to "Theater and Ecology." More recently, the art critic Suzi Gablik commented on the social and ecological concerns of contemporary visual artists in her essay "Arts and the Earth: Making Art as if the World Mattered," published in the Autumn 1995 issue of *Orion*:

> In Western art today, we have an aesthetic framework for those who believe the world is composed of discrete objects, and who are fascinated with the individual self, but we do not yet have a process-oriented framework for those for whom the world consists of dynamic interactions and interrelational processes. Such a framework would entail a transformation of aesthetic traditions based on individual autonomy and technical mastery into artistic practices based on the interdependent, ecological, and process character of the world, and implies a different level of interaction and permeability with the audience. (p. 44)

In other words, the development of a truly ecological aesthetic in the visual arts and other media (including literature) will require nothing short of a revolution in our notion of what art is. Preceding this revolution, though, must come a rethinking of the purposes of art. In 1990, Glen A. Love offered an eloquent statement about literature and ecology in his essay "Revaluing Nature: Toward an Ecological Criticism": "The most important function of literature today is to redirect human consciousness to a full consideration of its place in a threatened natural world" (p. 213). Since then, Love has commented that he wishes he had written "the most important function of literary criticism today" rather than "the most important function of literature," emphasizing the moral/ecological dimension of scholarship. Actual literary artists, in many cases, have never forgotten that values are at the heart of literature. Literary scholars cannot afford to shy away from the issue of human values and attitudes—this is the proper domain of literary studies (and such fields as philosophy, religious studies, and art history), and it is one of the reasons why the arts and humanities are gradually becoming central components of university programs in environmental studies.

Thoreau seemed to anticipate the social function of literature when he commented in *Walden* on the difficulty of expressing complex and subtle ideas. He wrote:

> The greatest gains and values are farthest from being appreciated. . . . We easily come to doubt if they exist. We soon forget them. They are the highest reality. Perhaps the facts most astounding and most real are never communicated from man to man. The true harvest of my daily life is somewhat as intangible and indescribable as the tints of morning or evening. It is a little stardust caught, a segment of the rainbow which I have clutched. (p. 145)

Likewise, the lessons of modern environmental science—including the work of ecologists, environmental historians, and environmental anthropologists—are often extremely abstract and difficult for the public to believe, difficult even to decipher. What is an "ecosystem" and why is it so delicate? Does the "ozone layer" that protects the Earth from the sun's ultraviolet rays really have a hole in it? How do we know that hundreds and hundreds of animal and plant species are disappearing each year, becoming extinct? Why does this matter, especially if extinction itself is a natural process? It is easy for people in urban, industrialized countries, such as the United States and Japan, simply to live from day to day, to satisfy our immediate needs and trust that there will always be a tomorrow for our species. The challenging task of the people I refer to as "nature writers" or "environmental writers" is both to create an interest in nature among their readers and to impress these readers with the necessity of living with discipline and a long-term vision of our relationship to nonhuman nature. It is the job of these writers to communicate the subtleties of this relationship that are often, as Thoreau puts it, "farthest from being appreciated."

The Practice of Ecocriticism: A Brief Example

Lest this essay operate solely as a metacritical commentary on the goals of environmental literature and ecocriticism, and on the process of developing an academic audience for American nature writing in Japan, I would like to offer an ecocritical reading of one brief example of contemporary environmental writing, an example that illustrates some of the genre's important traits: attentiveness to the physical world beyond human beings and stimulus for ethical reformation. Without a specific demonstration of ecocritical reading and environmental writing, it will be difficult for many readers to appreciate what precisely is involved in the art and scholarship I have been outlining above.

Gary Snyder's *No Nature: New and Selected Poems* was nominated for a National Book Award in 1992. The final poem in the collection, entitled "Ripples on the Surface," reads as follows:

> Ripples on the surface of the water—
> were silver salmon passing under—different
> from the ripples caused by breezes
>
> A scudding plume on the wave—
> a humpback whale is
> breaking out in air up
> gulping herring
>   —Nature is not a book, but a *performance*, a
> high old culture
>
> Ever-fresh events
> scraped out, rubbed out, and used, used, again—
> the braided channels of the rivers
> hidden under fields of grass—
>
> The vast wild
>   the house, alone.
> The little house in the wild,
>   the wild in the house.
>   Both forgotten.
>
>   No nature
>
> Both together, one big empty house. (p. 381)

Close reading of this text will draw the audience initially into an apparent passage from the poet's journal, an entry devoted to detailed observation of an ocean scene. We follow the poet's mental processes in discerning one set of water ripples ("silver salmon") from another ("caused by breezes"). Our attention is next directed toward the "scudding plume" of a surfacing whale, which leads to the realization that "nature is not a book, but a *performance*." Nature, in other words, is movement, patterns, physical material, something other than the staticity and abstractness of a written text. The following stanza confirms the idea of nature as active and changeable: "Ever-fresh events/scraped out, rubbed out, and used, used, again." Where does such a revelation lead? To the poet's concluding dissolution of the classic Western distinctions between "domestic" and "wild," "culture" and "nature." Although the poem opens with the human mind noticing subtle differences between superficial things, it moves toward the profound conclusion that every-thing—culture ("little house") and nature ("wild")—belongs "together," that the universe is "one big empty house." The inclusively defined "house" (as in the Greek root, "oikos," for the word "ecology") of the poem's final line implies habitat for the "performance" of active phenomena, human and nonhuman. This house is empty of distinctions, free from such ideas as culture and nature; it is a realm of "no nature" (and implicitly a realm of "no culture," except the "high old culture" of physical performance). The repetition of the word "both" in two of the final three lines reinforces the idea of connection rather than separation.

The point of walking through a close reading of Snyder's "Ripples on the Surface" is to demonstrate, in brief, the experience of interpreting a work of environmental literature that enacts what the author may consider an exemplary mental process (careful perception of the world) and then pursues the subtle didactic strategy of imagining a worldview from which such polarized concepts as culture and nature have been abolished. Such an interpretative procedure, whether conducted in writing or in a lecture, does not mandate that the critic's audience agree with the interpretation or even sympathize with the apparent perspective of the literary text. Rather, literary analysis is a process of exploration and reflection, and anyone who participates thoughtfully in this process is likely to work through a set of ideas that will lead to an enriched consciousness of language, mind, and world.

To push the above reading further, I could have established various connections between Snyder's language and ideas and those of other artists and thinkers. This is what commonly occurs in the practice of literary criticism. Ecocritics and teachers of environmental literature seek to offer readers a broader, deeper, and more explicit explanation of how and what environmental literature communicates than the writers themselves, immersed in their particularized narratives, can offer. Crucial to the ecocritical process of pulling things (ideas, texts, authors) together and putting them in perspective is our awareness of who and where we (readers and analysts of literature) are. Our awareness, literally, of where we stand in the world and why we are writing. In order to force myself to rethink such basic questions—Who am I? Where am I? Why am I doing what I do?—I routinely put myself in disorienting situations and then claw my way back to familiarity. Thus, in September 1993, I arrived with my family at Narita Airport in Japan, speaking hardly a word of the language. "Here are two words for you," said my friend as he greeted us. "'Hai' means 'yes.' And 'shizen' means 'nature.'"

Haiku, the Transient Frog, and Jump-starting an Academic Movement

What does any of this have to do with creating a constituency for environmental literature in the United States and Japan, the issue posed in the title of this article? Let me respond to this question with a poem and a few interpretive comments. To be perfectly honest, I am a specialist in American environmental literature, not Japanese literature. So when I went to Japan in 1993, my purpose was to teach the work of American nature writers, from Edward Abbey to Ann Zwinger, at several Tokyo universities. By the end of my eleven-month stay, I had not only taught at the University of Tokyo, Sophia University, and Rikkyo University, and offered an intensive course at Kanazawa University, but crisscrossed the Japanese islands giving nearly thirty lectures on environmental literature at scholarly conferences, universities, and gatherings of environmentalists and interested members of the public, from Sapporo to Naha. Toward the end of my stay in Japan, shortly after I had given an overview of American nature writing at the annual meeting of the Chu-Shikoku American Literary Society, a professor from Matsuyama University approached me at dinner and said, "Look, if you're going to spend nearly a year in Japan, you've got to memorize at least one haiku poem by Basho. In Japanese." He proceeded to recite the famous poem about a frog that jumps into an old pond, leaving behind the sound of water. To make sure I took my assignment seriously, he wrote down the following transliteration of the poem:

> Furuikeya
> Kawazu tobikomu
> Mizu no oto

The English translation is as follows:

> Old pond
> A frog jumps in
> The sound of water

My purpose in mentioning Basho's poem in this essay is not to offer a reading within the precise context of seventeenth-century Japanese poetry. Instead, I respond to these words as a twentieth-century American reader, seeking to derive meaning from literature in a way that clarifies and illuminates my own experience of the world. For instance, one way of reading this poem is to notice how it focuses on a small natural phenomenon and on the ideas of change and continuation. Frequently, in America especially, we think of nature with a capital "N" as something vast and pristine, something remote from clusters of human population. Basho's poem, on the other hand, attends to the familiar, old pond, possibly a pool of cloudy water no wider than the poet's own body is tall, located in the midst of a city. Tokyo, Kyoto, and other Japanese cities, even today, are full of such ponds. And full of frogs, too. So the poem reminds us to pay attention to small, familiar, and even urban aspects of the natural world. The abrupt movement of the jumping frog serves as an emblem of change, while the resultant sound of splashing water and the implied ripples in the water's surface represent duration, represent what lasts. It is this temporal aspect of the poem that reminds us of the concept fundamental to the entire genre of haiku poetry, expressed through the Japanese word "aware," meaning something like the sweet sadness of fleeting things, of transience. The physical world changes, leaving the human observer with the emotion of longing. Autumn and spring, the two seasons of most noticeable change, provide the most common settings for haiku. Some scholars believe that seasonal references in Japanese haiku are pro forma responses to the genre's requirements rather than genuine perceptions of nature, but American writers who have adopted the genre (from Ezra Pound to Gary Snyder) have typically viewed haiku as a verbal representation of moments of intensified engagement with the natural world.[1]

One could notice and benefit from all of these possible meanings of the poem, but I choose to read it in a more autobiographical way. To me, the old pond signifies Japan, a country whose ancient culture has demonstrated in various ways close attunement to natural creatures and processes for many centuries, despite its current reputation as an environmental culprit; I myself am the transient frog, appearing and disappearing in almost the same instant; and the "sound of water" is the consequence of my hectic stay in Japan, my efforts to jump-start the interest in environmental literature among Japanese scholars, journalists, editors, and writers. Japanese interest in both foreign and domestic environmental literature, which was at best tepid and skeptical in 1993, has become rampant within the past few years, especially among scholars of American literature, environmental journalists, and publishers. In the following section, I will explain the initial skepticism of the Japanese toward environmental literature and ecocriticism and provide an overview of the rapid process by which scholars and writers in Japan have committed themselves to the environmental view of literature.

The Formation of ASLE-Japan

There is an extended and important tradition of interest among American literary scholars in the field we now call "literature and environment." Even Perry Miller, who did so much groundbreaking work on colonial and nineteenth-century American literature in the 1930s and 1940s, could be called a "proto-ecocritic" because of his appreciation of the importance of nature to early American writers. Other active scholars during the early years of this field include Norman Foerster, who published *Nature in American Literature* in 1923, and Philip Marshall Hicks, the author of a 1924 dissertation at the University of Pennsylvania entitled "The Development of the Natural History Essay in American Literature." Isolated scholars cultivated the field in the ensuing decades.[2] In the 1980s, responding to the flowering of environmental literature that began in the late 1960s (Edward Abbey, Wallace Stegner, Wendell Berry, Annie Dillard, and so forth), more and more scholars and students began to take notice of the fascinating and important connections between literature and our understanding of nature, so that by the early 1990s there appeared to be sufficient "critical mass" to create an academic organization that would foster the continued development of this field.

The Association for the Study of Literature and Environment (ASLE) was launched in October 1992 with a friendly mob of fifty-four professors, writers, and graduate students crowded into a small meeting room at the Sands Regency Casino Hotel in Reno, Nevada. In its first four years, ASLE's membership grew to nearly 1,000, spanning several continents. ASLE publishes *ASLE News* (formerly *The American Nature Writing Newsletter*) and *ISLE: Interdisciplinary Studies in Literature and Environment*. It also produces an annual bibliography of new scholarship and primary literature in the field, distributes a handbook for prospective graduate students in literature and environment, sponsors numerous ASLE sessions at local and national conferences, holds an annual business meeting during the Western Literature Association Conference each October, and organizes a major conference every two years and a smaller symposium during off-years. The goal of the association is to stimulate and support discussion, research, and new artistic work in environmental literature and various ancillary fields. My summary of ASLE's work is intended as a demonstration—a very quick and superficial one—of how the academic community in the field of literary studies, especially in the United States, is responding to the challenge of our environmental predicament, a predicament (some would use the word "crisis") that we will likely never resolve or overcome in any final, simple way.

I mention all of this as a way of leading up to a discussion of how the Japanese academic, literary, and publishing communities have, with rather uncharacteristic swiftness, overcome their conservative, cautious impulses and taken to this field. I vividly remember the day I met my first group of students at the University of Tokyo in September 1993. I was teaching a class, "Rivers in American Literature," for graduate students and advanced undergraduates in American literature. Most Japanese literary scholars are extremely canonical (i.e., devoted to familiar, mainstream authors), and typical classes in American literature focus on such authors as Nathaniel Hawthorne, Emily Dickinson, Herman Melville, or William Faulkner. I believe the English faculty allowed me to present such an unconventional subject as "river literature" for the fluky reason that Professor Toshio Watanabe (the senior Americanist at the University of Tokyo and one of the senior scholars of American literature throughout Japan) had recently translated Norman Maclean's *A River Runs Through It*. He later told me that, although he had come to Tokyo many years earlier as a student and had remained as a professor at one of Japan's most prestigious universities, he had grown up in a fishing village on Sado Island, off the western coast of Honshu—thus his interest in Maclean.

But the students at the University of Tokyo were initially unconvinced that nature writing was a legitimate literary genre. I gave an introductory presentation on the idea of environmental literature and ecocriticism, asking a question inspired by Love's 1990 article: Could it be that, as Love put it, "the most important function of literature today is to redirect human consciousness to a full consideration of its place in a threatened natural world" (p. 213)? Most of the students were lifelong "Tokyojin"—inhabitants of a place where the rivers have all been straightened and lined with cement and where the buildings tower on all sides, a city that sprawls and spreads laterally as far as the eye can see. One student smirked as I spoke and then, when I had finished, raised his hand with surprising boldness, especially for a Japanese student: "But, sir," he said, "sir, you seem to forget that nature is obsolete and irrelevant in Japan today." I wished that the major earthquake many experts have been waiting for had struck Tokyo at that moment—so much for the irrelevance of nature. But that student's semiserious comment was indicative of the initial dubiousness with which my presentations, and American nature writing in general, were often received in Japan.

Although, as I mentioned above, Japanese culture is widely known for its traditional veneration of nature, the students and scholars I worked with in Tokyo and throughout Japan had long since abandoned their daily, conscious involvement with nature to become indoor people, "city people." In his article "The Conception of Nature in Japanese Culture," historian of science Masao Watanabe provides the following overview:

> [In Japan there is] a love of nature which has existed from very early days. This love of nature has resulted in a refined appreciation of the beauty of nature in, for example, landscapes, miniature gardens (*hakoniwa*), miniature trees (*bonsai*), flower arrangement (*ikebana*), the tea ceremony (*chanoyu*), short poems called *haiku*, and even the art of cookery.
>
> Nature for the Japanese has not traditionally been an object of man's investigation or of exploitation for human benefit, as it has been for Westerners. For the Japanese and for other Oriental peoples, man was considered a part of nature, and the art of living in harmony with nature was their wisdom of life. (1974, p. 279)

Watanabe illustrates this stereotypical appreciation of nature by commenting on two examples from classical Japanese literature: the eighteenth-century female haiku poet Kaga no Chiyo and the thirteenth-century author Kamo no Chomei. Chomei, for instance, abandoned the civilized world to live in a mountain hut, where he wrote, "My only desire for this life is to see the beauties of the seasons" (quoted in Watanabe 1974, p. 280). However, Watanabe concludes his essay with the realization that contemporary Japanese society exists in an awkward quandary, suspended between Western science and traditional Oriental philosophy:

> Obviously, this kind of sentiment has been rapidly fading in Japan since the hasty introduction of modern science and technology. This traditional sentiment, however, has not been completely replaced by the idea of man and his relation to nature which underlies Western science. Still immersed in nature itself, the Japanese people do not quite realize what is happening to nature and to themselves, and are thus exposed more directly to, and are more helpless in, the current environmental crisis. (p. 282)

Actually, the environmental movement in Japan has been active since the early twentieth century, helping to set aside the Oze Wetlands north of Tokyo as a national monument in 1930. The country's major environmental organization, the Nature Conservation Society of Japan, was established in 1951, specifically to monitor such preserves as the Oze Wetlands and Mount Meakan in Hokkaido's Akan National Park.[3] However, until the mid-1990s, most Japanese literary scholars viewed their own work as unrelated to the environmental movement or any other social movements in Japan or abroad. When I began teaching in Japan in 1993, the concepts of ecocriticism and environmental literature were unknown to all but a handful of scholars who had recently studied in the United States.

It is a rather interesting case study in "academic sociology" to consider how the Japanese scholarly community—particularly the community of American literature scholars in Japan—has reshaped itself around the genre of environmental literature. In October 1993, within a month of my arrival in Japan, the small Tokyo publisher, Fumikura Press, produced a special issue of its journal, *Folio A*, devoted to American nature writing. Professor Ken-ichi Noda of Kanazawa University and I spent the previous year assembling a minianthology consisting of samples of nonfiction nature writing by Loren Eiseley, Wallace Stegner, Wendell

Berry, Edward Abbey, Annie Dillard, Barry Lopez, Gretel Ehrlich, Robert Finch, and John Daniel, all translated into Japanese, plus introductory articles that Professor Noda and I prepared and a bibliography of American nature writing that had already been translated into Japanese. This issue sold out within a few months, and I was also able to distribute copies selectively as I traveled around the country, lecturing on nature writing. Word of mouth about nature writing spread quickly, aided by the availability of strong translations of selected texts.

In November 1993, there was a small gathering of Japanese scholars, mostly friends of Professor Noda, at the Chigusa ("Thousand Grasses") Bar in Shinjuku, the seedy, neon-and-cement heart of Tokyo that Snyder has referred to as "the 10,000 bars maze" (1992, p. ix). We spent three hours upstairs in a small, windowless, smoke-filled room, discussing "nature" as if it were a quaint abstraction, an amusing relic from the past. Japanese scholars wanted to know who the important American nature writers were, what their relation was to canonical figures in American literature (Henry David Thoreau, Nathaniel Hawthorne, Emily Dickinson, Mark Twain, William Faulkner, and so forth), and how the scholarly establishment in the United States viewed such literature and this environmental approach among literary critics. At first, it was not environmental concern that motivated the scholars at Chigusa to become interested in American nature writing; their primary attraction to the field resulted from the sense that this was fertile new territory for scholarship and, perhaps, from curiosity about the latest American academic "fad." To some extent, this may still be the case. I had trouble talking immediately after that first smokefest and despaired of triggering any widespread enthusiasm for environmental literature among the Japanese. But later that evening, as Professor Noda and I sat in a fast-food restaurant and ate french fries at midnight, he said: "That meeting went really well. I think there will soon be a Japanese branch of ASLE." Obviously, it can be difficult for an outsider to gauge the response of a new community.

Within a month, Professor Joji Okanda of Yamanashi Gakuin University had created the *ASLE-J Newsletter*, which he based loosely on *The American Nature Writing Newsletter*. Supported by the Japan-United States Educational Commission, the United States Information Agency, and various regional societies for the study of American literature and culture, I began sojourning to universities and academic meetings throughout the country—Sapporo, Kochi, Sendai, Fukuoka, Naha,

Miyazaki, Kofu, Hiroshima—and everywhere I went, I spoke to crowds of dozens, sometimes hundreds. I managed to make contact at each of my presentations with a handful of people interested enough to join the nature writing mailing list. A mere six months after the initial Shinjuku gathering, following additional formal planning meetings in Tokyo and Kyoto, a special session during the English Literary Society of Japan Conference (Japan's equivalent of the Modern Language Association) in Kumamoto on May 22, 1994, was devoted to the creation of "ASLE-Japan," with Ken Noda presiding. Thirty people attended the organizational session, but within months approximately 100 scholars, representing nearly every part of the country, had joined.

Since 1994, ASLE-Japan has held an annual meeting during the American Literary Society of Japan Conference. In February 1995, the distinguished journal *Eigo Seinen* (The Rising Generation), published an entire collection of articles on American nature writing. One of the central leaders of ASLE-Japan is Shigeyuki Okajima, a deputy editor and leading environmental journalist with *Yomiuri Shimbun*, Japan's largest daily newspaper. Okajima, who has written a book about American environmentalism and has also translated John Muir's *My First Summer in the Sierra* into Japanese, arranged for *Yomiuri Shimbun* to bring the prominent nature writer Terry Tempest Williams to Kanazawa and Hiroshima in 1995 for special ASLE-Japan symposia, resulting in Williams's essay about her emotional visit to Hiroshima (published in the May 15, 1995, issue of *The Nation*). At the Kanazawa meeting, prior to Williams's lecture and reading, the author Keizo Hino, winner of Japan's Akutagawa Prize (roughly the equivalent of the Pulitzer Prize in the United States), gave a talk in which he explained the daily influence of nature on his life in Tokyo. One of the goals of this meeting was to use the prominence of contemporary American environmental writing to help bring attention to similar work that is emerging in Japan.

A contingent of six ASLE-Japan members joined 300 other ASLE members at the first ASLE-US conference in June 1995 at Colorado State University in Fort Collins. Six weeks later, just a day before the fiftieth anniversary of the atomic bombing, ASLE-Japan sponsored another special symposium at Hiroshima University. Rick Bass, the important Montana nature writer, read from his work; I lectured about the future of ecocriticism; and fifteen Japanese scholars presented short summaries of their current research on nature writing. Many of the scholars who spoke at the August 1995 symposium in Hiroshima contributed to the collection of essays, *Environmental Approaches to American Literature: Toward the World of Nature Writing*, published in 1996 by Kyoto's Minerva Press. In July 1995, when Rick Bass and I first arrived in Tokyo, we went straight to the Chigusa Bar in Shinjuku for a reunion of ASLE-Japan members, sponsored by a half-dozen of the many Japanese publishers now actively interested in Japanese and American environmental literature: Takarajimasha, Hakusuisha, Yosensha, Minerva, Yama-Kei, *Shinra Magazine*, and *Yomiuri Shimbun*, to name a few. The room was crowded with scholars, writers, and editors talking animatedly about nature writing; only one or two were smoking. In February 1996, the popular Tokyo literary magazine, *Eureka*, published yet another collection of American nature writing in translation, followed by ten scholarly essays.

In August 1996, ASLE-Japan and ASLE-US joined forces to sponsor a symposium on Japanese and American environmental literature at the University of Hawaii-Manoa; fifty scholars and writers attended this meeting, including such leading Japanese and American authors as Keizo Hino, Michiko Ishimure, W.S. Merwin, David Quammen, and Linda Hogan. One of the oddities of this entire process of building a constituency for environmental literature in Japan is the fact that most of the Japanese scholars involved with ASLE are actually specialists in American or British literature. But perhaps this is not so surprising, as American environmental literature has undergone an extraordinary renaissance since the late 1960s, and scholarship in such fields as environmental ethics, environmental history, and environmental literature has followed suit. Japanese scholars whose work has brought them into regular contact with Americans studying environmental topics in literature have become the avant-garde ecocritics in their own country.[4] Gradually, prominent Americanists such as Takayuki Tatsumi of Keio University have drifted toward ecocriticism from their nonenvironmental work on canonical American writers. The real key to the deep and durable influence of environmental literature on the consciousness of the Japanese public will be the development of a new Japanese literature of nature, not merely the steady importation of American literature in translation.

It is still too early to comment on the links between environmental literature and grassroots environmental activism in Japan; in fact, we are only now beginning to see the mainstream consumption of environmental literature in the United States, despite decades of rich artistic and scholarly productivity.[5] However, it is clear that Japanese ecocritics and American ecocritics living in Japan are working today to identify native Japanese traditions of nature writing and to encourage contemporary Japanese authors whose work explores the natural world and the relation between nature and human culture. Japanese participants in the August 1996 ASLE Symposium on Japanese and American Environmental Literature discussed a wide range of traditional and contemporary environmental literature and philosophy from their country, including the bear stories of Hokkaido's native people, the trickster and regeneration stories in the *Kojiki*, and the writings of Nanao Sakaki, Takeshi Kaiko, Yasunari Kawabata, Uenish Haruji, Tokutomi Roka, Keizo Hino, and Michiko Ishimure.

My own goal in working to bring American nature writing to Japan was to inspire people to pay more attention to local, urban nature and to the ecological implications of Japanese literature; I accomplished this by explaining to various Japanese audiences my view that nature writing is meant not merely to absorb our attention, but to deflect it out toward the world.

Frankly, it is difficult to gauge the influence of literature on its audience; sometimes, the best literature does not merely guide readers toward a particular worldview, but instead aims to shake up readers' current worldviews, disrupting complacency and inspiring new reflection.[6] To monitor the effect of contemporary American environmental literature on my Japanese students, I asked them to keep daily journals of their natural observations and to take turns reading from these journals at our weekly meetings. I recall one particular student from Sophia University in Tokyo, a quiet young man who seldom spoke in class and wrote a few lackluster analytical essays for me early in the semester. Toward the end of the term, he read a journal entry about a butterfly that had flown into the train that morning as he traveled from his home in suburban Tokyo to the downtown campus, explaining how the commuters on the train had worked together to protect the butterfly from the air conditioner's fan and to usher it from the car with their books and newspapers when the doors opened at the next stop. This may seem like a small observation to make, marginal evidence of new awakening to the presence of nature in the world's largest city. But normally this is the closest we can come to documenting the influence of literature that we expect—that we hope—will have a constructive, stimulating effect on students and other readers.

Contemporary American nature writers, in many cases, have inherited Thoreau's appreciation for the immediate and local rather than the distant and exotic. For some writers, like Wendell Berry, this idea has become a crucial rallying point. In June 1989, Berry gave a speech to a group of graduating students at the College of the Atlantic in which he explained that "the question that must be addressed . . . is not how to care for the planet but how to care for each of the planet's millions of human and natural neighborhoods, each of its millions of small pieces and parcels of land, each one of which is in some precious way different from all the others" (1990, p. 200). The ability to evoke the subtle mysteries of specific "neighborhoods" is one of the great contributions of nature writing to American culture, and when this nature writing is exported to other cultures, its proper function is not simply to attract tourists to Edward Abbey's Arches National Park or Rick Bass's Yaak Valley or even to Walden Pond, but rather to offer models for the process of noticing—and caring about—the world wherever readers might live, even in Tokyo. In fact, one of ASLE's major tasks right now is cultivating an interest in home-grown environmental writing among Japanese writers and scholars of Japanese literature, including such contemporary writers as Michiko Ishimure (whose work on Minamata disease is comparable to Rachel Carson's *Silent Spring*) and Tomoske Noda (author of numerous books about Japanese rivers).

In July 1994, at the end of my first extended stay in Japan, I accompanied a dozen students from Rikkyo, Sophia, and Tokyo universities on a field trip to a mountainous area in Saitama Prefecture, just northwest of Tokyo, for a day of hiking and crawling through caves. Even Yuki, the Todai student from Tokyo University who had begun the year by cautioning me that nature is obsolete in contemporary Japan, joined the excursion and may have received a corrective to his own skepticism. I would not go so far as to suggest that environmental literature has entirely reformed the rigidly anthropocentric views of my Japanese students, but I do believe that reading and discussing such literature has contributed, in small, subtle ways, to the students' subconscious, sensory attunement to their daily contact with nature. And this may be an important first step toward environmental awareness and activism. As Snyder's poem "Ripples on the Surface" suggests, conceptual development may originate in something as mundane as physical observation.

In fact, even the teacher of environmental literature, who understands in principle the value of simple, sensory perception of the world, occasionally must be reminded of this lesson. A few weeks before the Saitama trip with my students, just after speaking in Matsuyama (on the southern island of Shikoku) and learning Basho's poem about the old pond, the frog, and the sound of water, I had the chance to travel with two ASLE-Japan members to visit eighty-four-year-old farmer and philosopher Masanobu Fukuoka, the author of *Shizen Noho Wara Ippon No Kakumei* (The One-Straw Revolution), which was published in Japan in 1975 and translated a few years later, with a preface by Wendell Berry. After spending a few hours walking around Fukuoka's jungle-like orchards in the mountains near Matsuyama, we went to have tea in a dusty, rundown hut. While drinking tea, we listened to Fukuoka talk about farming and nature. Then I asked him a question that I had been pondering during our entire visit. Did he think it might be possible for universities to contribute to our understanding of nature? In particular, what did he think of the three literature professors who had come to see him? Fukuoka seemed to look right past me, and then he said, "Listen to the bird sing." I thought he simply had not heard my question or that he found it unimportant. But everyone stopped talking and, sure enough, there was a nightingale calling outside the hut. Then Fukuoka's assistant leaned over to me and whispered, "He means, it is possible if you have a simple mind." In other words, those of us who work at universities might be able to contribute meaningfully to society's understanding and appreciation of nature if we remember to pay attention to nature itself, if we do not lose ourselves in lectures, theories, texts, and laboratories. A powerful admonition: ecocritics, and perhaps literary scholars and students in general, need contact not just with written texts and not just with each other, but with the physical world. This idea comes flashing back to me whenever I think of those discussions of nature writing at Chigusa, where the natural world, with all of its beauty and danger, all of its reality, becomes an abstraction, lost in smoke and windowless darkness.

It would be presumptuous to guess precisely the future trajectory of ecocriticism and environmental literature in the United States and other countries, such as Japan. What I have tried to offer in this essay, however, is my general view of what both literature and literary scholarship might contribute to the international environmental movement. Unlike other forms of environmentalism that tend to respond to specific problems in specific geographical locations, "literary ecology" (to use the phrase of Cheryl Glotfelty and Harold Fromm) typically plays an indirect, long-term role in social evolution, challenging readers to consider the just and sustainable relationship between their human communities and the planet. The report of my experience as a nature-writing ambassador from the United States to Japan, also summarized in this article, is intended to demonstrate that the work of academics need not simply disappear into library catacombs, but might serve to stimulate important cultural developments at home and abroad.

Notes

1. According to contemporary Japanese poet Mutsuo Takahashi: "Rigid custom made it mandatory to mention one of the seasons in the first verse. . . . It is obvious that the seasons are bound up with life, so the seasonal reference adds vitality to a poem" (1993, p. 27). Gary Snyder, on the other hand, adopts a haiku-like, abbreviated format in his poem "On Climbing the Sierra Matterhorn Again After Thirty-one Years": "Range after range of mountains / Year after year after year. / I am still in love" (1992, p. 362). But the purpose here is obviously to evoke the chiaroscuro effect of viewing successive ranges of mountains, and then to subsume the visual phenomenon within the concluding statement of emotion, suggesting that this feeling ("love") has been developed through years of contact. In sum, Snyder's haiku represents powerful contact with nature rather than a formulaic gesture.

2. Henry Nash Smith's *Virgin Land: The American West as Symbol and Myth* (1950), Marjorie Hope Nicolson's *Mountain Gloom and Mountain Glory* (1959), Leo Marx's *The Machine in the Garden* (1964), Paul Shepard's *Man in the Landscape: A Historic View of the Esthetics of Nature* (1967), and Joseph Meeker's *The Comedy of Survival: In Search of an Environmental Ethic* (1974) are some notable examples.

3. A useful summary of the environmental movement in Japan is provided in the booklet *Nature Conservation Japan*, published in March 1992 by the Nature Conservation Society of Japan (address: Toranomon-Denki Building, 4F, 2–8–1 Toranomon, Minato-ku, Tokyo 105, Japan).

4. It was a quirk of fate that Ken Noda happened to spend the 1989–1990 academic year at Brown University as an American Council of Learned Societies Fellow working on Emily Dickinson with my dissertation advisor, Barton St. Armand. St. Armand was in France most of that year, so he advised Noda to meet with me; that is how he came to be interested in nature writing and how I eventually arrived in Japan to be "the Johnny Appleseed of nature writing." ASLE-Japan evolved through layers and layers of personal networks in the Japanese scholarly community, with Ken Noda at the center.

5. In April 1996, Poet Laureate Robert Hass joined the Orion Society, the Library of Congress, the Academy of American Poets, the Association for the Study of Literature and Environment, and dozens of other literary and environmental organizations to sponsor "Watershed: Writers, Nature, and Community" in Washington, D.C. This event, which drew some thirty distinguished American nature writers to the Library of Congress for a week of readings and discussions, marked the newly recognized centrality of such writers within American culture. Also, a sign that ecocriticism is on the verge of breaking into the mainstream of American literary scholarship occurred when *The Chronicle of Higher Education* published a lengthy

cover story titled "Inventing a New Field: The Study of Literature About the Environment" in its August 9, 1996, issue.

6. For further discussion of the persuasive possibilities of environmental writing, see my essay, "Epistemology and Politics in American Nature Writing: Embedded Rhetoric and Discrete Rhetoric" (1996).

Bibliography

Berry, Wendell. 1990. *What Are People For?* San Francisco: North Point Press.

Foerster, Norman. 1923. *Nature in American Literature*. New York: Macmillan.

Fukuoka, M. 1978. *The One-Straw Revolution: An Introduction to Natural Farming*. Trans. Chris Pearce, Tsune Kurosawa, and Larry Korn. Preface by Wendell Berry. Berkeley, CA: Rodale Press.

Gablik, S. 1995. "Arts and the Earth: Making Art as if the World Mattered."*Orion* 14, no. 4 (Autumn): 44–53.

Glotfelty, C., and H. Fromm, eds. 1996. *The Ecocriticism Reader: Landmarks in Literary Ecology*. Athens: University of Georgia Press.

Hans, J.S. 1990. *The Value(s) of Literature*. Albany: State University of New York Press.

Hicks, Philip Marshall. 1924. "The Development of the Natural History Essay in American Literature. Ph.D. diss., University of Pennsylvania.

Kittredge, William W. 1987. *Owning It All*. Minneapolis, MN: Graywolf Press.

Lopez, Barry. 1987. "Contribution to Natural History: An Annotated Booklist." In *On Nature*, ed. Daniel Halpern. San Francisco: North Point Press.

———. 1990. *Alan Magee: Inlets*. Portland, ME: Joan Whitney Payson Gallery of Art, Westbrook College.

Love, Glen A. 1990. "Revaluing Nature: Toward an Ecological Criticism." *Western American Literature* (Fall): 201–215.

Marshall, I., and S. Slovic, eds. "Narrative Scholarship: Storytelling in Ecocriticism." Collection of nineteen papers presented at the Western Literature Association Conference, Vancouver, British Columbia, October 12, 1995.

Marx, Leo. 1964. *The Machine in the Garden*. New York: Oxford University Press.

Meeker, Joseph. 1974. *The Comedy of Survival: In Search of an Environmental Ethic*. Los Angeles: Guild of Tutors Press.

Miller, P. 1939. *The New England Mind: The Seventeenth Century*. Cambridge: Harvard University Press.

Nature Conservation Japan. 1992. Tokyo: Nature Conservation Society of Japan.

Nicolson, Marjorie Hope. 1959. *Mountain Gloom and Mountain Glory*. Ithaca: Cornell University Press.

Noda, K., and S. Slovic, eds. 1993. *Folio A* (Fall) (special issue devoted to American nature writing). Tokyo: Fumikura Press.

———. 1996. *Eureka* (February) (special issue devoted to American nature writing).

Shepard, Paul. 1967. *Man in the Landscape: A Historic View of the Esthetics of Nature*. New York: Ballantine.

Slovic, S. 1995. "Nature Writing: The New American Renaissance." *The Rising Generation* (February): 554–562.

————. 1995. *Worldly Words: An Anthology of American Nature Writing*. Tokyo: Fumikura Press.

————. 1996. "Epistemology and Politics in American Nature Writing: Embedded Rhetoric and Discrete Rhetoric." In *Green Culture: Environmental Rhetoric in Contemporary America*, ed. Carl G. Herndl and Stuart C. Brown. Madison: University of Wisconsin Press.

Slovic, S., and K. Noda, eds. 1996. *Environmental Approaches to American Literature: Toward the World of Nature Writing*. Kyoto: Minerva Press.

Smith, Henry Nash. 1950. *Virgin Land: The American West as Symbol and Myth*. Cambridge: Harvard University Press.

Snyder, Gary. 1987. Foreword. In *Break the Mirror: The Poems of Nanao Sakaki*, ed. N. Sasaki. San Francisco: North Point Press.

————. 1992. *No Nature: New and Selected Poems*. New York: Pantheon.

Takahashi, Mutsuo. 1993. "Haiku: Haiku Poetry." *The Sun* (August): 26–27.

Thoreau, Henry David. 1980 [1862]. "Walking." *The Natural History Essays*. Salt Lake City: Peregrine Smith.

————. 1992 [1854]. *Walden and Resistance to Civil Government*. Second Norton Critical Edition. New York: Norton.

Watanabe, Masao. 1974. "The Conception of Nature in Japanese Culture." *Science* 183 (January 25): 279–282.

Williams, T.T. 1995. "We Are All Hibakusha." *The Nation* (May 15): 661–664.

Winkler, K.J. 1996. "Inventing a New Field: The Study of Literature About the Environment." *The Chronicle of Higher Education* (August 9).

The Editors

Karen K. Gaul teaches cultural anthropology at Hendrix College in Conway, AR. She holds a master's degree (1989) and a doctorate (1994) in cultural anthropology (University of Massachusetts, Amherst) and a Masters of Theological Studies (1987, Harvard Divinity School). Her research focuses on symbolic understandings about and practical uses of forests in the Himalayan hills of North India. She was research associate at the Maureen and Mike Mansfield Center at The University of Montana from 1995–1997.

Jackie Hiltz was senior research associate at the Mansfield Center at The University of Montana from 1996–99. She coedited America's Wars in Asia: A Cultural Approach to History and Memory (1998). Her current research focuses on the political and cultural history of Sikkim (India). Recently, she spent nine months in the eastern Himalaya gathering archival materials and interviewing Sikkimese and Indian politicians, historians, and religious leaders. She is a graduate of Stanford University and The University of Montana and has taught courses on Asia at The University of Montana.

The Contributors

J. Baird Callicott is professor of philosophy and religion studies at the University of North Texas. In 1971 he designed and taught the nation's first course in environmental ethics at the University of Wisconsin–Stevens Point. In 1973 he helped to create, and from 1980 to 1986 directed, a multidisciplinary Letters and Science Environmental Studies program at UWSP. He was president of the International Society for Environmental Ethics from 1997 to 2000. His publications include the 1989 collection *Nature in Asian Traditions of Thought*, coedited with Roger Ames, and *Earth's Insights* (1994), a cross-cultural examination of ecological ethics.

Dan Flores is A.B. Hammond Professor of Western History at The University of Montana where he teaches courses on the American West, American environmental history, Native American history, and art and the American West. He has authored numerous articles on the environmental history of the Southwest and the Rocky Mountain West. Among his books are *Horizontal Yellow: Nature and History in the Near Southwest* (1999), *Caprock Canyonlands: Journeys into the Heart of the Southern Plains* (1990), and *Jefferson and Southwestern Exploration* (1984). *The Natural West: Environmental History in the Rockies and the Plains* will be published in 2000. He received his bachelor's (1971) and his master's (1972) degrees in history from Northwest State University of Louisiana, and a doctorate in history from Texas A&M University (1978).

Allan G. Grapard is International Shinto Foundation Professor of Shinto Studies in the Department of East Asian Languages and Cultural Studies at the University of California, Santa Barbara. He received a doctorate from the National Institute for Oriental Languages and Civilizations, Paris (1977) and studied at both Kyoto National University and Shuchin Buddhist University in Kyoto, Japan. He is the author of *The Protocol of the Gods* (1992) and has written extensively on Shinto religion, religious geography of Japan, and environmentalism. His latest work is *The Religion of Space and the Limits of Religion* (forthcoming).

Daniel Kemmis, director of the O'Connor Center for the Rocky Mountain West, served as mayor of Missoula, speaker and minority leader of the Montana House of Representatives, and Montana legislator for four terms. He is the author of two books: *Community and the Politics of Place* (1990) and *The Good City and the Good Life* (1995). He has had articles published in national magazines and journals on such topics as community and community building, city design, bioregionalism, and the economy and politics of the West. In 1997 President Clinton awarded Kemmis the Charles Frankel Prize for outstanding contribution to the field of humanities. He is a graduate of Harvard University and the University of Montana Law School.

William L. Lang is professor of history at Portland State University and director for the Center for Columbia River History. He received his bachelor's degree in history from Willamette University (1964), a master's degree in American history from Washington State University (1966), and a doctorate in American history from the University of Delaware at Newark (1974). His publications include *Montana: A History of Two Centuries* (1991), *Confederacy of Ambition: William Winlock Miller and the Making of Washington Territory* (1996), and *Great River of the West: Essays on the Columbia River* (1999). He teaches courses on historiography, public history, environmental history, and ethnic history with an emphasis on the Pacific Northwest and the American West.

Alan Graham McQuillan is professor of forest management in the School of Forestry at The University of Montana. He currently teaches courses titled "Timber Management" and "Ethics and the Management of Public Lands," and has taught forest planning operations research, integrated management, and forest valuation. His research areas include primarily land use ethics and aesthetics, along with American Indian land management, forest planning techniques, sustainable development, and ecosystems management. McQuillan earned his bachelor of science degree in economics with technology from the City University of London (1970), a master of science degree in forestry (1972), and a doctorate in forest management from the University of Montana (1981). In 1998, together with Ashley Preston, he coedited the book *Globally and Locally: Seeking a Middle Path to Sustainable Development.* He is currently finishing a book titled *Forest Beauty and the Forester.*

Cliff Montagne is associate professor of soil sciences at Montana State University (MSU). He received a bachelor's degree in geology from Dartmouth College (1969), a master's degree in geology/earth science (1971) and a doctorate in crop and soil sciences from MSU (1976). He is Codirector of the Bioregions Program at MSU. Montagne teaches and leads field courses in soil sciences, soil conservation, and holistic management. The bioregions program facilitates community-level decision making and exchange between similar bioregions in the greater Yellowstone area, Mongolia, northern Japan, and Nepal. Montagne also has lectured in universities in Japan, Thailand, and New Zealand and travels regularly to Asia.

Karen G. Mumford is a doctoral student in the graduate program in conservation biology at the University of Minnesota and is also a visiting assistant professor at Emory University. She is conducting research with J. Baird Callicott to examine how values and ethics have influenced the use and management of natural resources in the North American Great Lakes region. She received a master's degree in fisheries biology from Iowa State University, Ames, and a master's degree from the graduate program in urban and regional planning at the University of Iowa, Iowa City. She has worked in the office of the governor of the State of Illinois as a Dunn Fellow and for the Iowa Department of Natural Resources.

Rhoads Murphey is professor of history at the University of Michigan, Ann Arbor. He received a bachelor's in history (1941), a master's in history (1942), a master's in regional studies/China (1948), and a doctorate in Far Eastern history (1950) all from Harvard University. He has served as a visiting professor at National Taiwan University, the University of Pennsylvania, Tokyo University, Sichuan University, Cambridge University, and Oxford University. He is the author of fourteen books, including text books for Asian studies courses, and some sixty articles in scholarly journals. Murphey has been a Fellow with the Social Science Research Council, the Ford Foundation, Guggenheim Foundation, and the National Endowment for the Humanities.

Nancy Lee Peluso is associate professor of environmental social science in the Department of Environmental Science, Policy, and Management at the University of California, Berkeley. She received her doctorate in rural sociology at Cornell University in 1988. Peluso has conducted field research in Java; East and West Kalimantan, Indonesia; and Sarawak, Malaysia. Her 1992 book *Rich Forests, Poor People: Resource Control and Resistance in Java* won the annual award of the Rural Sociological Society in 1995 for outstanding scholarly contribution. She has also coedited a volume with Christine Padoch, *Borneo in Transition: People, Forests, Conservation and Development* (1996). Her most recent projects include *Violent Environment*—a collaboration with Michael Watts (forthcoming)—and a collaboration with Peter Vandergeest, *Forest Laws and Customary Rights in Southeast Asia* (forthcoming).

Scott Slovic is associate professor of literature and the environment at The University of Nevada, Reno, where he also directs the Center for Environmental Arts and Humanities. The author of numerous publications on American, German, and Japanese environmental literature, he has also written or edited seven books, including most recently *Reading the Earth: New Directions in the Study of Literature and the Environment* (1998) and *Literature and the Environment: Readings on Nature and Culture* (1999). His anthology of contemporary Southwestern environmental writing is due to appear in the fall of 2000. Slovic served as founding president of the Association for the Study of Literature and Environment (ASLE) from 1992 to 1995. Currently, he edits ASLE's journal, *ISLE: Interdisciplinary Studies in Literature and Environment.*

Vaclav Smil was born in Plzen, Bohemia, and studied in an interdisciplinary program at the Faculty of Natural Sciences of Carolinum University in Prague. In 1969, after the Soviet invasion of Czechoslovakia, he left the country for the United States. In 1972 he received a doctorate from the College of Earth and Mineral Sciences at Pennsylvania State University. Since 1972 he has been at the University of Manitoba where he is now a Distinguished Professor. He has published 18 books and over 200 papers on interdisciplinary topics related to energy, economics, Asia, and global environmental conditions. He has been invited to speak at conferences and workshops worldwide and served as a consultant to the Academy of Arts and Sciences, the Center for Futures Research, the International Research and Development Center, the Office of Technology Assessment of the U.S. Congress, Project 2050, the Rockefeller

Foundation, the U.S. Agency for International Development, the U.S. Academy of Sciences, the World Bank, and the World Resources Institute. He is a Fellow of the Royal Society of Canada (Science Academy).

Jack Ward Thomas is Boone and Crockett Professor of Wildlife Conservation at The University of Montana. He was the chief of the United States Forest Service from 1993 to 1996. He worked as a wildlife biologist in Texas from 1957 to 1966, and then as Research Wildlife Biologist for the U.S. Forest Service in West Virginia and in Massachusetts from 1966 to 1974. From 1974 to 1993 he was Chief Research Wildlife Biologist and Project Leader on Range and Wildlife Habitat Research for the Forest Service in Oregon. Thomas received a bachelor of science degree in wildlife management from the Texas A&M University, a master of science degree in wildlife ecology from West Virginia University (1969), and a doctorate in forestry from the University of Massachusetts (1972). He has approximately 300 publications on elk, deer, and turkey biology; wildlife disease; wildlife habitat; songbird ecology; northern spotted owl management; ecosystem management; and land use planning. He has collaborated on wildlife management projects in India and Pakistan.

Xiaoshan Yang received a doctorate in Comparative Literature from Harvard University (1994) and is currently an assistant professor of Chinese in the Department of East Asian Languages and Literature at the University of Notre Dame. His publications include *To Perceive and to Represent: A Comparative Study of Chinese and English Poetics of Nature Imagery* (1996).

Index

Aesthetic construction
  complexity theory and, 188, 211n.10
    determinism, 197, 199, 215n.50
    order, 191
    regimentation, 192–93
  criterion for, 206–10
    Taoist *wu-wei*, 206–10
    Taoist *yu-wei*, 206–7, 208
  global context, 186
  interest level and
    beauty, 193–95
    patterns, 193, 214n.31
  order and, 190–93
    complexity theory, 191, 192–93
    creation of, 191–92
    regimentation, 192–93
  polarity and, 202, 203–5, 216n.62
  potency and, 205–6
    Taoist *li*, 206, 207–8, 217n.78
    Taoist *te*, 205–6
  principles of, 187, 200–203
    creativity, 187, 202
    disclosure, 187, 201
    harmony, 187, 200
    rightness, 187, 202–3
    sensitive dependence, 187,
      195–200
    universal characteristics, 187,
      201
  sensitive dependence, 187, 195–200
    aesthetic sensibility, 198

Aesthetic construction
  sensitive dependence *(continued)*
    boundary conditions, 196,
      215n.46
    butterfly effect, 196, 200,
      215n.45
    chaotic determinism and, 197,
      215n.47
    complexity theory and, 197,
      199, 200, 215n.50
    determinism and, 197, 199,
      215n.50
    minimalism and, 198–99
Western ecology
    abstraction, 186, 187
    aesthetic criterion, 208–9
    aesthetic sensibility, 198
    development of, 187–88, 204
    logical construction, 186–87
    modernism, 187–88
    nature knowledge, 188–90,
      212n.13
    planning failure, 185–86, 209
    polarity, 203–5
    potency, 205–6
    reductionism, 186, 187, 204
Afforestation program, China, 169–74
    assessment of, 169–74, 180n.5
    planting rates, 170–71, 172–73, 180n.5
    political influence, 169
    Western perspective of, 169–70

Afforestation program, China *(continued)*
  See also Deforestation, Asia; Forest
    management, Indonesia
Agent Orange, 53
Agriculture, deforestation and, 36–37, 38
  maize, 40
  rice, 36–37
  shifting cultivation, 39
  soil alkalinization, 44
  soil salinization, 44
  tea, 40
Air pollution, Asia, 43–44, 52–53
Association for the Study of Literature
    and Environment
  Japan, 233–35
  United States, 228–37
        conferences of, 229
        development of, 228–29
        publications of, 229

Biodiversity preservation, 64, 71–72
Boone and Crockett Club (Montana),
    10–12
Buddhism, 93
  See also Mount Hiko, Japan
Burma, 53

Chamba, India, xvi–xviii, xxi–xxii
China
  afforestation program, 169–74
        assessment of, 169–74, 180n.5
        planting rates, 170–71, 172–73,
          180n.5
        political influence, 169
        Western perspective of, 169–70
  deforestation, 37, 38–39
        air pollution and, 43, 44
        endangered species, 37
        erosion, 45
        flooding, 37–38, 45–46
        historically, 39–43, 45–46
        population growth and, 36,
          40–41
        water pollution and, 44
  food production, 174–79
        dairy, 179

China
  food production *(continued)*
        dietary changes, 175–76,
          178–79
        farmland depletion, 175–76
        fertilization, 178
        grain, 175, 176, 178
        improvement strategies, 177–79
        irrigation, 177–78
        pork, 178
        statistical errors, 176–77
        waste reduction, 178
        Western perspective of, 174–75,
          176
  medieval poetry
        ancient poetry contrast, 93–94
        Buddhism and, 93
        communism and, 104–5
        Confucianism and, 92
        cultural change and, 104–6
        Daoism and, 92, 93, 106n.3
        of fields/gardens, 91, 100–104
        historical emergence, 91–94
        of mountains/water, 91, 97–100
        of seclusion, 91, 94–97
  Western perspective of, 167–69, 174,
      180
        afforestation program, 169–70
        Maoism, 168–69
Clean Air Act, 23
Clean Water Act, 23
Columbia River
  cultural identification, 131–32
  Euro-American contact, 132–33,
      136–43
        descriptive maps, 136–37,
          140–41, 145n.16
        Hudson Bay Company, 141–42
        Lewis/Clark expedition, 137–41
        utilitarian perspective, 137,
          139–43
  geography of, 130
  Native Americans and, 131
        creation stories, 134–36
        cultural diversity, 133
        decline of, 142

Columbia River
  Native Americans *(continued)*
    descriptive maps, 133–34,
      140–41
    spiritual perspective, 135–36,
      139, 140–41
  protective legislation, 131–32, 143
Communism, 104–5
Confucianism, 92
Conservation
  complementary philosophy, 70–72
    community ecology, 70
    ecosystem ecology, 70
  conservation biology, 58, 62–70
    agricultural zone, 70
    appropriate technology, 65, 69,
      70, 71
    biodiversity preservation, 64,
      71–72
    ecological integrity, 64–65
    ecological rehabilitation, 65,
      67–68, 70
    ecological sustainability, 65,
      68–69, 70, 71, 72
    ecosystem health, 65, 68–69, 70
    ecosystem management, 65, 69,
      70
    integrationist school, 63, 64,
      65–69, 70–71
    project examples, 72
    segregationist school, 63–65, 70
    sustainable development, 65, 68,
      70, 71
    urban-industrial zone, 70
  Earth Summit (1992), 58
  historically, 58–60
  philosophy of, 59–60
    nature preservation, 59–60, 61,
      62, 64, 69–70, 72
    resource conservation, 59–62,
      68, 69–70, 72
  practice of, 58–59
Culture
  cross-cultural study, xxi–xxiii
    China, xxii, xxiv
    India, xxii

Culture
  cross-cultural study *(continued)*
    Japan, xxii, xxiv
    Pacific Northwest, xxiii, xxiv
    Southeast Asia, xxii
  mountain ecology, 79
  U.S. forest management, 30–31
  See also Mount Hiko, Japan;
    Spirituality

Dam projects, India, 48
Daoism, 92, 93, 106n.3
Deforestation, Asia
  agricultural impact, 36–37, 38
    maize, 40
    rice, 36–37
    shifting cultivation, 39
    soil alkalinization, 44
    soil salinization, 44
    tea, 40
  China, 37, 38–39
    air pollution, 43, 44
    endangered species, 37
    erosion, 45
    flooding, 37–38, 45–46
    historically, 39–43, 45–46
    population growth, 36, 40–41
    water pollution, 44
  elite perspective, 35–36, 41, 43, 45, 55
  endangered species, 37, 47, 48, 54
    China, 37
    India, 37, 47, 48
    Japan, 54
    Southeast Asia, 37
  erosion, 45, 48
  fires, 39
  flooding, 37–38, 45–46
  India, 37, 38–39, 46–50
    air pollution, 43–44
    dam projects, 48
    endangered species, 37, 47, 48
    erosion, 48
    historically, 46–49
    Nepal, 49–50
    population growth, 36
    protest movement, 49

Deforestation, Asia
 India *(continued)*
   tourism, 49–50
   water pollution, 44
 Japan, 39
   air pollution, 52–53
   endangered species, 54
   historically, 50–51
   industrial pollution, 52–53
   population growth, 36, 41
 Korea, 37, 51
   population growth, 36
   water pollution, 44
 pollution
   Agent Orange, 53
   air, 43–44, 52–53
   industrial, 52–53
   pesticide usage, 44, 54
   water, 44
 population growth and, 36, 40–41,
   55–56
   China, 36, 40–41
   India, 36
   Japan, 36, 41
   Korea, 36
   Southeast Asia, 36
 siltation, 37–38, 45–46
 Southeast Asia, 37, 53–55
   Burma, 53
   endangered species, 37
   eucalyptus, 53–54
   Java, 53
   Malaya, 53
   Philippines, 54, 55
   population growth, 36
   Thailand, 53
   tropical forests, 54–55
   Vietnam, 53
 Taiwan, 51
 terracing, 37–38, 42, 44
 wooden construction, 39
 See also Afforestation program, China;
   Forest management, Indonesia
Drummond, Montana, 8–9

Earth Summit (1992), 58

Ecological integrity, 64–65
Ecological rehabilitation, 65, 67–68, 70
Ecological sustainability, 65, 68–69, 70,
   71, 72
Ecosystem health, 65, 68–69, 70
Ecosystem management, 65, 69, 70
Emerson, Ralph Waldo, 59, 61
Endangered species
 China, 37
 India, 37, 47, 48
 Japan, 54
 Southeast Asia, 37
Endangered Species Act, 23, 24, 29
Environmental study
 cross-cultural approach, xxi–xxiii
   China, xxii, xxiv
   India, xxii
   Japan, xxii, xxiv
   Pacific Northwest, xxiii, xxiv
   Southeast Asia, xxii
 forest management
   Chamba, India, xvi–xviii,
     xxi–xxii
   Libby, Montana, xvi, xvii–xviii,
     xxi–xxii
   Shimokawa, Japan, xvii–xviii,
     xxi–xxii
 interdisciplinary approach, xviii–xxi
   history, xxi
   literature, xx–xxi
   philosophy, xxi
   science, xx
   social science, xx
 Montana symposium, xxiii–xxiv
Erosion, Asia, 45, 48
Eucalyptus, 53–54

Fires
 Asian deforestation, 39
 U.S. forest management, 21
Flooding, Asia, 37–38, 45–46
Food production, China, 174–79
 dairy, 179
 dietary changes, 175–76, 178–79
 farmland depletion, 175–76
 fertilization, 178

Food production, China *(continued)*
  grain, 175, 176, 178
  improvement strategies, 177–79
  irrigation, 177–78
  pork, 178
  statistical errors, 176–77
  waste reduction, 178
  Western perspective of, 174–75, 176
Forest management
  Chamba, India, xvi–xviii, xxi–xxii
  Shimokawa, Japan, xvii–xviii, xxi–xxii
Forest management, Indonesia
  Java teak forests, 147–48, 150–53
        black market, 151
        degradation of, 148, 153
        government role, 148, 150–53,
          164
        historical perspective, 152–53t
        property rights, 151, 153
  Kalimantan ironwood forests, 148–49,
    153–57
        chainsaw usage, 157
        government role, 148–49,
          153–57, 164
        historical perspective, 153–54
        privatization, 156
        property rights, 149, 153–54,
          155–57
        taxation, 155–56
  West Kalimantan forests, 158–64
        government role, 149, 158,
          159–65
        historical perspective, 158–63
        property rights, 149, 159–64
        rubber production, 160, 161,
          162–64
Forest management, United States
  improvement strategies, 25–29
        annual sale projections, 25–26
        court decisions, 28–29
        economic markets, 27
        funding, 26
        legislation, 28–29
        personnel, 26
        process complexity, 28–29
        public opinion, 27

Forest management, United States
  improvement strategies *(continued)*
        regulatory agencies, 27–29
        scientific knowledge, 26
        technological development,
          26–27
        wood substitutes, 26–27
  Libby, Montana, xvi, xvii–xviii,
    xxi–xxii
  ownership transference, 1, 29–31
        cultural heritage and, 30–31
  stability feasibility, 20
  stability influences, 21–25
        court decisions, 24
        disease, 21
        drought, 21–22
        economic markets, 23
        federal budget, 24
        fire, 21
        funding, 22
        global warming, 22
        legislation, 23–24, 32n.1
        management actions, 22
        personnel quality, 22
        pesticides, 21
        process complexity, 24–25
        public opinion, 23
        regulatory agencies, 23–24
        scientific knowledge, 22–23

Hokkaido, Japan
  Ainu population, xi, xiv(n.5)
  development of, ix, xi–xii
  environmental destruction, xi, xiv(n.6)
  government control, xi–xii
Hong Kong, 4–5, 14

India
  Chamba, xvi–xviii, xxi–xxii
  deforestation, 37, 38–39, 46–50
        air pollution and, 43–44
        dam projects, 48
        endangered species, 37, 47, 48
        erosion, 48
        historically, 46–49
        Nepal, 49–50

India
  deforestation *(continued)*
      population growth and, 36
      protest movement, 49
      tourism and, 49–50
      water pollution and, 44
Indonesia. *See* Forest management,
    Indonesia
Interdisciplinary study, xviii–xxi
  history, xxi
  literature, xx-xxi
  philosophy, xxi
  science, xx
  social science, xx
Ironwood forests. *See* Forest manage-
    ment, Indonesia

Japan
  deforestation, 39
      air pollution and, 52–53
      endangered species, 54
      historically, 50–51
      industrial pollution and, 52–53
      population growth and, 36, 41
  Shimokawa, xvii–xviii, xxi–xxii
  See also Mount Hiko, Japan
Java
  deforestation, 53
  teak forests, 147–48, 150–53
      black market, 151
      degradation of, 148, 153
      government role, 148, 150–53,
          164
      historical perspective, 152–53t
      property rights, 151, 153

Kalimantan. *See* Forest management,
    Indonesia
Kinoshiro-Taisetsu (KST) homes, ix–xiii
  ferroconcrete foundation, x, xii
  innovative features, x–xi, xii–xiii
  lamination process, xi, xii, xiii(n.4)
  multigenerational living, x–xi
  petchka stove, x, xiii, xiv(n.7)
  snow-duct roof, x, xii
  Total Systems approach, ix, x–xi

Korea, deforestation, 37, 51
  population growth and, 36
  water pollution and, 44

Leopold, Aldo, xx
Libby, Montana, xvi, xvii–xviii, xxi–xxii
Literature, environmental
  Association for the Study of Literature
      and Environment, 228–37
      conferences of, 229
      development of, 228–29
      Japan, 233–35
      publications of, 229
  critique of, 224–26
  future of, 237–38
  interdisciplinary approach, xx–xxi
  Japanese haiku, 226–28, 238n.1
  Japanese interest in, 229–37
      Association for the Study of
          Literature and Environ-
          ment, 233–35
      environmental movements, 231
  role of, 219–23
      environmental importance,
          235–38
      environmental understanding,
          223
      ethical component, 220
      social dimension, 221–23
  See also Poetry, Chinese medieval
Louisville, Kentucky, 16, 17–18

Maize, 40
Malaya, 53
Marsh, George Perkins, 60
Missoula, Montana
  city-environment synergy, 1, 6–15
      Boone and Crockett Club, 10–12
      cluster industries, 9–10
      Drummond, 8–9
      economies and, 6–7, 16–17
      ecosystem management, 13
      Forest Service, 12–14
      organic ecosystems, 14, 17,
          19n.5
      Seattle, 17

Missoula, Montana *(continued)*
  environmental symposium, xxiii–xxiv
  Forest Service, 12–14
      ecosystem management, 13
  nation vs. city state, 3–6
      Hong Kong, 4–5, 14
  open space designation, xv
  rural vs. urban America, 15–19
      Louisville, Kentucky, 16, 17–18
Missoula Area Economic Development
    Corporation, 14
Missoula Economic Development
    Corporation, 9–10, 14
Montana. *See* Drummond, Montana;
    Libby, Montana; Missoula,
    Montana
Mountain ecology
  global perspective, 79–84
      Eastern spirituality, 80–81
      economic influence, 83–84
      European spirituality, 81–82
      Western spirituality, 81, 82–83,
        85
  Western characteristics, 75–79
      aridity, 75–76
      human influences, 78–79
      indigenous cultures, 79
      individual ecologies, 78
      latitude, 78
      public domain, 83, 84–86
      scholarly perspectives, 75–76,
        77, 79
      slope, 77
      spirituality, 81, 82–83, 85
      variability, 76–77
Mount Hiko, Japan
  administrative history, 119–25
      Meiji destruction, 123–25
  body symbolism, 117–19
  early history, 109–10
  Four Lands Perimeter, 110–11, 112–15,
    128n.4
      first zone, 111, 113
      second zone, 111, 113
      third zone, 111, 113–14
      fourth zone, 111, 114

Mount Hiko, Japan
  Four Lands Perimeter *(continued)*
      symbolism of, 114–15
  global influences, 125–26
  Lotus Blossom Ritual, 111–12,
    129n.5
  mountain ascetics, 108, 114–15,
    123–25, 127n.1
  social status and, 115–17
  tourism, 127
  women and, 120
Muir, John, 59, 61, 63
Multiple-Use Sustained Yield Act, 23

National Forest Management Act, 23, 29
Nature Conservancy, 61

Organic ecosystems, 14, 17, 19n.5

Pesticides
  Asian pollution, 44, 54
  U.S. forest management, 21
Philippines, 54, 55
Pinchot, Gifford, 60, 63
Poetry, Chinese medieval
  ancient poetry contrast, 93–94
  Buddhism and, 93
  communism and, 104–5
  Confucianism and, 92
  cultural change and, 104–6
  Daoism and, 92, 93, 106n.3
  of fields/gardens, 91, 100–104
  historical emergence, 91–94
  of mountains/water, 91, 97–100
  of seclusion, 91, 94–97
Pollution, Asia
  Agent Orange, 53
  air, 43–44, 52–53
  industrial, 52–53
  pesticide usage, 44, 54
  water, 44
Population growth, Asia
  China, 36, 40–41
  deforestation and, 36, 40–41, 55–56
  India, 36
  Japan, 36, 41

Population growth, Asia *(continued)*
  Korea, 36
  Southeast Asia, 36
Public Land Law Review Commission,
  29

Rescission Bill (1995), 24
Rice, 36–37, 71
Rubber, Indonesia, 160, 161, 162–64

Salinization, soil, 44
Seattle, Washington, 17
Shifting cultivation, 39
Shimokawa, Japan, xvii–xviii, xxi–xxii
Sierra Club, 61
Siltation, Asia, 37–38, 45–46
Southeast Asia, deforestation, 37,
  53–55
  Burma, 53
  endangered species, 37
  eucalyptus, 53–54
  Java, 53
  Malaya, 53
  Philippines, 54, 55
  Thailand, 53
  tropical forests, 54–55
  Vietnam, 53
  See also Deforestation, Asia
Spirituality
  Chinese medieval poetry
    Buddhism and, 93
    Confucianism and, 92
    Daoism and, 92, 93, 106n.3
  mountain ecology and
    Eastern, 80–81
    European, 81–82
    Western, 81, 82–83, 85
  Native Americans, 135–36, 139,
    140–41
  See also Mount Hiko; Japan
Sustainable development, 65, 68,
  70, 71

Taiwan, 51
Tao Qian, 100–104
Tea, 40
Teak forests. *See* Java
Terracing, Asia, 37–38, 42, 44
Thailand, 53
Thoreau, Henry David, 59, 61, 63, 219,
  223
318 sales, 24, 32n.1
Tourism, India, 49–50
Tropical forests, 54–55

Vietnam, 53

Water pollution, Asia, 44
Webb, Walter Prescott, 75–76
Wild and Scenic Rivers Act, 23
Wilderness Act, 23
Wilderness Society, 61

Xie Lingyun, 97–100

Yamaguchi, Akira, ix–xiii
  childhood, ix–x
  construction origins, x
  Hokkaido
    Ainu population, xi, xiv(n.5)
    development of, ix, xi–xii
    environmental destruction, xi,
      xiv(n.6)
    government control, xi–xii
  Kinoshiro-Taisetsu (KST) homes, ix–xiii
    ferroconcrete foundation, x, xii
    innovative features, x–xi, xii–xiii
    lamination process, xi, xii,
      xiii(n.4)
    multigenerational living, x–xi
    petchka stove, x, xiii, xiv(n.7)
    snow-duct roof, x, xii
    Total Systems approach, ix, x–xi

Zuo Si, 94–97